New Religions and the Theological Imagination in America

MARY FARRELL BEDNAROWSKI

INDIANA UNIVERSITY PRESS
Bloomington and Indianapolis

Manufactured in the United States of America

Library of Congress Cataloging-in-Publication Data

Bednarowski, Mary Farrell.
New religions and the theological imagination in America
/ Mary Farrell Bednarowski.
p.   cm. — (Religion in North America)
Bibliography: p.
Includes index.
ISBN 0-253-31137-3
1. United States—Religion.   2. Sects—United States.   3. Cults—
United States.   I. Title.   II. Series.
BL2525.B44 1989

291.2–dc19   88–46038
                                                                            CIP

ISBN 0-253-20952-8 (pbk.)

2 3 4 5 6 00 99 98 97 96 95

New Religions and
the Theological Imagination
in America

Religion in North America

Catherine L. Albanese and Stephen J. Stein, editors

CONTENTS

For Keith, Betsy, and Paul

Foreword

In this volume Mary Farrell Bednarowski breaks new ground in the comparative study of alternative religious movements in America. She is among the first to offer a sustained description and analysis of the religious thought of these communities without reflecting the normative bias of an apologist, an opponent, or an apostate. Bednarowski takes very seriously the theological efforts of these "new religions." She directs our attention to their attempts to make sense out of daily experience, to find meaning in life, and to live consistently. In this way we gain insight into their theological views.

Bednarowski focuses on six religious groups, three with nineteenth-century origins, three others coming on the American scene in the twentieth century. Mormonism, Christian Science, Theosophy, the Unification Church, Scientology, and the New Age movement are the chosen "new religions." Each has attracted substantial numbers of followers in America. Each possesses innovative theological ideas that arouse curiosity and interest, and all six are still present on the contemporary scene. The juxtaposition of these groups from different centuries reveals fundamental continuities in American religious thought.

Bednarowski's "conversational" mode of discourse, deceptively simple, carries us to the center of religious thinking in these groups. She examines the views of the six on the universe, the deity, human nature, the good life, and the destiny of persons after death—classic issues theologians standardly address under the categories of cosmology, metaphysics, ethics, and eschatology. Bednarowski demonstrates the intellectual integrity of these new religions and their potential significance in the world of religious thought.

Despite that integrity, it is virtually impossible to overstate the prevailing disdain these new religious movements receive in contemporary theological circles. The religious thought of these groups is frequently dismissed because of its base in special revelations given to the movements' founders, its association with social and ethnic outsiders, its lack of traditional intellectual sophistication, and its pragmatic orientation reflected in concern for the mundane aspects of life such as healing and material prosperity. This opposition is, in part, a reflection of the academy's unwillingness to consider the religious ponderings of a non-elite, non-professional group of writers and thinkers who have not been trained at a seminary or in a university. These uncredentialed voices represent a kind of "do-it-yourself" theology that gives free reign to the theological imagination and knows few of the restraints imposed by Western theological and philosophical traditions. Bednarowski turns these criticisms on end and suggests that the homespun quality and even the inconsistencies contribute to the appeal and influence of these alternative religious communities.

The new religions are openly critical of the more established, culturally powerful denominations in American life, and yet the former enjoy remarkable success in a society supposedly dominated by the latter. (It could be argued that it is sociologically or psychologically useful to retain distinction.) In this context, Bednarowski's instructive account raises serious questions about the *theological* usefulness of the distinction between mainline and fringe religious movements since both address the same issues. On intellectual grounds, therefore, there is no cause for treating the two in different ways.

Implicit in Bednarowski's study is the judgment that the theological reflections of these new religions have been overlooked too long, and that the losers in this oversight are not simply those excluded from contemporary theological conversation but also those who have done the excluding. She and we think that several of the writings cited extensively in her account, including the *Book of Mormon*, *Science and Health with Key to the Scriptures*, and *Divine Principle*, are too infrequently read by students of American religious thought. This study demonstrates the growing importance of these writings. There is every reason to believe that in the twenty-first century these and similar writings will figure significantly in every attempt to describe the development of American theology. Bednarowski's inclusion of the New Age movement, lampooned in cartoons and on television talk shows, demonstrates her willingness to grapple with the newest forms of popular religious thought in America.

The reader of this volume should not expect to find some kind of handbook for religious dialogue or guide to "your neighbor's" religion. This work has a sophistication about it that precludes such approaches. Rather, Bednarowski is a patient, insightful guide who leads us into the intricacies of theology. Her study is likely to appeal to the curious and uninitiated as well as to the established members of the academy. After this book, it should no longer be possible to discuss American theology comprehensively without bringing into the picture the distinctive contributions made by Bednarowski's six new religious movements and other alternative groups.

Catherine L. Albanese
Stephen J. Stein, *Series Editors*

Preface

This book is the product of many years of interest in new religious movements in nineteenth- and twentieth-century American culture. In broad terms, it is an effort to put forth and interpret manifestations of the theological imagination that have emerged in religious movements other than the established traditions, specifically Mormonism, Christian Science, Theosophy, the Unification Church, Scientology, and New Age thought. The project has its origins in one of those chance encounters in academic life that change the shape of a career.

Almost twenty years ago I began research for a Master's thesis in American literature. My task was to analyze the poetry of a nineteenth-century Spiritualist medium, Lizzie Doten, who claimed that her poems had been dictated to her by the spirits of Edgar Allan Poe, William Shakespeare, Lord Byron, and Robert Burns. It did not take long to discover that the poetry itself could not withstand much in the way of intense analysis, but I became very interested in the religious movement, nineteenth-century American Spiritualism, which had inspired Lizzie Doten's poetry and provided the theological assumptions that informed the content of the poems.

In my search for information about Lizzie Doten, I turned more out of desperation than wisdom to the writings published by the Spiritualists after the beginning of the movement in 1848. I read their biographical writings, their pamphlets and periodicals, and their interpretations of the theological implications of the movement. Through these writings I found myself in theological conversation with the Spiritualists, and I began to comprehend that for them, the spirit manifestations that had attracted so much attention to the movement were not ends in themselves. They provided the physical evidence of life after death necessary for the formation of a scientific religion—a new religion that did not contradict the findings of science but at the same time promised the consolations of religion. In reading descriptions of the religious doubts that occasioned their conversion to Spiritualism as well as the renewal of faith that followed, I came to understand the Spiritualists as entering a culture-wide conversation about the criteria a religious-belief system must meet in order to make sense, to cohere with human experience and intellectual developments in disciplines outside theology, in the middle of the nineteenth century.

The contributions of the Spiritualists to nineteenth-century theological discourse were more derivative than original and barely sophisticated enough to survive into the twentieth century. But their efforts made it clear to me that theological discussion in the United States goes on in arenas not confined to the institutionalized ponderings of the established religions and the academy. This early experience with Spiritualism, in fact, prompted my move from the study of literature to the study of religion in American culture, particularly new religions and their beliefs. It convinced me that to concentrate on the beliefs of new religions is to enter a three-way conversation about theological concepts—with the new religions, with the established traditions, and with the larger culture—conversations in which the voices of the new religions are loudest rather than piping up now and then from the periphery. The more I learned about the theologies of new religious movements, the more I became convinced that, whatever the combination of historical, sociological, and psychological complexities that have contributed to the formation and growth of new religions in America in the last hundred and fifty years, the theological dimensions of these religions must also be taken seriously.[1]

As a student of religion, my understanding of what comprises "theology" is quite broad as I apply it to the new religions. I am drawn to contemporary definitions of theology that tie its work not to the explication and interpretation of specific doctrines, particularly Christian doctrines, but to the more general task of ordering reality in light of that which the particular system understands as the ultimate measure of all things—that which is the measure of everything else. I find ethicist James Gustafson's interpretation particularly helpful, because it makes room for a variety of definitions of God or ultimate reality and because it takes seriously the cultural dimensions of theology. "Theology," Gustafson says, "is an effort to make sense out of a very broad range of human experiences, to find some meaning in them and for them that enables persons to live and to act in coherent ways." Theology, he says, "speaks to the limit-questions of not only human experience, but also our knowledge of nature." For Gustafson, theology is both practical and "speculative." If its ways of construing the world cannot be tested in the same ways as those of science, nonetheless its adequacy can be judged "by the kind of direction it gives to human action, by the degree of coherence it provides for understanding the meaning of human life in the presence of 'ineffable mystery' or 'being itself' or the 'God who acts in history' or what have you."[2]

I am also compelled by Gordon Kaufman's speaking of theology as "human work," as an imaginative and constructive enterprise. "Theology," he says, "is done by men and women for human purposes, and theological work is always assessed, therefore, by human standards invoked by human beings." Kaufman denies that theology has ever been "simply the translation and handing on of tradition."[3] Both Gustafson and Kaufman are Protestant theologians who do their work within particular communities of faith, but their definitions of theology provide the student of religion with perspectives about the nature of theology that are useful in looking at religious movements that fall outside the boundaries of what is considered orthodox Christianity.

In order to look at the new religions as contributors to theological reflection in American culture, this book is organized as a series of theological conversations in which the voices of the six new religious movements mentioned above predominate. The purpose of these conversations is threefold. The first is to provide information about the beliefs of the new religions, to ask, simply, "What do we have here, theologically speaking?" The second is to use that information in order to interpret the ways in which the new religions have understood themselves as providing alternative answers to theological questions—about God or ultimate reality, evil, human nature, the world, death, and the requirements for living a moral life. The third is to speculate about some of the cultural influences that have enlivened the theological imagination in America to the point where, according to the founders and subsequent interpreters of new religions, it can no longer be contained within the boundaries of orthodoxy.

If the term "conversation" seems too naively genteel a word to apply to the subject of new religions, a topic that has been characterized by a great deal of acrimony in the popular press and in much scholarship as well, I am consciously attempting to set a more moderate tone for this work without trying to deny the controversy which has attended many discussions of new religions. I am guided in this enterprise by the discussions of theologian David Tracy, who has done extensive work on the subject of theological conversation in a pluralist culture. In his own interpretation of the need for theological conversation, Tracy assumes that the partners will emerge from among the world religions, "the classic expressions of the human spirit," not from among religious movements which have been around for relatively few years. But his description of the requirements for genuine conversation, that we reach out to the "hard concreteness of the other" and that the conversation partners let the subject matter take over, cannot help but be useful criteria in a more volatile situation. "Conversation occurs," says Tracy, "only when we free ourselves for the common subject matter and free ourselves from the prison of our vaunted individualism (expressed in either the timidity of self-consciousness or the indecent desire for self aggrandizement)."[4]

Tracy does not use the term "conversation" to refer to exchanges in which very little is at stake. For him genuine conversation is both serious business and an infrequent occurrence. "A conversation," says Tracy, "is a rare phenomenon even for Socrates. It is not a confrontation. It is not a debate. It is not an exam. It is questioning itself. It is a willingness to follow the question wherever it may go."[5] For Tracy conversation does not preclude confrontation. In fact, it demands confrontation as part of the whole, and I have included in the conversations within the following chapters arguments of many sorts—arguments which follow from letting the theological questions guide the conversations.

In order to accomplish my task—to find out what is going on theologically in the new religions and "to reach out to the hard concreteness of the other"—I have concentrated on an analysis of primary sources, although I have benefited greatly from a variety of secondary sources that will be cited along the way. I have tried to stay as much as possible with interpretive sources that the new religions have intended for their own members as much as for outsiders, but I have also made use of pamphlets, question-and-answer booklets, and home-study courses published primarily for inquirers. As far as volume of sources is concerned, there is unevenness. The amount of excellent material, both primary and secondary, about Mormonism, for example, is overwhelming. By comparison, there are many fewer scholarly treatments of Christian Science written either by members or by outside interpreters. Sources for the study of Theosophy, particularly contemporary interpretations, are becoming more plentiful all the time, and there is a great deal of material to be found on Unification beliefs, written both by members and by outside interpreters, primarily because the Unification Church sponsors so many conferences in order to make known its beliefs and to solicit responses to its emerging theology. By contrast, whereas there are many works available on Scientology by its founder, L. Ron Hubbard, there are almost no interpretive sources written by other Scientologists; the few outside studies are sociological in emphasis. New Age materials are abundant, but they emerge from a variety of religious movements rather than just one, and they vary greatly in depth of treatment. A large number of the interpretations of New Age thinking that take it seriously and attempt to articulate its theological assumptions come from Roman Catholic theologians, and this pattern is reflected in the sources cited.

Something needs to be said, also, about the various interpreters quoted, for they vary in their relationships to the movements of which they are a part. I have made every effort to cite those interpreters from inside each movement who speak about particular beliefs with the greatest clarity and intensity and in ways I have judged to be characteristic rather than idiosyncratic. To put this a little differently, I have looked for those spokespersons who have best been able to get to the heart of a theological point. In some cases this requires letting the most traditional and the most liberal voices be heard within a single paragraph or section. For example, a discussion of issues of sexuality in Mormonism may require that I quote persons with very different perspectives in order to deal adequately with the complexities of a particular matter— the President of the Church speaking officially as well as a Mormon scholar writing in a journal that is considered so liberal as to be nearly outside the tradition.

In other cases, I often cite the founder or another early interpreter of a movement on a particular point along with a very contemporary interpreter. This approach has the drawback of blurring issues of historical development especially in regard to those groups with their origins in the nineteenth century. On the other hand, citing interpreters from various times in a movement's history has the advantage of pulling together themes that have persisted over the period of time in which a movement has existed. In any case, where developmental issues are significant for my own task of letting various voices be heard, I try to point that out.

Further, with regard to sources, my own interpretations of various doctrines were influenced by discussions I've had with members of new religious movements in different parts of the country—places like Wheaton, Illinois; Clearwater and Cassadega, Florida; Lake Geneva, Wisconsin; Tahlequah, Oklahoma; Pasadena, California; Charlevoix, Michigan; and Minneapolis and St. Paul, Minnesota. These discussions were not interviews; they were informal in nature. Nor were they consistently structured, although I always asked people what it was that first drew them to a particular movement or what made them stay if they were life-long members. I inquired about what beliefs or insights most moved them, what mattered most to them—what beliefs were coherent with their own life experiences and their understandings of how the universe operates. The people I talked to were theologically articulate, willing to interpret their beliefs, and happy to point me in the direction of the sources that had been helpful to them.

Acknowledgments

I have received a great deal of help in my research from members of new religious movements, particularly Alice Fleisher and Jack Corley of the Unification Church, Mary Lynne Wolfe of the Church of Scientology of Minnesota, the Reverend Barbara Everett of the Aquarian Light Church, the Reverend Carol Parrish-Harra of the Light of Christ Community Church, and David Fossum of the Church of Jesus Christ of Latter-day Saints. They were willing to assist me, even though I indicated that, although I would do my best to be as accurate as possible about beliefs, I might not always end up describing their movements as they hoped I would. I would also like to express my thanks to Kelly McShane, who introduced me to Common Ground, a fellowship of Christians and Jews in northern Illinois that describes itself as guided by New Age thinking. I am indebted to the Association of Theological Schools for a travel grant and to United Theological Seminary of the Twin Cities for a six-month sabbatical. I am grateful to Jeanne Schaaf Strickland who pored through social-science research on new religions looking for studies whose results might affect my understanding of theological matters. I have had stimulating discussions about new religions with friends and colleagues in American studies and in various branches of theology and religious studies, among them James B. Nelson, Bruce Forbes, and Wilson Yates. Mary Potter Engel, Jean Ward, and Clyde Steckel read parts of the manuscript and made many helpful comments. Catherine L. Albanese and Stephen J. Stein read the entire manuscript and not only made excellent suggestions but helped to restore the kind of perspective that flies out the window when one has worked on a project for a long time. Roberta K. Gladowski also read the whole manuscript and helped to make the process of early revision not only useful but fun. Paul and Irene Bednarowski made many trips to Minneapolis to babysit while I made use of my travel grant, and Sara Bednarowski, our niece, spent a summer being companion and chauffeur to our children. As always, Keith, Betsy, and Paul make sense of everything else.

ONE

Introduction

New Religions and the
Theological Imagination

This book is a comparative study of the theologies of selected new religions in nineteenth- and twentieth-century American culture: Mormonism, Christian Science, Theosophy, Unificationism, Scientology, and New Age thought. It is also a pursuit of the workings of the theological imagination in American culture across the boundaries of the established religious traditions.

I define the theological imagination as a creative human capacity—and an inclination—to formulate meaning systems, models of the universe, by which men and women are able to orient and interpret their lives. Broadly, the task of the theological imagination is twofold: to articulate an understanding of our circumstances as human persons in the world, including our relationship to whatever power orders the world, and to formulate the proper response to these circumstances.[1] The constructs—the meaning systems—that emerge from the creative work of the theological imagination must have the capacity to touch the heart as well as to compel the intellect and to suggest ways of being in the world.

The work of the theological imagination in American culture is grounded in certain universal questions as they have been expressed in Western culture. What is the nature of the divine or the ultimate? How is the divine made known, if at all, in the world? What is the make-up of the cosmos? What are the origins of evil and suffering? What does it mean to be human? What are the limits and the possibilities of human nature and of human knowledge? What is the meaning of death, and why do we have to die? What happens after the death of the body? What must we do to live a moral life, one which accords with the nature of reality as we understand it?

At the same time, the theological imagination is culture-bound. It must formulate its answers to universal questions within the context of particular times and places. It is tied not only to pivotal historical events, scientific discoveries, and economic and political developments but also to the concepts of the predominant religious traditions of a culture. As Gordon D. Kaufman points out, "the idea of God with which any particular individual works is always a qualification and development of notions inherited from earlier worshipers and prophets, poets and thinkers."[2]

To say that the theological imagination is tied to the religious traditions of a particular culture does not mean that it operates only within the established traditions of that culture. The theological imagination is unfettered by orthodoxies. The point of this study, in fact, is to demonstrate that new religious movements cannot be seen as emerging from "the margins" of cultural conversation about theological matters. Instead, their founders and interpreters must be seen as participants who choose to join in theological conversation in the culture. They join in because they understand themselves as having new revelations to offer, new models of the universe that will address the inadequacies of those meaning systems, religious and secular, that are presently available.

What are the cultural circumstances from which the religious movements in this study as well as other new religions have emerged? Those movements with their origins in the nineteenth century could not escape an awareness of growing religious pluralism in American culture. Joseph Smith, for example, chronicled his own difficulties with competing denominations in the early part of the nineteenth century as he attempted to find one which adequately responded to his own religious seeking: "priest contending against priest, and convert against convert; so that all their good feelings one for another, if they ever had any, were entirely lost in a strife of words and a contest about opinions."[3] Among so many religions, people asked, can one be right or true? Can any be right or true? Adding to this problem of pluralism by the latter end of the century was growing knowledge about the nature of religion itself as a human phenomenon that tended to relativize the truth claims of any particular religious movement.

Neither could the founders and interpreters of new religions ignore the rapidly increasing power and prestige of the sciences, the emergence of evolutionary thought as a system for explaining the workings of the natural world, and the growing prominence of a materialistic world view. For many, all these factors pointed to unbelief as a more intellectually respectable and even morally preferable option to religion for understanding the nature of reality and the meaning of life. Science provided evidence for its statements about the nature of reality. Religion demanded faith in that which could not be demonstrated. "Suffice it to say," said nineteenth-century minister George Chainey, "that the time came when the principal doctrines of Methodism became to my mind false, to my conscience immoral, and to my heart utterly repulsive."[4]

The religious movements that have come into existence since the second half of the twentieth century have inherited these realities and have others to contend with as well. Among them are the development of psychology to explain human nature and motivations; the continuing power of science but also a growing disillusionment over its promises and fears that its dangers might outweigh its blessings; medical advances that have extended human life but have also raised questions about the actual definition of "life"—when it begins, when it ends, and what is meant by "quality of life"; grave concerns for the environment; terror over continuing ideological conflicts of a global nature, which could result in global war and our own extinction.

The theological interpreters of both centuries have experienced wars, economic depressions, disillusionment, and even despair about the mission of a nation whose birth and continuing identity has been tied to the workings of God's providence. And they have had to continue to interpret, likewise, those experiences of human limitation and powerlessness—death, sickness, oppression, natural disasters—that are part of all human history.

All of these factors, the particular and the universal, have acted as catalysts for the theological imagination in the last hundred and fifty years of American culture. They have called for interpretations of God, human nature, and the world that make sense in the face of intellectual, historical, political, economic, sociological, and psychological developments which seem to call into question the insights religion has been able to muster in order to interpret human existence adequately.

For the established traditions, the interpretive task has required grounding not just in the traditional theological questions but in the symbols of the tradition as well. In an on-going process the Christian denominations in particular have needed, first, to articulate and re-affirm the truths that each considers absolutely essential to its identity, the "kerygma" of the tradition as some theologians refer to it. And, in doing so, each denomination has also had to struggle to accommodate its body of doctrine to the demand that it "make sense" even if in a metaphorical way at this time in history. These interpreters have needed to call on the theological imagination to give new life to the traditional symbols, to counteract what many have seen as the bankruptcy of theological language. Process theology, various liberation theologies—feminist, black, Latin American—even the "death-of-God" movement of the 1960s, can all be seen as efforts of the theological imagination to retain the coherence of the established traditions. At bottom, the established traditions have had to argue even for the relevance of membership in a religious faith community at a time when religion has become one among many different meaning systems available in the culture.

By contrast, the new religions must exercise the theological imagination in order to draw out the implications of new revelations. Their founders and interpreters say, in effect, "We cannot make sense of the universe nor can we adequately answer questions of an ultimate nature or interpret human experience without new information or insights or perspectives about what God or the ultimate is like and about who we are as human persons—revelations that go beyond that which is contained in the Hebrew and Christian scriptures and the traditional interpretations of them by the established religions." Thus, the interpretive task of the new religions is to systematize the revelations of their founders, to elucidate the potential of these new revelations to offer alternative interpretations of terms such as "salvation," "redemption," "enlightenment," "atonement," and "sin," to say nothing of "God" or the "Absolute." The new systems not only incorporate the essential insights of the founder but also contain both explicit and implicit refutations of the beliefs of the established religious and secular models of reality.

There is another dimension to the theological imagination as it is enlivened by its encounter with the universal questions of Western religion and with the circumstances of American culture. That is the tendency to ponder theological concepts in terms of polarities. Deconstructionist theologian Mark C. Taylor speaks of the Western theological tradition as resting upon "a polar or, more precisely, a dyadic tradition." Taylor claims that "the history of religious thought in the West can be read as a pendular movement between seemingly exclusive and evident opposites." As Taylor describes it, the theological treatment of polarities has been different from that of philosophy, which has tended to see the polarities as equal in value. Theology, on the other hand, establishes a hierarchy among the opposites, "an asymmetrical hierarchy in which one member governs or rules the other throughout the theological, logical, axiological, and even political dimensions."[5] Thus the polarities, among them God/world, divine/human, good/evil, spirit/matter, body/soul, sin/salvation, determinism/freedom, and individual/community, are in tension with each other. For some theologians, Paul Tillich, for example, this tension can be creative. For others, like Taylor, this hierarchical polarization has rendered theological thinking incapable of the kind of fundamental change necessary to contemporary circumstances. From my perspective, as a student of religion and particularly of new religions, I would claim that dyadic thinking continues to stimulate the theological imagination in American culture.

If dyadic thinking is characteristic of Western theological thought, that tendency has been reinforced in American culture and particularly in regard to religion. I do not want to argue that this inclination is uniquely American. Like many of my colleagues in American studies and in American religious history, I am increasingly finding assumptions of American exceptionalism more contrived and constraining than liberating.[6] But I do want to maintain that this mode of thinking is at least intensely American.

Even a superficial reading of American religious history yields a lengthy list of encounters within and among religious groups that are framed in terms of a dyadic framework: Puritanism and Arminianism, Puritanism and Quakerism, Calvinism and Unitarianism, deism and revivalism, Unitarianism and Transcendentalism, the "warfare" between science and religion, modernism and fundamentalism, creationism and evolutionary thought, and liberalism and conservatism. In broader terms, theologians speak of the Protestant and Catholic sensibilities. The Protestant sensibility, as Sallie McFague describes it, is "metaphorical" in nature, and "tends to see dissimilarity, distinction, tension and hence to be skeptical and secular, stressing the transcendence of God and the finitude of creation." The Catholic sensibility is inclined to be "symbolical" or "analogical" and thus "tends to see similarity, connection, harmony and, hence, to be believing and religious, stressing the continuity between God and creation."[7]

American scholarship in the field of religion is animated, also, by the contemplation of polarities. Catherine L. Albanese has written a well-received textbook on American religion in which she draws on the energy created by thinking about religion in American culture in terms of the one and the many.[8] In *Religious Outsiders and the Making of Americans*, R. Laurence Moore plays on the ways in which a religious identity and an American identity emerged for a variety of American religious groups—Mormons, Catholics, Jews, Christian Scientists, fundamentalists, Blacks, millennialists—by means of a transvaluation of the values typically associated with "insiders" and "outsiders."[9] Proceeding from a sociological perspective, Robert Bellah and four colleagues in *Habits of the Heart* posed the struggle between individualism and commitment to community as one of the most fundamental in the shaping of the American character.[10] In the analysis of a specific religious group, the Seventh-day Adventists, Jonathan Butler charts historical development in terms of the metaphors of boundlessness and consolidation. "Adventist development," he says, "has benefited both from periods of movement, spontaneity and disorder, and from those of stability and structure."[11]

I maintain that both the creative and the receptive aspects of the theological imagination in American culture have been shaped by dyadic thinking. In the chapters to follow, it becomes apparent very quickly that the new religions are caught up with assessing the relative values of head and heart, faith and reason, God and human, immanence and transcendence, spirit and matter, body and soul, good and evil, science and religion, freedom and determinism, sin and salvation, individual and community. The capacity of the new religions to speak convincingly to these tensions among the various polarities that tax the credibility of answers provided by the established traditions and by the secular culture has a great deal to do with which new religions have been sophisticated enough to survive and to grow.

The following chapters are concerned with the answers the new religions provide to universal questions as they have been articulated in nineteenth and twentieth-century American culture. The chapters are arranged not so as to cover each group separately but, instead, are based on pivotal questions. The second is devoted to conversation about God or ultimate reality, the third to human nature, the fourth to death and afterlife, and the fifth to ethical reflection and moral living. To organize chapters thematically around fundamental questions has several advantages. First, such an approach reinforces the idea of the new religions as participants in American theological discussion and as participants who pay serious attention to those polarities that have shaped Western theological thinking. When they articulate the details of their belief systems, the new religions are not doing so in a cultural void, and they are speaking not just to their own members. When they claim the need for new revelations or restorations or revitalizations, the new religions are usually very clear about what inadequacies in the established traditions and in the secular culture have occasioned their need to do so.

The thematic approach has the further advantage of providing an opportunity to intensify the questions themselves—to frame them in a variety of ways. Thus, the very questions common to many religious traditions—about the nature of God or ultimate reality and the deity's relationship to the world, for example—as they are asked and answered by the new religions can add their own dynamic to conversations about new belief systems in American culture in relation to the established traditions and to the secular culture.

Finally, to juxtapose the various answers of the new religions to common questions makes it possible to discern not only differences in their teachings but also overlapping patterns or themes that go beyond specific doctrinal differences and periods of time. Such a process can provide at least some historical perspective, particularly on those groups that have emerged in the last thirty-five years.

As far as the actual participants in these conversations are concerned, a word about their selection is necessary before going on to a brief historical account of each. First, I looked for variety of movements, although not in overwhelming quantities. I did not want just to analyze "positive-thinking" religions, for example, or occult groups. I was also concerned to include groups that have attracted thousands rather than hundreds of followers and have produced substantial written materials which can be analyzed both for unique doctrines and for common themes. In the case of the nineteenth-century movements, it seemed wisest to choose religious movements which have survived to the present, particularly since I am concerned with making comparisons that cut across historical periods.

From a more theoretical standpoint, I sought out groups from the nineteenth century that displayed differing cosmologies—that is, different understandings of what the cosmos looks like and the relationship of the cosmos to whatever power sustains it. Different cosmologies suggest the possibility of varying understandings of the value of spirit and matter, of body and soul, of the nature of the ultimate and its relationship to the world. In this respect, Mormonism, Christian Science, and Theosophy appeared to be excellent candidates. Furthermore, I wanted to pair up the nineteenth-century groups with cosmological counterparts in the twentieth century, not in order to say, "Look, history repeats itself," but to provide a basis for suggesting that common theological themes have emerged and reemerged over the course of one hundred fifty years, in spite of significant differences among the new religions in origins and specific doctrines. Thus, the cosmological partners I've chosen for Mormonism, Christian Science, and Theosophy are, respectively, Unificationism, Scientology, and New Age thought.

To explain further, Mormonism and the Unification Church both posit the existence of elaborate spiritual realms in addition to the material world. They hold that God is made known in history by means of special revelation as well as in the creation. To study the natural world, they say, is to learn something of God's nature, as well. Both maintain that special revelation did not end with the Bible. In both cosmologies, the world is looked on as the arena for salvific action on the part of men and women, not as a temporary abode to be denigrated for its impermanence. In fact, the eschatology of both these religious movements teaches that the earth will become as heaven and a dwelling place for the righteous.

By contrast, both Christian Science and Scientology make radical statements about the need for humankind to escape from the spiritually deadening and illusory bonds of earth and the flesh. In such world views, the constant quest is for the knowledge and understanding of the true nature of reality, with the assumption that the material world is not the place in which to achieve it.

Theosophy and New Age thought provide yet another cosmological view—the intertwining of the material and the spiritual. These religious movements speak of the dual process of evolution and involution, of the world issuing forth from the divine source in its many different manifestations and then returning to the source, the All. In this cosmological framework, the divine is immanent in the world and in human nature. The material world is not permanent and will eventually be subsumed into the One; nonetheless, as the world unfolds, every atom of it, animal, vegetable and mineral, is filled with the divine life.

These cosmologies, although by no means new in the history of the West, have been shaped in their specific details by the revelations of the founders of the six religious movements under consideration. Understood as new models of the universe by their members, they imply a critique of other models, and as will become clear in the following conversations, they have given rise to specific beliefs about the nature of God, the reality and the relative value of the material and the spiritual worlds, and the roles and obligations of humanity in these worlds. They provide excellent arenas for the exercise of the theological imagination on those polarities that undergird Western theological thinking.

The Church of Jesus Christ of Latter-day Saints, the Mormons, is the oldest of the groups under consideration. It is also the largest of the religions in these conversations, and it is growing, with perhaps five million members in the United States and more than a million in other countries.

It is elaborately and hierarchically organized.[12] Its teachings and practices, which have evolved over the more than one hundred fifty years of its history, have their basis in the series of visions that its founder, Joseph Smith (1805–1844), experienced in the 1820's, visions which gave rise not only to a new revelation, but to new scriptures and a new religious tradition as well.[13]

Influenced by both deism and revivalism, Joseph Smith's religious seeking began as a personal quest to discover which of many competing denominations contained the fullness of God's truth. Inspired by the biblical Book of James "to ask of God" if one were lacking wisdom, Smith sought divine assistance for his "extreme difficulties." He learned in a vision of the Father and the Son, who appeared as two separate male personages, that he must join no presently existing denominations, for "they draw near to me with their lips, but their hearts are far from me, they teach for doctrines the commandments of men, having a form of godliness, but they deny the power thereof."[14]

Joseph Smith also experienced subsequent visions during which he was informed of the existence of the golden tablets from which he translated the Book of Mormon—a history of the migrations of Near Eastern peoples to America in Old Testament times and of the eventual appearance of Jesus in America. For Smith, these visions constituted a mandate to form a new religion, a restoration, that would truly be an embodiment of the church founded by Jesus Christ, the teachings of whose true church had been obscured and lost by the corruptions and apostasies of multiple versions of Christianity. In 1830, according to the literature which the Church of Jesus Christ of Latter-day Saints distributes to those interested in understanding the movement, "the Almighty restored his church to earth again. He has raised up modern prophets and apostles to direct the work."[15]

I do not see evidence in the history of Mormonism that Joseph Smith set out to devise a new model of the universe—his concern was to restore the true church of Jesus Christ—but a new model emerged nonetheless based on what Sterling McMurrin calls a materialist metaphysics, one which by no means denies the existence of heaven or of spirits but sees the stuff of spirit as different only in degree from that of matter.[16] Based on this metaphysics, Mormonism gave rise to a belief system that uses many of the terms and concepts of Christianity, but which interprets them from a materialist or "common-sense" or "literal-minded" perspective, which de-mystifies traditional doctrines.[17] In Mormon theology, spirit is not some incomprehensible essence unavailable to human understanding but instead it is invisible matter. Eternity is not timelessness; it is endless time. God is not simply pictured in anthropomorphic images for the instruction and comfort of the faithful, but is, in fact, understood as an "exalted man" who has achieved divinity through his own efforts. The universe and its inhabitants are not created out of nothing but from pre-existing matter. Humankind is not depraved, existing conditionally, and destined for damnation unless saved by God's mercy but is capable of achieving godhood.

As a new model of the universe, Mormonism seems to have an unusual capacity to function as a kind of metaphysical tension breaker when it comes to putting together the components that make up its world view. It is a view which is grounded in "matter," in the practical and the earth-bound but which at the same time insists on the reality of the spiritual de-fined on its own terms. As an alternative world view in American religious history, Mormonism has demonstrated a powerful ability to generate val-ues and actions characterized as intensely American, while at the same time providing a theological system that sees itself as set apart from all other attempts, American or otherwise, to establish the kingdom of God on earth.

A variety of historical sources chronicle the way in which Mormonism, a kingdom set apart for various peculiarities in the nineteenth century, the-ological, social, and political, has become by the end of the twentieth cen-tury (and long before) an assimilated denomination.[18] But through that process, the thirteen articles of faith of the Church of Jesus Christ of Latter-day Saints, some of which will figure prominently in the following chap-ters, have remained the same since they were written by Joseph Smith and published in the *Pearl of Great Price*.

As Thomas O'Dea has pointed out, the Mormon theology and world view can be described as secularizing the sacred or as sacralizing the secu-lar. There is evidence for both interpretations.[19] When the voice of Mor-monism is heard in the conversations to follow, it will demonstrate more clearly the ways in which this new religion of the nineteenth century con-tinues to reconcile certain tensions that have obtained in traditional Chris-tianity.

The cultural context that produced the Unification Church, Mormon-ism's counterpart in this study, was not the United States but Korea. The movement's foundation rests on the revelation that its founder, the Rever-end Sun Myung Moon (b. 1920), received on a Korean hillside on Easter morning in 1936 at the age of sixteen, a rather striking parallel to Joseph Smith's first vision. According to Moon, Jesus appeared to him in spirit and asked him to be his instrument for bringing about a new age for hu-manity and to complete the work of redemption that Jesus had left unfin-ished when he was crucified. Moon's family became Presbyterian when he was ten, which helps to account for the Christian content of the vision.

Over the next nine years Moon developed his theological system, which was eventually published as *Divine Principle*. Like the *Book of Mormon* and Mary Baker Eddy's *Science and Health with Key to the Scriptures*, *Divine Principle* is perceived as an amplification of the Hebrew and Christian scrip-tures. Described as a combination of Eastern thought, Christianity, and Moon's own insights, the book is a systematic theology that presents a view of God and the world, of human nature, and of the human fall from the original perfection of creation. *Divine Principle* speaks to the purpose of history and categorizes historical periods in relation to their struggle to restore the creation to perfection. It also puts forth Moon's interpretation of the Second Advent.

The cosmology, the new model of the universe, which undergirds Unification theology and its understanding of reality, is based on a concept of the spiritual and material worlds as overlapping circles. This cosmology is esoteric and complex and involves an elaborate schema of the relationships among polarities: subject and object, spirit and matter, inner and outer, male and female, visible and invisible, cause and effect, and mind and body. In the relational dynamic of "give and take" among these polarities there is an intersecting of the physical and spiritual worlds, and the human is described as having both spiritual and physical bodies and senses.

This strong belief in the dual nature of reality in Unification theology helps to clarify the Unification interpretation of the human situation and what must be the proper response to it. According to Unification theology, history is the working out of a plan to restore a fallen creation to the dominion of God and to deliver it from the power of Satan. Jesus as the second Adam brought about the spiritual redemption of creation. The crucifixion, however, which Unificationists interpret as a tragedy rather than as the fulfillment of God's will, prevented a physical redemption. This is up to the Reverend Moon who must establish a perfect family on earth as Jesus was unable to do.

Out of the need for a restored creation and the physical redemption of the institutions of the world come most of the values espoused by the Reverend Moon and his followers: God-centered, traditionally structured families; an intense antagonism toward communism (this also comes out of Moon's prison experiences in Korea), which Unificationism sees as an amoral, godless political system dominated by Satan; and the need for unceasing, sacrificial work in the world.

The Reverend Moon's revitalization movement was one among many that arose in Korea during a time of political and religious turmoil. But Moon was the only prophet to see America as the logical arena for what he understands as the fulfillment of God's work on earth. The first Unification missionary came to the United States in 1959 to establish a study center, and Moon himself arrived for the first time in 1972. Moon has spelled out the connections he sees between the religious movement he founded and the destiny of America as a nation chosen by God to do salvific work for the rest of the world, both physically and spiritually. According to Moon, "America was formed to be the new flag bearer of God's will to move towards world salvation through cooperation between religion and state. . . . It is not by accident that America's founding spirit is described in the motto 'one nation under God.' This was already destined in the will of God." [20] As did Joseph Smith, Moon sees the American continent itself as playing a unique and essential role in the working out of God's will.

Joseph Smith had been dead for twenty-two years and the Mormons were long established in Salt Lake City with Brigham Young as their leader, when Mary Baker Eddy (1821–1910) injured herself in a fall on the ice in Lynn, Massachusetts, in 1866. If Joseph Smith's religious quest began in a personal search for assurance of religious truth, Eddy's journey was shaped by a desire for healing, both physical and emotional. Raised as a Calvinist but exposed in her searching to the healing methods of Phineas P. Quimby, Eddy went her own way in constructing the concepts of Christian Science. She was indeed healed of the injuries from her fall as she read a biblical account of one of Jesus' healings, and, in that experience, came to the insight, or discovery as she described it, that was to form the basis of Christian Science. What is wrong with the world and with our individual lives has its origins in a radical mistake of cosmic proportions about the nature of reality—that it is dual in nature, both spirit and matter, or, worse, that reality is comprised of matter alone.

According to the new understanding of Eddy, "there is not life, truth, intelligence, nor substance in matter." [21] Over and over again, throughout her writings, she stated her radical premise that matter does not exist. That which our senses seem to detect is illusory, because the material senses cannot detect Spirit and therefore give false testimony about the nature of reality. If matter is unreal, then, likewise, evil, sickness, pain, and death are unreal.

Like the visions of Joseph Smith, Eddy's experience of injury and recovery gave rise to a new revelation, a new scripture—*Science and Health*—and a new religious tradition. For Eddy, however, Christian Science was more than just a new understanding of how the universe operates—it provided a means to the healing of both sin and sickness. She had made a second discovery during her recovery in 1866: her ability to heal herself and others of pain, both physical and mental. As the implications of her discovery began to unfold, she described herself as apprehending "for the first time, in their spiritual meaning, Jesus' teaching and demonstration, and the Principle and rule of spiritual science and metaphysical healing,—in a word, Christian Science." [22]

Christian Science, like Mormonism, called for a new interpretation of traditional theological concepts. To say that Christian Science is in some way the opposite of Mormonism is obviously simplistic, but there is some validity in that judgment. Mormonism derived much of its theological and practical energy in the nineteenth century and continues to do so by embracing a materialist metaphysics and the evidence of experience and the senses as conducive to discovering ultimate truth. Christian Science has found that same kind of energy in its equally fervent embracing of spirit and rejection of matter. That these two movements have survived as they have into the twentieth century offers testimony that we have not yet finished with metaphysical concerns in American culture. The movements have not survived to the same extent, however, for it is apparent that while Mormonism has expanded greatly since its beginnings and continues to grow, Christian Science has never been a large church and is at the present time losing members. Stephen Gottschalk, an editor and consultant for the Church of Christ, Scientist, likens the process to a similar loss of membership taking place in the liberal Protestant denominations.[23] Christian Science does not publish its membership statistics, but a realistic estimate for the 1980's might be somewhere between 200,000 and 250,000.

There is a seventy-five year gap between the founding of Christian Science and the emergence in American culture of what was to become Scientology. If Eddy looked to the healing message of the Bible and her own metaphysical insight to provide the building blocks for her new model of the universe, L. Ron Hubbard (1911–1986), the founder of Scientology, turned instead to more contemporary sources. Scientology has its origins in a system of self-help that is spelled out in early form in *Dianetics: The Modern Science of Mental Health*, which Hubbard published in 1950. The book itself is a treatise on the workings of the human mind, the "anatomy" of the mind as Hubbard calls it. *The Basic Dictionary of Dianetics and Scientology* defines Dianetics as a system of thought in the following way: "Dianetics is *not* psychiatry. It is *not* hypnotism. It is . . . defined as what the soul is doing to the body. Dianetics is a system of analysis, control, and development of human thought which also provides techniques for increased ability, rationality, and freedom from the discovered source of irrational behavior stemming from the mind."[24]

Dianetics quickly began its evolution from what was chiefly a self-help method to a more specifically religious system known as Scientology and was registered for the first time as The Church of Scientology in California in 1954. The movement's critics continue to dispute Scientology's assertion that it is a religion, and the fact that the movement directs some of its strongest indictments against mental health professionals rather than the established religions reinforces this interpretation. But church publications are specific and pointed in their descriptions of Scientology as a religion. In "The Scientology Catechism," Scientology is defined as religious in all the traditional understandings of the concept including ritual, creed, and a "religious philosophy in its highest meaning as it concerns itself with Man and his relations to the Supreme Being and life, bringing Man to total freedom and truth."[25]

But, Scientologists explain, theirs is an "applied" religious philosophy that sees past traumas, physical or mental, as the barriers to rational behavior, spiritual development, freedom, happiness, and success. Scientology calls these past traumas "engrams." When engrams began to emerge in the auditing process—the question and answer procedure by which Scientology methods are used to elicit memories of past traumas—not just from the present life of Scientologists, but from past lives as well, Hubbard expanded the cosmology of Scientology to take this new information into account. It grew to encompass vastly complex hierarchies whose development had occurred over trillions of years of human history on the spiritual plane. At large in this cosmos are "thetans," defined by Scientology as spiritual beings who are free of the influence of cause and effect and of the restrictions of the physical world, but who are often not aware of these capacities and have become trapped in MEST (matter, energy, space, time). The goal of Scientology is the restoration of knowledge of the thetan's true identity. Important for understanding the cosmological scheme of Scientology are the Eight Dynamics, pictured as concentric circles, the innermost concerned with survival of self and the outermost with "the urge toward existence as Infinity."[26]

The esoteric vocabulary and the anti-matter elements of Scientology are present but muted in the movement's description of itself as a practical religious system. In *Scientology: What Is It?*, an advertising supplement inserted recently in the Sunday edition of large metropolitan newspapers, Scientology is described as "a study of knowledge" but on a fairly mundane level: "It is knowledge about why people have the problems that they have, about why people sometimes have trouble communicating with others, about the causes of upsets in life, about things that stop people from using all the abilities they do have."[27]

Hubbard died in January, 1986, a fact which suggests that Scientology will face over the next years the reality of that period of adjustment which follows the founder's death. Scientology publications continue to cite Hubbard not just as the founder but as the primary interpreter of the movement. The consequences of Hubbard's death are not yet discernible in the literature of Scientology, and whether there will be significant changes in the movement is not yet clear.

In terms of cosmology, Theosophy has taken a more moderate course, at least metaphysically speaking, than have the four movements thus far discussed in its pronouncements about the nature of reality and the relationship between spirit and matter. Theosophy in America had its origins in the founding of the Theosophical Society by Helena P. Blavatsky (1831–1891) and Colonel Henry Olcott (1832–1907) in 1875, the same year Mary Baker Eddy published *Science and Health*. The Theosophical Society in America was chartered in October 1886. Theosophy does not denigrate earthly life or life in the physical body as wholly illusory and useless for spiritual development. Theosophy holds that earthly life is an essential but less spiritually aware existence than is possible on more ethereal, less dense planes of reality. It does not teach, on the other hand, a thoroughgoing materialism, since it sees both spirit and matter as equal manifestations of the Absolute.

When founded, the Theosophical Society had three objectives as described by Blavatsky: "(1) To form the nucleus of a Universal Brotherhood of Humanity without distinction of race, colour, or creed. (2) To promote the study of the world's religion and sciences. . . . (3) To investigate the hidden mysteries of Nature under every aspect possible, and the psychic and spiritual powers latent in man especially."[28] A recent history of the Theosophical Society echoes these words of Blavatsky: ". . . this history of the Theosophical Society in America is, in a very real sense, the history of a small group of spiritually dedicated individuals; people determined to establish a nucleus of universal brotherhood and to encourage a search for truth in this world of illusions, dilemmas, sufferings, and satisfactions."[29]

It has been the aim of Theosophy to reclaim the ancient wisdom that Theosophists understand as having once formed the foundation of a civilization in which science and religion were united. By the late nineteenth century bits and pieces of this wisdom were thought to be scattered throughout the religions, sciences, and philosophies of the world. Theosophy works to revive and reassemble the ancient beliefs into a coherent system which mitigates the intellectual inadequacies, superstitions, and tyrannies of traditional religions and at the same time puts the reins on the arrogance of science. In the eyes of Blavatsky, science professed no need for the ancient past and rejected the reality of the spiritual. " . . . There must be somewhere," said Blavatsky in *The Key to Theosophy*, "a philosophical and religious system which shall be scientific and not merely speculative," and she claimed that "such a system must be sought for in teachings far antedating any modern faith."[30] It is a system that assumes a model of the universe in which the spiritual and the material are so entwined that it is possible to discern laws that apply to both. In their search for the laws that govern both the spiritual and material aspects of the universe Theosophists have devoted themselves particularly to the study of Eastern religions and the occult but to the sciences and philosophy as well.

Theosophy has survived into the twentieth century in spite of several scandals in the history of the movement and schisms from the original organization. It has also exerted considerable influence on contemporary New Age thought described below. In fact, the term "Perennial Philosophy" used frequently by New Age thinkers is also applied by some Theosophists to Theosophy itself as manifesting one particular form of the Perennial Philosophy. In 1980, Bruce F. Campbell estimated the membership of the three chief groups, the Theosophical Society in America (Wheaton, Illinois, with international headquarters in Adyar, India) , The Theosophical Society International (Pasadena), and the United Lodge of Theosophists (Los Angeles), at more than thirty-five thousand, the Adyar group being by far the largest (most of the materials for this study have come from this branch of Theosophy).[31] Today Theosophy continues to look to the past for knowledge about ultimate truth, but, as it did in the nineteenth century, it seeks to apply the ancient wisdom to contemporary issues.

Theosophists occasionally describe themselves as participating in the coming of the New Age, but it is not a term that is typically applied to that movement. "New Age," in fact, is not a new term in American culture. Christians have used it for centuries as a synonym for the kingdom of God, and the concept is well known among a variety of American religious movements—Swedenborgianism, for example. Since the 1960s, however, and particularly in the 1970s and 1980s, "New Age" has come to refer to an amorphous group of ideas and religious movements concerned with an evolving higher consciousness in humankind.

The difficulty of listing with confidence groups that can accurately be called "New Age" becomes apparent as soon as one looks at lists of New Age groups that others have already made. Writing for *Update: A Quarterly Journal on New Religious Movements*, which is directed primarily at Christians, but is also for scholars interested in new religions, Mark Albrecht applies the term New Age to a lengthy list of specific religious movements, which includes not only such groups as the Theosophical Society, the Anthroposophical Society, the Lucis Trust, the Church Universal and Triumphant, and Silva Mind Control but also, startlingly, Unitarianism.[32] In *The Encyclopedia of American Religions*, J. Gordon Melton devotes two chapters to "The Psychic and New Age Families" and includes the Swedenborgians, the Spiritualists, the Theosophists and various off-shoots of Theosophy, UFO groups, and drug-oriented groups.[33] In a recent article in *The New York Times Magazine*, Fergus M. Bordewich speaks of New Age movements as "a protean phenomenon that embraces cults like the Church of Scientology and the Unification Church. . . ."[34] From my perspective, categorization this broad makes it difficult to get at any of the distinctiveness of New Age thought.

For the purposes of this study, I take my cue on which groups to include from David Spangler, an acknowledged spokesperson for New Age thought, who defines New Age groups specifically as "intentional spiritual communities [which] espouse explicitly the idea of an emerging planetary culture based on human transformation."[35] As examples he lists the Findhorn Foundation in Scotland, which he calls the "grandmother of new age groups," the Chinook Learning Community in Washington state, the High Wind Association in Milwaukee, Lindisfarne in Massachusetts, and the Lorian Association in Madison, Wisconsin, with which Spangler is associated. My own list includes the Light of Christ Community Church of Tahlequah, Oklahoma, a group which refers to itself as both New Age and esoteric Christian in its teachings and which has affiliates in different parts of the country, among them the Aquarian Light Church in Minneapolis, Minnesota; the Institute in Culture and Creation Spirituality in Oakland, California, founded by Dominican priest Matthew Fox, which conveys New Age concepts from within the Roman Catholic tradition; and Common Ground, a fellowship of Christians and Jews in northern Illinois.

I want to concentrate on groups that have formed the intentional communities, whether residential or not, of which Spangler speaks and which articulate a concern for the furtherance of a planetary culture. Spangler, in fact, maintains that in the New Age communities about which he is knowledgeable, the phrase "emerging planetary culture" is replacing the phrase "emerging new age." Spangler defines "planetary culture" as the "possibility of a human culture . . . existing side by side in a complementary way with the different historical cultures of humanity, both enriching and being enriched by them. . . ."[36]

To see an emphasis on the formation of spiritual communities as an essential part of New Age thought in combination with the need for furtherance of a planetary culture and individual spiritual transformation sets aside for the purposes of this study those manifestations of New Age thinking which dominate the popular understanding of what New Age means and which Spangler refers to as "glamour," for example actress Shirley MacLaine's writings or the thoughts of Ramtha, the 35,000 year-old warrior chanelled by JZ Knight. By "glamour" Spangler means what he calls "the shadow side of the Age of Aquarius," which he sees associated with the "private world of ego fulfillment and a consequent withdrawal from the world." At this level, Spangler contends, New Age thinking "is populated with strange and exotic beings, masters, adepts, extraterrestrials . . . psychic powers and occult mysteries . . . conspiracies and hidden teachings."[37] Although such manifestations may be found in many New Age groups, they are only incidental, as Spangler sees it, to the more pressing concerns of a planetary culture. This is the stuff of best-sellers, of well known personalities, and Doonesbury cartoons, and it is not part of this analysis except in passing, primarily because these manifestations of New Age thinking do not yield the level of theological discussion necessary for inclusion in this study.

The cosmology that undergirds the New Age understanding of a planetary culture emerges from an understanding of the immanence of the divine. Depending on the particular group, the concept of immanence may find expression in an occult or Eastern world view reminiscent of Theosophy. Or, it may take form within the framework of a Roman Catholic or Anglican understanding of the sacramental nature of reality and of the relationship between the spiritual and material worlds.[38] Whatever the origins of their immanentist cosmologies, New Age theorists have in common a perception of this particular time in history as one of drastic change—paradigmatic change—that will affect all the institutions of the culture, not just organized religion. In *The Aquarian Conspiracy*, a widely popular book describing some of these changes, Marilyn Ferguson speaks of "a leaderless but powerful network . . . in the United States. Its members have broken with certain key elements of Western thought and they may even have broken continuity with history."[39] Ferguson refers to this network as the "Aquarian conspiracy," which she defines as a "benign conspiracy for the ecology of everything: birth, death, learning, health, family, work, science, spirituality, the arts, the community, relationships, politics."[40]

To aid the "ecology of everything," New Age thinkers call for the reform of most of society's institutions. They base this call on their indictment of the essentially dualistic view of reality they see as being imprinted on the psyches of those who participate in Western culture. This dualistic view that separates spirit from matter, male from female, body from soul, science from religion, reason from feeling has caused the fragmentation of cultural institutions and values in modern times. The New Age response to this fragmentation is a constant looking toward wholeness—individual, communal, national, and planetary. This emphasis on wholeness helps to account for the wide range of concerns addressed in New Age literature: healing, nutrition, comparative religions, ecology, physics, brain research, feminism, politics, the sociology of knowledge, and spirituality. Many New Age thinkers emphasize the urgency of perceiving reality in these more holistic ways.

New Age thinkers accuse the established traditions of contributing to dualistic thinking by walling off the sacred in a variety of ways—by depriving church members of access to spiritual experiences, by stressing an empty morality over transformation, and by preaching a doctrine of human sin that keeps men and women from recognizing the presence of God within. In protest, they claim for humankind the possibility of experiences on more spiritual planes of reality and of guidance from those both living and dead who are more advanced spiritually than we are (Spangler speaks at length of "John," the spirit being from whom he learns). While more traditionally Christian New Age groups, such as the Institute in Culture and Creation Spirituality, do not speak of spirit guides, they nonetheless offer instruction in a variety of techniques for seeking the divine within such as meditation, yoga, massage, and fasting.

Like Theosophy and Spiritualism in the nineteenth century, the New Age movement is particularly interested in the development and reform of science and the scientific method and in its appropriation for matters of the spirit. For New Agers, science functions in revelatory ways, not just as the dispenser of knowledge about the laws on which the physical universe operates, but as the supporter of New Age theories about wholeness and meaning in the physical universe.[41]

For anyone familiar with Theosophy and even with nineteenth-century Spiritualism, the New Age and its ideas do not, in fact, seem to be very new. But at this juncture in history there are two features that set this latest manifestation of what some have called the Perennial Philosophy apart: first, the application of New Age concepts to contemporary issues of a global nature, such as ecology, world hunger, and, particularly concerns about nuclear warfare and world peace, all of which have implications for the formation of a planetary culture; and, second, the broadening of a concept of immanence from one which must necessarily be tied to an occult or Eastern world view to one which, according to James Parks Morton, Dean of the Cathedral of St. John the Divine, makes it possible for "one to be an orthodox, incarnational Christian and at the same time become a 'universalist' (a 'catholic'), recognizing one's fellowship (one's communion) in the sisterhood and brotherhood of all creation."[42]

Contemporary New Age thought is both a continuation and an expansion of many of the theological and philosophical concepts that Theosophy pulled together and began offering to American culture in the last quarter of the nineteenth century. It captures the spirit of Theosophy's three objects—to establish a Universal Brotherhood of Humanity; to encourage the study of comparative religion, philosophy and science; and to investigate unexplained laws of nature and the powers latent in man—and reinterprets them for the last quarter of the twentieth century in terms of a planetary culture,[43] a coming together of religion and science, and a charge to humankind to recognize and to act out of its own participation and that of all creation in the divine reality that is made immanent in the world.

In the conversations that follow, the religious movements described above will provide many different answers to questions of an ultimate nature—different from each other and from the established traditions—but their motivation to do so proceeds from the same assumption, that is, that we need to think about both questions and answers in new ways which go beyond a reinterpretation of the theological concepts as they have been articulated in the established religions.

In the answers of the new religions it is possible to observe the work of the theological imagination as it responds to the stimulation of universal questions, to the circumstances of the particular cultural contexts of nineteenth- and twentieth-century America, and to the creative energy produced by the dyadic thinking which is so ingrained both in Western theological thinking and in American culture.

Who or What Is God Like?

Concepts of Deity in the New Religions

The theological imagination in the West and in American culture has been dominated by the concept of God put forth by the Hebrew and Christian scriptures and further shaped by what has come to be known as classical theism. Anthropomorphized as "Father," this deity's characteristics have been described in terms of polarities: just and merciful, loving and angry, rewarding and punishing, sovereign and good, capricious and constant, jealous and accepting, forgiving and judging, immanent and transcendent. Classical theism has ascribed to God's nature omnipotence, omniscience, omnipresence, and immutability. Contemporary theological literature, however, both scholarly and popular, questions whether this concept of God can bear up under the weight of human experience and modern science.

In 1972 the theologian Gordon D. Kaufman published a book called *God the Problem*.[1] In the first chapter Kaufman catalogued ten issues that face religious movements or individuals concerned with conceptualizing the "idea" of God or of ultimate reality at this time in history in the West. Some of the issues are theoretical in nature, among them linguistic, epistemological, and methodological concerns as to whether one can by any means know something about the referent of the term "god" and thereby engage in cognitively meaningful talk about God. Others are more existential and have to do with the contemporary experience of the "hiddenness" of God, particularly in the face of terrible evil and suffering, and the problems associated with traditional interpretations of God's power and sovereignty in view of the human desire for moral autonomy. Kaufman also raises questions of an intellectual nature posed for the modern person by doctrines of Christian theology such as the Trinity and the Incarnation.

If Kaufman sets forth issues facing the contemporary person who thinks about God and wants to talk about God and to live in accordance with a coherent understanding of God's nature, Charles Hartshorne, the process theologian and student of Alfred North Whitehead, gets to the heart of the matter in a different way. He claims in *Omnipotence and Other*

Theological Mistakes that we are faced by so many issues about the nature and knowledge of God because we have made grievous errors in continuing to interpret God's nature as it has been described by classical theism. Hartshorne particularly refutes classical theism's insistence on God as "Absolutely perfect and therefore Unchangeable," God as omnipotent, meaning "perfect in power," and God as omniscient, or knowing every detail of what will unfold until the end of history. Hartshorne refutes these "mistakes" in his book, which he intended for lay people as much as for professional theologians, and says that he was motivated to write it because of discussions with two educated women who were troubled by their experience of "absurdities in the idea of God" as put forth by classical theism.[2] He claims that this concept of God does not make sense, given what we know of how the universe operates and how we experience our own lives.

Kaufman and Hartshorne are academic theologians, but their observations are not so abstruse that they cannot be recognized in the concerns about the nature and knowledge of deity expressed by the six religious movements under consideration. All of them are engaged in making their own contributions to a culture-wide conversation that has taken place over at least the last two centuries as millions of Americans have struggled to define the meaning of "God" or of ultimate reality as those terms have been understood and interpreted in scripture and church tradition, in theological treatises, and in the prayers of the faithful. And they have, likewise, struggled to reconcile these interpretations with their own life experiences.

Just as do academic theologians and interpreters and defenders of the established traditions, the founders of new religious movements ask questions about the nature of deity or ultimate reality. Who or what is God and what are the deity's characteristics? Is God knowable or unknowable? Is God transcendent or immanent? Is ultimate reality personal in nature or impersonal? Is God just or merciful? Limited or omnipotent? Immutable or changing?

In putting forth their own answers to these questions, the new religions are spared the challenge of having to remain within the bounds of Judeo-Christian orthodoxy. But no less than the established traditions, a new religion must be watchful that its doctrine of deity or ultimate reality does not ask for a greater suspension of disbelief than the modern or post-modern intellect can tolerate and that it does not, either, appall the heart or the conscience. New doctrines of the divine must speak to the doubts occasioned by one of the most pressing dilemmas of classical theism: that an omniscient, omnipotent, unchanging, all-good, and transcendent deity has created what seems to be an ever-changing world filled more with pain than joy. They must respond also, at least in some fashion, to the question that the contemporary person knows too much not to ask: Is the knowledge of God that we have traditionally claimed simply knowledge of self and world, a creation of human longing?[3]

The reality of religious pluralism is testimony to the fact that there is no one way to meet these challenges, to answer these questions. There are only more or less satisfactory interpretations for individuals and communities. The accounts that follow are of the efforts of six new religious movements to define God or ultimate reality in response to the challenges—to formulate concepts of deity that deal with the dilemmas of classical theism and are acceptable to their followers both intellectually and affectively.

As an aside before proceeding, I would like to clarify that I do not intend to argue that in formulating new concepts of deity the new religions articulate their task as that of resolving the dilemmas of classical theism. Rather, as will become more apparent in the following pages, the understanding of God which emerges from classical theism is so dominant in American culture that it seems nearly impossible to discuss "God" or ultimate reality without at least alluding to it.[4]

MORMONISM AND UNIFICATIONISM: GOD AS LOVING FATHER

Given the differences of their origins in time and in space—early nineteenth-century western New York and mid-twentieth-century Korea— and taking into account very significant, even drastic, differences in their specific doctrines, Mormonism and the Unification Church come together at a surprising number of places in their understandings of who God is and how God can be known. In both religious movements, God is a father[5] who has been motivated by love to create the world and his human children. Both movements acknowledge that God's nature is revealed in the natural world; by studying nature we can learn something of God. Both also claim the necessity of special revelation through emissaries divinely chosen to transmit saving knowledge which is beyond the capacity of humankind to discern or acquire on its own. No matter what we can learn of God from the laws of nature and of science, says Bruce R. McConkie, one of the best known contemporary Mormon theologians, "God stands revealed or he remains forever unknown."[6]

But, by contrast with the traditional Biblical religions, Mormonism and the Unification Church claim that special revelation has not ended—that it was given to their founders, Joseph Smith and the Reverend Sun Myung Moon, and will continue to be given as needed throughout the unfolding of human history. In making this claim, neither movement rejects the Bible. They insist, rather, that all revelation is not contained in it. They hold that common sense, if nothing else, dictates that special revelation given thousands of years ago is not sufficient for modern times. "Wherefore, because that ye have a Bible," says the *Book of Mormon*, ye need not suppose that it contains all my words; neither need ye suppose that I have not caused more to be written."[7] Unification sources agree: "Naturally, the quality of teaching and the method and extent of giving the truth must vary according to each age, for the truth is given to people of different ages, who are at different spiritual and intellectual levels."[8] Therefore, these two movements state, there must be new revelations for new historical circumstances.

Mormons and Unificationists are well aware that to claim a dispensation, a special revelation from God in modern times, is to ask for both controversy and ridicule. Further, it imposes an intellectual burden on followers that one might think would exceed the capabilities of contemporary people—to believe, as Mormonism puts it, that "the heavens are open" and that the divine continues to make itself known to those on earth. A contemporary Mormon interpreter, Hugh Nibley, considers that the claim to a new revelation has aroused much more hostility in the last century and a half than polygamy ever did: "The ferocious denunciations from press and pulpit, the incitement of mobs, and the stampeding of legislatures always rested on one thing alone—that incredible fact that in an age of modern enlightenment, universal education, and scientific supremacy there should be found co-existing with Christian civilization a community of primitives so ignorant, deluded, and depraved as to believe in revelation from heaven and the operation of charismatic gifts."[9]

If incredulity greeted nineteenth-century claims of a revelation from heaven and continues to do so as Mormonism has developed into the late twentieth century, so, likewise, has the claim of Moon and his followers of special and direct revelation been rejected by the established traditions and by the secular culture. In fact, given the controversy that has surrounded the Unification Church in the United States, the following statement from *Divine Principle* sounds like understatement: "It may be displeasing to religious believers, especially to Christians, to learn that a new expression of truth must appear" (p. 9).

Mormons and Unificationists are both admonished to expect skepticism from the culture at large and from the established religions and even to feel no surprise at encountering it in their own hearts. In each case members are counseled to guard against it by means of prayer, for in each system, faith in the founder's revelation precedes certain knowledge of the truths of the movement. "If we believe that what Joseph said was true," says one Mormon writer, "we can again possess the simple essentials for an understanding of God."[10] To make the same point, the Unification Church cites New Testament stories about persons who were healed by Jesus. First they believed in Jesus's power, and then they were healed: "Faith was the condition that allowed God's healing energy to work. Without that faith, no healing was possible. Likewise Matthew tells us that Jesus promised people seeking for answers that they would find them, but urged them first to do their part."[11]

What is the saving knowledge about God's nature or character that has been revealed in Mormonism and Unificationism? For Mormons the revelation centers around the fact that God is a man and has a body. The Father God who was revealed to Joseph Smith in his first vision in 1820 is an actual male person with "body parts and passions" who shared the Godhead with Jesus, his son, another distinct personage with a body who also appeared to Joseph Smith at the same time. The Holy Ghost is a third personage who has a spirit body but no physical body. This god is a deity who is transcendent, but not totally "other." He is the literal father of our spirit bodies, as he is the literal father of Jesus. And this is a god who was once human and is now, in the famous phrase, "an exalted man who sits enthroned in yonder heavens."[12]

Mormons interpret Joseph Smith's vision of God the Father and God the Son as functioning to clear away centuries of obscurantist Christian theology, the product of church councils and deliberately mystifying theological interpretations of the doctrine of God. These had served to conceal the fact that God has a body and is a former human person who has achieved divinity. Thus, Joseph Smith's vision served not just as a revelation, but as a restoration—in fact, as the foundation for the restoration of the Church of Jesus Christ. At the moment of Joseph's vision, says Mark E. Peterson, "for the first time in many centuries, a mortal being knew what God looked like, and heard his spoken words. It is only with this sure knowledge that Joseph Smith was able to proceed with his great assignment."[13]

If the Mormon concept of God as a male person who continues to reveal himself in history seems to the contemporary person to ask more by way of faith than is tolerable, at another level logical difficulties fall away, as is the case with most systems, if one is able to accept the major premises. Mormons can dispense with the effort to ponder God's absoluteness and immutability, for theirs is a god that changes and develops—that exists in time and space and who operates, as Sterling McMurrin explains in his discussion of the "finiteness" of the Mormon God, "within the ongoing processes of the universe."[14] Further, the understanding of Father, Son, and Holy Ghost as separate personages, enables Mormons to hold on to the trinitarian language and concepts of traditional Christianity without imposing the immense intellectual difficulty that the doctrine of the Trinity has presented for Christians—that they accept the mystery of three persons in one God. McConkie explains that "there are three *Gods*—the Father, Son, and Holy Ghost—who, though separate in personality, are united as one in purpose, in plan, and in all the attributes of perfection."[15] Mormon writings indicate, also, that it is not an error to think of the persons of the Trinity in a hierarchical way. If the three persons are united in purpose, plan, and perfection, Jesus, who is understood as the creator of this world and as the Jehovah of the Old Testament, nonetheless has fewer responsibilities than God the Father, and the Holy Ghost has fewer responsibilities than Jesus.[16]

Perhaps even more important at the affective level is the capacity for the Mormon doctrine of deity to dispense with what Charles Hartshorne names as another of the "mistakes" of classical theism, and that is what he calls God's "unsympathetic goodness." God's love for us "does not . . . mean that God sympathizes with us, is rejoiced or made happy by our joy or good fortune or grieved by our sorrow or misery."[17] By contrast, the god of Mormonism *feels*—not just love, but empathy, for this god was once human and knows what the mortal life is like. "Mortals are not traveling a course unknown to God," says David Yarn. "He knows mortality not merely analogically but by his own experience."[18]

"Is this not a God who is limited?" traditional Christianity has asked of Mormons. Such is indeed the case, concedes Mormonism, if we are comparing the god of Mormonism to the omniscient, omnipotent, never-changing god of classical theism. Mormons, too, use the terms "omniscient, omnipotent, and omnipresent" to refer to God, but such attributes are relative in the ever-changing, ever-progressing cosmos of Mormonism. It is, in fact, Mormonism's very willingness to accept a concept of deity that appears limited by contrast with classical theism that helps it to formulate a theodicy which dissociates God from the origin and continuing existence of evil. Mormons do not have to ask: "If God is so good and so powerful, why is there so much evil in the world?"

In the Mormon understanding, God co-exists in a cosmos of many worlds and many gods and eternally existing elements with which he must contend. In fact, the Mormon god is not the creator of the universe out of nothing, but its organizer out of chaotic elements. Thus God must deal with certain realities which have been given from all eternity. Among these givens is evil which, as Bruce McConkie explains, "had its beginnings in pre-existence." Evil is an eternal part of the Mormon cosmos; it does not have to be explained away by means of a doctrine of deity. As Sterling McMurrin elaborates, it is not so much that evil *must* exist in the Mormon system as that it *does* exist, and God, like the rest of us, must struggle against it.[19] Mormons also understand much of the pain and suffering in the world as issuing from bad choices, the product of agency, or free will, which has been misdirected or misinformed. McConkie attributes evil to "false worship" and seems to be speaking primarily in this instance of what might be called moral evil—"unrighteousness, fornication, wickedness, covetousness, maliciousness, etc." He claims that "the reason for all this evil is that men no longer worship the true and living God."[20]

Whatever the causes of evil, God is not responsible for them; certain things are beyond his power. And, far from diminishing the devotion of Mormons to a god who cannot do away with evil completely, such an understanding seems to forge an even stronger bond of identity with and devotion to the divine. As will become more apparent below, a similar situation prevails in Unificationism.

Like Mormonism, Unification theology understands God's nature as reflected and made known in human nature, but it would disagree with Mormonism on its doctrine of God as a deity of flesh and bones. The Unification concept of God derives not from a materialist and finitist metaphysics that seems to have been at least in part a product of the American frontier, but from a more Eastern orientation toward the nature of reality. Yet both religions agree that God's nature can be discovered in the physical universe: "We will determine what God's nature is like by finding the characteristics common to all entities in his Creation," says *Divine Principle*.[21]

Unificationists can discern God's nature in the things of the world because they understand both God and the creation as made up of dual characteristics that do not exist independently of each other but in harmonious, reciprocal relationship. Chief among these dualities—or better—polarities, are *sung sang* and *hyung sang*, Korean words which are translated to mean the inner and outer aspects of each being. In addition, there are the polarities of positivity and negativity and of male and female. The reciprocal action among these polarities emerges from God, the First Cause, as the creative energy which produces humankind and the world. Unification theology speaks of the relationship of God to creation as that of subject to object, and it sees this relationship, in turn, as pervasive throughout creation: in atoms, in the individual human person, in families, and in nations. Those same polarities which constitute God's nature exist in every particle of the universe.

There is intense emphasis in Unification theology on harmony as well as creative energy among polarities, for at its best, the subject-object relationship at every level is characterized by "give-and-take action." As it is explained in *Divine Principle*, "when the subject and object aspects within a being and between beings are engaged in give-and-take action, all the forces necessary for its existence, reproduction, and action are generated."[22] As Unificationists understand it, since the human fall men and women have been engaged in give-and-take action with Satan rather than with God. This relationship with Satan accounts for the state of the world at this time in history, and it introduces a strong element of tragedy into the Unification understanding of the nature of God that is completely absent from Mormon theology.

This focus on a distorted relationship between God and humanity helps to make clear why it is that the concept of God's heart is at the center of the affective appeal of Unification's doctrine of deity, just as the understanding of God as a male personage is so essential to Mormonism. "In the Bible," says one Unification source, "we find that more fundamental than God's intellect and will is God's heart for humans."[23] It was heart, God's capacity for love, that motivated him to form us and the creation in the first place in order to experience reciprocal love in a subject-object relationship. It was also heart that prompted God to make us free to accept or reject the divine love. Thus, it was heart that resulted in God's making himself vulnerable to the possibility that we might be tempted away from his love and that "his tender, sensitive" heart would be left "grieving over a lost relationship of love."[24]

As it turned out, we did indeed misuse our freedom, succumb to the temptation of Satan, and reject God's love. In doing so, we have limited our capacity to receive and respond to God's love. And, according to Unification theology, we have also limited God's ability to reach out to us. The truth about God, then, as Unificationists understand it, is that "God has been hurt more than man. God feels crushed by the historic betrayal of His loved ones—as any lover would be. The injured heart of God, the suffering of the Heavenly Father, is beyond measurement and human comprehension."[25]

Just as is the case in Mormonism, the god of Unificationism is a god who feels. He is not a deity immune to the suffering inflicted on him by humanity's transgressions; he is not a deity characterized by "unsympathetic goodness." Because of God's suffering, we are tied to God, not just as children are connected to a loving parent but as radically disobedient children who must restore their father to the happiness of which they have deprived him and which is rightfully his.

Is a god who truly suffers in this way not a weaker god than the god of classical theism, of traditional Christianity, who feels no pain? Most Unificationists would testify that this is not how they understand their God. In Unification theology, a God who suffers is greater than one who has no feelings.[26] Unificationists acknowledge that their concept of a god who suffers from human failings and who does nothing to interfere in the tragic errors of men and women might be seen as a god with limited powers, but they see these limitations as self-imposed in the interest of human freedom: "So it is not that God *cannot* fulfill his will by himself; we should understand that he *will* not fulfill it without his children's cooperation."[27]

The understanding of God's broken heart and self-imposed limitations has more than an affective function in Unification theology. Along with the doctrine of the Fall, it also provides the basis for this movement's theodicy. Whereas the god of Mormonism is up against evil as one of the eternally existing elements which he did not create, Unification theology introduces evil into the system as the result of the human fall from the original creation. Unificationists feel strongly the need "to defend God against the accusation that God is responsible for evil, has unnecessarily allowed evil to exist, and either willingly or helplessly will allow extreme suffering to exist forevermore."[28] It is humankind and not God who are responsible for the evils and sufferings of the world, although, as will become more clear in the following chapter, it is within the capabilities of human nature to restore the creation to the perfection that existed before the Fall: "However evil man may have been through all ages and in all places, he at least has the power of conscience remaining in his inmost self. . . . If there were no conscience left in fallen men, God's providence of restoration would be impossible" (*Divine Principle*, p. 30). Thus, however dire and tragic the circumstances of the world as brought about by human sin, God in Unification theology is still with us and for us.

In summing up some of the common themes in the Mormon and Unification doctrines of God, it is easily possible to do so in such a way that these two new religions seem merely to be adding their voices to those of traditional Christianity. Since both consider themselves Christian[29]—Mormonism as a restoration of Christianity and Unificationism as a revitalization—this is not surprising. Both movements claim the Biblical mode of revelation in that they understand God as made known through the creation and by means of special revelations in history to chosen prophets. They proclaim God as a personal deity, a loving father, and they use traditional God language—omniscience, omnipotence, omnipresence—to describe a deity who is a god of history—one who puts forth a plan for salvation that shapes individual human lives and integrates all of human history as well into the divine purpose. If asked whether the god we know is only self and world, Mormons and Unificationists would answer with an emphatic negative. Their god is a transcendent deity with being apart from that of humankind, and, if asked whether God is responsible for evil, their answers, although emerging from different metaphysical assumptions, would be negative again.

But Mormonism and Unificationism maintain their agreement with these broad outlines of traditional Christianity precisely by departing from the tradition at other crucial points, particularly in the matter of God's nature. The theological imagination as it is manifested in these two movements finds much of its grounding in the outlines of the Judaeo-Christian story of the loving God who is active in history, but that same imagination has been stimulated by the new revelations of its founders to reconceptualize this god so as to escape some of the dilemmas of classical theism.

Both movements refute the once-for-all character of special revelation in traditional Christianity: for Mormons and Unificationists, a God who continues to reveal himself in specific ways in modern times is more comprehensible and defensible than the god whose special revelation ended during apostolic times. And they have intensified, again by different means, God's personal characteristics in order to bring a transcendent deity closer to earth and to forge a stronger bond of affection between God and humanity. In intensifying and elaborating on the personal characteristics of God, both movements are willing to give up deities who are unlimited in their powers, at least as compared with the god of classical theism. And, in a kind of transvaluation of values, both of these new religions make of God's limitations a source of greatness rather than weakness.

CHRISTIAN SCIENCE AND SCIENTOLOGY: GOD OUTSIDE THE WORLD

Christian Science and, to a much lesser degree, Scientology set for themselves the same task as Mormonism and Unificationism: to make the experience of God available and comprehensible to humankind. But they do so by putting forth radically different understandings of what God is like and how God is related to the world. Both movements see the material world as that which obscures the knowledge of God rather than reveals it, and it has been one of the primary tasks of their founders to demonstrate that this is the case. Christian Science and Scientology speak of their founders (and their founders speak of themselves) not as having been granted a special revelation of supernatural origin which imparts information either forgotten or heretofore unknown but of having discovered or gained insight into the principles and laws upon which the universe operates. Such knowledge, rather than faith in the sense in which Mormonism and Unificationism and traditional Christianity use the term, becomes the basis for understanding the nature of God, particularly in Christian Science, and for the healing practices of both religions.

This much said about common themes, it needs to be indicated at this point that, in contrast with Mormonism and Unificationism, the similarities in the understanding of God in Christian Science and Scientology are exhausted very quickly—and this in spite of their cosmological agreement that the physical universe obscures rather than reveals knowledge of a spiritual nature. This is the case primarily because Christian Science is a system which radically reinterprets, but nonetheless retains, the language of traditional Christian theology. It is also a system in which an understanding of the doctrine of God is essential for comprehending the entire world view. Scientology, on the other hand, leaves the language of theology behind and develops the vocabulary of L. Ron Hubbard, which has its own unique characteristics as well as much in common with the language of psychology. Further, the doctrine of God in Scientology is of minimal importance for understanding the rest of the system; the chief emphasis is on the working of the human mind and the nature of the thetan.[30]

It is almost impossible to overestimate the importance of understanding what Christian Science means by "God," if we are to comprehend all the other aspects of Christian Science, but it is also important to know what the movement rejects of traditional Christian concepts of deity. First, just as intensely as much of traditional Christianity, Mormonism and the Unification Church defend their belief in a personal God. Christian Science, on the other hand, rejects both the possibility and the desirability of an anthropomorphic deity.

"A corporeal God," says Mary Baker Eddy, "as often defined by lexicographers and scholastic theologians, is only an infinite finite being, an unlimited man,—a theory to me inconceivable."[31] It is just this cosmic and tragic error on the part of traditional Christianity, according to Christian Science—its insistence that God is anthropomorphic in nature and can be apprehended at least in part by the senses and by study of the world—that has trapped us into unnecessarily perpetuating both sin and sickness. As Eddy explains in "The People's Idea of God," the worship of God as "form" has led to all of the limitations that our false understanding places on human experience: "Idolatry," she says, "sprang from the belief that God is a form, more than an infinite and divine Mind; sin, sickness, and death originated in the belief that Spirit materialized into a body, infinity became finity, or man, and the eternal entered the temporal."[32]

Second, Christian Science denies that God is the creator of the material world and that we can understand at least something of God's nature by observing it. Matter is not real, according to Christian Science, and God did not create the world of matter as we know it. Because the material world is illusory, fragmented, limited, filled with suffering and death, it tells us nothing of God, who is none of these things. And our senses, thought by those who hold to the reality of the material world to supply us with genuine knowledge of reality and of God, in truth lead us badly astray for they convince us that the material world is something other than an illusion. As Eddy puts it, "on the theory that God's formations are spiritual, harmonious, and eternal, and that God is the only creator, Christian Science rejects the validity of the testimony of the senses, which take evidence of their own—sickness, disease, and death."[33]

While the members of many other religious traditions are advised to look around them at the world and to discern from what they observe at least something of God's nature, Christian Scientists are admonished to refrain from doing exactly that.[34] DeWitt John, a twentieth-century interpreter of Christian Science, explains that "Christian Science does not start with the material world and then try to discover what kind of God would have made it. Right here it parts company with rationalist theories, human philosophies, and, indeed, most religions. Christian Science starts solely with God as the infinite, all-pervading, supreme, eternal, omnipotent, original Cause of all that truly is. . . ."[35]

What, then, is the definition of God with which Christian Science starts? In *Science and Health*, Eddy answers the question, "What is God?" in the following way: "God is incorporeal, divine, infinite Mind, Spirit, Soul, Principle, Life, Truth, Love."[36] This definition incorporates what are called the seven deific synonyms in Christian Science, and they are in no way intended to indicate that God is divisible or many-parted. She goes on to say, these synonyms "refer to one absolute God. They are also intended to express the nature, essence, and wholeness of Deity" (p. 465). Neither are these synonyms intended to indicate that God is so abstract as to lack love for humankind. If God is not a person in Christian Science, God nonetheless has personal characteristics, chief among them Love. It is Love that speaks to the nurturing aspects of God in Christian Science, the means by which we know God as both mother and father. "Love," as DeWitt John explains it, "is not simply an attribute of God, but the very essence of the divine Being; Love is the fountain of infinite goodness."[37]

Because God is one and indivisible, it is erroneous in Christian Science to speak of God as "in" the world or humankind. "Science," says Eddy in *Science and Health*, "reveals Spirit, Soul, as not in the body, and God as not in man but as reflected by man" (p. 467). God's creation is not "the world" as we know it in all its imperfections. Nor is the physical human body part of God's creation. Because God is perfect, the creation, which is God's reflection, is also perfect. Therefore, it is beyond possibility that the world as we know it could be God's creation, and it is a distortion of Christian Science teaching to say that God is "in" the world.

It is the definition of God as Mind, Spirit, Soul, Principle, Life, Truth, and Love, that undergirds the theodicy of Christian Science, for it totally dissociates God from any connection with evil and human suffering. On the other hand, it leaves unanswered, at least at first glance, the question as to how God is revealed. If God cannot be known in the world, then how can God be known at all? The answer lies in the nature of Christian Science healing. In Christian Science theology there is a reciprocal relationship between healing and the knowledge of God which emerged from Eddy's own experience of healing and revelation in 1866: to be healed is to understand the true nature of God, and to understand the true nature of God is to be healed. Eddy not only recovered from the injuries of a fall, she gained essential insight into the nature of God, the true meaning of the Bible, and the role of Jesus Christ in Christianity.

The implications of her discovery of God's nature were not instantaneously made known to her. Over the course of three years and using the Bible as her "textbook," Eddy describes herself as growing in her understanding that God was not a personal being responsible for the ills of the world; that the Bible was not an account of supernatural healings which occurred outside the parameters of divine law; and that Jesus was not a miracle worker but a "natural and divine Scientist" who understood the perfection of God's creation. And she learned, above all, that God does not create or intend or permit evil and pain.

Christian Science literature is filled with testimonials of healings that demonstrate this understanding of the nature of God, from the final chapter (one hundred pages long) of *Science and Health* to the sections called "Testimonies of Christian Science Healing" in the *Christian Science Sentinel*, a weekly journal, and *The Christian Science Journal*, a monthly publication. The weekly Wednesday-night services in Christian Science churches serve the same purpose—to demonstrate the efficacy of the Christian Science understanding of deity.

In spite of all the emphasis on healings, Christian Scientists and students of the movement are warned that the healings which take place, both from sin and from suffering, must not be the primary focus in Christian Science, for their true purpose is to reveal God. As Stephen Gottschalk explains, "the purpose of this healing is not human improvement so much as it is the renewed God-experience it makes possible. Thus, the complaint that some people use Christian Science in order to attain secular ends of health, wealth or success is a wholly valid one from the point of view of Christian Science itself."[38] Robert Peel, the well-known Christian Scientist and biographer of Eddy, reinforces this point in *Spiritual Healing in a Scien-*

tific Age by saying that "the healing of disease is incidental to the progressive spiritualizing of one's whole life and thought."[39]

Christian Scientists, however, are not asked to "believe" before they can be healed. Eddy herself was healed without knowing at first why her healing had occurred. And in *Science and Health*, she cites cases of people being healed before they knew anything about Christian Science. For example, a man cured of "valvular heart disease" testified: "I was completely healed before I had met a Scientist, or one who knew anything about Christian Science, and before I had read a line of any other Christian Science literature except one leaf of a tract" (p. 609). This is not to say that Christian Science discounts the need for constant and continuing study of the Bible and of *Science and Health*, for these are the primary acts of piety of the movement. Greater knowledge of God results in more healing.

Because they understand healing from sin and sickness as emerging from the experience or knowledge of God, Christian Scientists do away with that form of piety which expresses itself in Christianity as "petitionary prayer," or asking God for assistance or for favors. Christian Science maintains that we cannot ask God to free us from suffering, for, if we only knew it, we cannot be in bondage to something which does not exist. Further, such a prayer implies that God has something to do with evil. John explains that "it is never the Christian Scientist's aim in prayer to somehow change God, or to obtain His special intercession in some human situation. Rather, it is to bring human consciousness into communion with Truth, which annihilates discord."[40]

In spite of the promise of healing associated with Christian Science's doctrine of deity, and in spite of its divorcing God from any connection with evil and suffering, Christian Science acknowledges that its concept of deity may appear to many, both inside and outside the movement, as too abstract to touch the heart. As one member put it, "many believe it to be a transcendental, ascetic, or joyless attitude of thought."[41] In refuting this interpretation, the same member, a Sunday-school teacher, spoke of a teenager and her friends who admitted that they didn't want to get "too spiritual." The instructor responded by reminding the students of the basic teachings of Christian Science: "That it reveals the allness and infinitude of good and the nothingness of evil; that God is the only creator and that man is His child, wholly good and spiritual, the object of His love and care . . . that God is the all-wise and loving Father-Mother of us all and provides for each one everything he needs. No one who turns to God is deprived of any good thing; he loses only false material beliefs which are harmful."[42] To know these things about God, says Christian Science, is to be healed.

In articulating its doctrine of deity, Christian Science asks of its members what would seem to be an overwhelmingly difficult task—to disregard the evidence of the senses and of what the rest of the world agrees to be the nature of reality in order to come to an understanding of who God is and what God does. Christian Science, in fact, has not lessened the intensity of that demand in the years since its founding. On the other hand, Christian Science, as it explains itself, does not ask what traditional Christianity has historically required: that we incorporate into our understanding of God's nature some explanation for the existence and persistence of evil in the world.

The healing that takes place in Scientology is of a different order from that of Christian Science. It can similarly be looked on as deliverance from ignorance, in this case from the power of engrams, the unremembered pain of earlier traumas, but in Scientology healing is not directly dependent on the knowledge of God's nature. In fact, Scientology is something of a wild card among the religious movements in this study, because it claims that God, who is identified with the Eighth Dynamic, the farthest out of the concentric circles of existence and survival, is not yet very well known, at least not by means available through Scientology. "In Scientology," say the members, "we believe that God exists. As to the form in which He exists, we do not yet have dogma. As the Church of Scientology evolves, who can say what might be discovered."[43] Lack of precise knowledge about God's nature does not keep Scientology from affirming the importance and social necessity of believing in a divine being. "The Scientology Catechism" quotes Hubbard as saying that "no culture in the history of the world, save the thoroughly depraved and suffering ones, has failed to affirm the existence of a Supreme Being. It is an empirical observation that men without a strong and lasting faith in a Supreme Being are less capable, less ethical, and less valuable to themselves and society."[44]

How does Scientology interpret its unwillingness to elaborate on a definition of God's nature? One response is to emphasize what it sees as the narrowness and exclusivity of any one definition, for "of necessity any definition of God must be subjective, and we make no attempt to define God as a reality for all people. It would only be possible, theoretically, to be totally aware of God, in all manifestations, when one was spiritually advanced."[45] Such a stance reinforces Scientology's description of itself as a "pan-denominational applied religious philosophy" which urges its members to remain, if they wish to do so, in denominations of which they are already members.

Stronger, though, than the sense that God's nature has yet to be discovered in its entirety or that one definition of God is too narrow to serve the variety of constituents that Scientology wishes to attract is the contention that it is up to the individual to discover for himself or herself an understanding of God that makes sense. Scientologists see a contrast between traditional theologies that depend on "a revelation or disclosure which is directed towards a specific object—the nature of God and His will for men" and the process of self-discovery in Scientology, by which "a person expands across the dynamics to the 8th or God dynamic, which he reaches through his spiritual advancement."[46]

References to the Eighth Dynamic are the closest one is likely to come in conversations with Scientologists about God. It is a phrase that comes from the cosmology of Scientology and its understanding that "survival . . . the basic single thrust of life through time and space, energy and matter," is divided into eight dynamics or fundamental urges that motivate and structure human conduct. Organized in concentric circles, the dynamics expand outward to the eighth, "the urge toward existence as infinity. This is also identified as the Supreme Being." Again, Scientologists do not claim to be able to say much about the Eighth Dynamic, other than that it exists. They caution that "the science of Scientology does not intrude into the dynamic of the Supreme Being."[47]

In spite of an absence of systematized writings about God's nature, there are some clues about general perceptions. In an interview granted for a book on Scientology, the Reverend Robert H. Thomas, identified as a "leading authority in Scientology in the U.S.," stressed that it is up to the individual to discern "the relationship of God to the community of souls," but, he expressed his own opinion: "God, I think, is to be considered infinite potential." The limits on that potential, according to Thomas, are imposed by the individual's particular viewpoint and understanding.[48]

In such a description there may be some coincidence of understanding with the concepts of insight and discovery into the nature of God or Mind as they are articulated in Christian Science, as well as common themes relating to the individual's ability to know the nature of God depending on spiritual advancement, but Thomas speaks of his own source of speculation on this subject as coming from Tibetan Tantrism: "As the Tantric conceives it, mind is the noumenal source of all phenomena. All aspects of creation, regardless of how tangible and objective they may seem to be in the physical world, are only thought images projected by God or by other entities."[49]

Another clue to Scientology's understanding of God's nature, as much as there is a common understanding, comes from Robert H. Thomas's writing in another source, a twentieth-anniversary booklet on Dianetics and Scientology. In the introduction Thomas says: "Awed by the immensity of the natural world around him, Man has, for aeons, yearned to discover in himself a cosmic origin nearer to his Gods. Can there be some imprisoned divinity in him which survives the suffering and erosions of time?"[50]

There have also been some references to Scientology's understanding of God in recent newspaper articles about Hubbard's death and about court cases in which the Church of Scientology has been involved. These articles contain bits of information, apparently compiled from court documents, which indicate that Scientology teaches its more advanced members "that Earth was called Teegeeach 75 million years ago and was among 90 planets ruled by Xemu, who spread his evil by thermonuclear bombs." Xemu destroyed selected inhabitants of these planets and "implanted seeds of aberrant behavior to affect future generations of mankind."[51]

Thomas's reference to the possibility of "imprisoned splendor" in humankind in addition to stories of Xemu as an ancient and powerful ruler of the world suggest a gnostic flavor in Scientology that is intensified by its anti-matter stance, which will become more apparent in the next chapter, on human nature. It may be the case that, as Scientology makes its teachings about God more public, there will be illuminating parallels between this movement and the mythology of gnosticism, with its emphasis on a dualistic cosmology of concentric circles, its understanding of the world as created by a malignant deity who is inferior to the true but unknown God, and its understanding of men and women as ignorant of the spark or fragment of divinity that dwells within.

At the moment, an attempt to converse with Scientology about its doctrine of deity yields the reminder that, in this belief system, vastly more emphasis is given to the god-like nature of the human person and to the workings of the human mind than to the nature of God. It follows, then, that discerning the nature of God as it is implied in occasional sources in Scientology might better be accomplished indirectly through a study of its teachings on human nature than by interpolating a cohesive definition of God that may not have much cogency for Scientologists. As a result, Scientology's theodicy, if that is even an accurate word here, can only be inferred from the interpretation of human nature to follow in the next chapter as Scientology provides its answers to questions about the cause of human unhappiness and suffering in the world.

In popular assessments of both Christian Science and Scientology, it is frequently suggested that both these movements are, in fact, modern gnosticisms. This is a claim upheld primarily because both movements concur in their understanding of the material world as yielding error, negative rather than positive knowledge. I have already indicated my suspicion that looking at Scientology from a gnostic perspective in order to understand better its concept of deity might be a productive exercise. But, in attempting to understand what alternative interpretation of God Christian Science offers, to describe it as "gnostic" is misleading.

Whereas gnosticism and Scientology are dualistic systems, positing the reality, if not the equality, of spirit and matter, the theology of Christian Science is monistic in nature. A study of Christian Science yields no concept of a demiurge who has created the material world as a trap for humankind. If there is anything villainous in Christian Science, it is mortal mind; but mortal mind refers to a false mode of thinking rather than to a cosmic antagonist of God. Further, the god of Christian Science is not a radically transcendent, "unknowable" god as is the god of gnosticism. Nor is this god immanent. As Stephen Gottschalk points out, these concepts that are so meaningful in orthodox Christianity are not very illuminating when it comes to talking about Christian Science.[52] Because the creation—which is not synonymous with the material world—is a reflection of God, it is not something separate and apart from God. There is nothing for God to be

transcendent from or immanent in. There are no concentric circles of existence or reality, as in gnosticism, which separate God from the creation.
Finally, there is no hint in Christian Science of "imprisoned splendor" in
humankind—of bits of the divine broken off and lodged in human persons
who are ignorant of their true natures. Rather, the knowledge of God is
present, but it must be ever more realized through repentance, prayer, and
study and made manifest through healing of both sin and sickness.

This comparison with gnosticism, which is fruitful in the case of Scientology but misleading as a way of understanding Christian Science, reinforces the conclusion that Christian Science and Scientology offer alternative interpretations of God that are not only different from that of the
established traditions and from the concepts of deity in Mormonism and
the Unification Church. They are also very different from each other, as is
the relative emphasis they place on the need for a well-defined doctrine
of God. For Scientologists such a doctrine need not be elaborate. For Christian Science, there is no more important concept—the rest of the system
is unintelligible without it. In the matter of theodicy, Scientology does not
provide us with enough information to do more than speculate about how
God in this system might or might not be related to evil. Christian Science, on the other hand, in separating God from all connection with the
illusory world of matter, sin, and suffering, devotes a major part of its theological creativity to clarifying its insistence that God is "All-in-All." There
is no room in the universe for evil. But, however different they may finally
be from each other, Christian Science and Scientology offer alternatives to
all those religious traditions that find God or ultimate reality at home in
the material world. They have constructed systems in which God and the
world must be seen as apart from each other and, thus, each must be interpreted in that light.

THEOSOPHY AND NEW AGE THOUGHT: GOD WITHIN

In presenting another set of alternatives to understanding the nature and
knowledge of God, Theosophy and New Age thought demonstrate some
kinship with Christian Science and, to an extent, Scientology in putting
forth a non-anthropomorphic concept of deity. H.P. Blavatsky echoes
Mary Baker Eddy in her denunciation of the limitations of the anthropomorphic God of the Biblical religions. "Theosophists," Blavatsky says, "reject the idea of a personal or an extra-cosmic and anthropomorphic God,
who is but the gigantic shadow of *man*, and not man at his best, either.
The God of theology, we say, is a bundle of contradictions and a logical
impossibility. Therefore we will have nothing to do with him."[53]

But the resemblance between the Theosophical and New Age concepts
of God and that of Christian Science, particularly, cannot be sustained be-

yond their agreement that God is one, unlimited, absolute, and non-anthropomorphic. Theosophy and New Age thought go on immediately to make known their understanding that the ultimate reality referred to as the One, the Absolute, the All, is made manifest not just as spirit, but also in matter: "The One Reality," say the Theosophists, "is everywhere, in everything, from atom to universe. There is nothing that is not in some degree a part of this life."[54] Thus, that which is emphatically and absolutely denied by Christian Science—that God is "within" the material world—constitutes the major affirmation of how the ultimate is known in Theosophy and in New Age thought.

As Blavatsky puts it, the Absolute cannot be depicted at all. It is "inconceivable, indescribable . . . unconditioned, unlimited in any way whatsoever. This Absolute is always unmanifest, eternal, infinite, and with no attributes. Possibly the only positive thing that can be said about it is that it IS, and that it is ALL Potentiality."[55] The Absolute pours itself out, manifests itself, in the polarities of spirit—or consciousness—and matter. The interaction between these polarities has created not just the universe we know, but many universes. Why such interplay happens in the first place we have no way of understanding. As Robert Ellwood interprets it, such a question is beyond the reach of Theosophy or cosmology to explain, but he sees Theosophy as supplementing the speculations of the physical sciences which posit that in the coming into being of the universe, consciousness is present immediately along with matter. "Consciousness," says Ellwood, "wants to experience awareness, to know. . . . Consciousness needs to set part of itself outside itself, so to speak, so that there can be knower and known, subject and object. The universe, then, is a mirror in which the Absolute—God, if you wish—knows itself."[56]

There seems at first to be some parallel here with Unification theology's understanding of the creation as brought into being by God's desire to have an object for his love; but the pouring forth of the One into the Universe is not understood in Theosophy as bearing any resemblance to the doctrine of creation in Judaism or Christianity. Theosophists see the One as the cause of the universe, but not as its creator. When asked who it is that created the universe, Blavatsky responded that, "No one creates it. Science would call the process evolution; the pre-Christian philosophers and the Orientalists call it emanation; we, Occultists and Theosophists, see in it only the universal and eternal *reality* casting a reflection of *itself* on the infinite Spatial depths."[57]

The Theosophical view of the coming into being of the universe as a manifestation of the One has obvious implications for the possibility of experiencing the divine. If God, or the One, is made manifest in every atom of the universe, then it is also manifest in us as human beings. In fact, according to Theosophy, the One is most intensely present in men and women, because Theosophy understands consciousness of the Absolute, or the "rootless root," as Blavatsky sometimes called it, as developing through an evolutionary process. God-consciousness in the rock is not nearly so developed as it is in the Higher Self of human consciousness.

Theosophy does not claim that knowledge of the One is total. The One is not only immanent in the world; it is also a transcendent Absolute never totally manifested. A contemporary Theosophist, Shirley Nicholson, explains: "According to theosophical teaching, this transcendental Source is not identical with nor exhausted by creation; only a portion of the All becomes involved in the process of manifestation." She goes on to say that, "While we can never fully know the unreachable Divine Source in its purity, we can approach it in its numberless manifestations, as it 'thrills throughout every atom and infinitesimal point of the whole Kosmos.'"[58] In other words, Theosophists are not pantheists, and interpreters of the movement take pains to make that clear.

Nonetheless, Theosophists accept the reality of "God within," and the experience of God is accessible to us precisely because we are human beings whose consciousness has developed to the extent that a knowledge of God within is therefore available to us. As another contemporary source puts it, "Virtually all normal people have the possibility of a conscious, even if limited, contact with the eternal spirit which is their inmost centre and essence. The contact may be dim, confused, uncertain, but it exists. . . . and it can be reinforced and strengthened, or starved and impoverished."[59]

How can we, in fact, reinforce and strengthen our experience and knowledge of God within rather than starve and impoverish it? In one sense, Theosophists would answer, the gradual acquisition of such knowledge is inevitable as spirit and matter, the manifestations of the divine, evolve over the billions of years required for the dual process of evolution and involution: the outpouring of the One into the many and the return journey back to the One. But the development of Higher Consciousness, of God-experience, can also be hastened and intensified.

Ellwood refers to of the search for the "great path," which moves us in the direction of fuller being and greater wisdom and joy. The search for our true natures, for God within, begins with the acknowledgment that we are not simply matter and that, indeed, we are manifestations of the One. He describes this knowledge as "an awareness greater than words, awareness which begins with awareness of one's own true nature as one with the true nature of the universe in which we are embedded. . . ." We must find our way further on the path by means of the "twin pillars" of wisdom and compassion. According to Ellwood, wisdom is concerned with that very capacity to recognize the indwelling of the One in our own consciousness, and he defines compassion as "the recognition of the oneness of my life with another's, that what the other suffers I must suffer, and that what I do for the other I do for myself, since our lives are bound together and share the same nature."[60]

Theosophy tells us that we are not totally on our own in our search for the path and our true natures, for we are assisted by each other and by the Masters or Mahatmas, defined by Blavatsky and other Theosophists as those who have achieved the wisdom, compassion, and spiritual advancement sufficient to free them from the earthly cycle of birth, death, and reincarnation. They have chosen, however, to serve as guides for those still on the path to union with the One.

However optimistic Theosophy may be about our innate capacity for the experience of God, the development of higher consciousness in all aspects of reality, and the evolution of the entire cosmos toward the One, it nonetheless acknowledges the existence of evil and speculates about its origins. Theosophy denies that the One or the Absolute is in any way responsible for evil or that it inflicts senseless suffering on men and women.

Ellwood writes of evil in terms of "disharmonies," or things that "ought not to be," or development that is being obstructed. Sometimes, in fact, what appears to be evil is simply a matter of misinterpretation—in other words, that which seems to be evil to us may make sense if we know the whole cosmic plan, or, if we at least have confidence that there is such a plan. Death, for example, which seems to us to be a tragedy, "may really be greater life." In a system that is evolutionary in principle, that which seems to us to be evil may have its own function in the over-all scheme: "The blockage of one creature or species may be only for the sake of allowing a more advanced form to take its place as evolution moves forward."[61]

Ellwood finds in Blavatsky's *Secret Doctrine* suggestions that when the One pours itself out into consciousness and matter and is manifested in the many, the possibility for discord and lack of harmony becomes real, "For when many different entities—atoms—molecules, and the rest—are put into play, any number of possible combinations will emerge, not all benign to one another."[62]

As Ellwood points out, however, and as other Theosophists indicate, all evil, particularly moral evil, cannot be attributed to the laws of evolution, karma, or dualities. Christmas Humphreys quotes A. P. Sinnett in *The Mahatma Letters* as attributing evil to human origins: "The real evil proceeds from human intelligence. . . . Humanity alone is the true source of evil. Evil is the exaggeration of good, the progeny of human selfishness."[63] Blavatsky reinforces both the concept of human responsibility for evil and evil as disharmony in *The Key to Theosophy*. In a discussion of karma, she reiterates the Theosophical understanding of the oneness of reality and evil as the result of discord: "We say that 'Good' and 'Harmony,' and 'Evil' and 'Disharmony,' are synonymous. Further we maintain that all pain and suffering are results of want of Harmony, and that the one terrible and only cause of the disturbance of Harmony is *selfishness* in some form or another."[64]

Whatever the various origins of evil and suffering in the world, Theosophy does not attribute them to the Absolute. To understand the nature of evil in this system does not require explanations for how it is that God either causes evil or permits it to occur, because the unchanging, limitless Absolute does not participate in those processes from which evil emerges. At the same time, Theosophy's understanding of God as the Absolute One provides the means for eradicating evil. This will be accomplished not just by the inevitable working out of the evolutionary journey on the part of human persons and the cosmos but because such an understanding of the One demonstrates on "logical, philosophical, metaphysical, and even scientific grounds that . . . all men have spiritually and physically the same origin, which is the fundamental teaching of Theosophy."[65] This knowledge, say Theosophists, must eventually move us to accept that we can do nothing without affecting every other dweller, animate or inanimate, in the cosmos, and, because that knowledge is within us, we must eventually come upon it. Sooner or later—and needless suffering is caused if it is later—we must acknowledge that, if we do evil to another, we do it to ourselves as well.

New Age thought follows very much in the footsteps of Theosophy in affirming a doctrine of God's immanence and of its inevitable implications: the interrelatedness of all aspects of nature and human culture and their eventual reunion in the One. New Age thought is similar to Theosophy, also, in its inclination to pay more attention to the implications of immanence than to elaborate on the attributes of the Absolute. New Age thought, nonetheless, is much less systematized than Theosophy, and its basic themes must be sought in a variety of disparate sources and religious movements. They have not coalesced into a body of materials equivalent to *The Secret Doctrine*, nor are there one or two persons, such as Blavatsky, whose written works provide the basis for most other interpretations. Still, to one familiar with the themes of Theosophy, particularly in reference to ultimate reality, the similarities with New Age thought are apparent.

The immanence of the One in the universe and particularly in human consciousness is one of the most dominant themes of New Age thought. In *The Aquarian Conspiracy*, Marilyn Ferguson speaks of the concept of "God within" as "the oldest heresy," in which "God is experienced as flow, wholeness, the infinite kaleidoscope of life and death, Ultimate Cause, the ground of being . . . the consciousness that manifests as *lila*, the play of the universe . . . the organizing matrix we can experience but not tell, that which enlivens matter."[66] New Age thinkers see themselves as yielding to the unassailable mystery which lies behind the origin of the One. Ferguson says that "we need not postulate a purpose for this Ultimate Cause nor wonder who or what caused whatever Big Bang launched the visible universe. There is only the experience."[67]

Such emphasis on experience alone leads some New Age writers to dispense with ontological distinctions between God and the manifested universe that Theosophists and many New Age thinkers are anxious to maintain, for serious New Agers do not see themselves as pantheists. One popular New Age author, Shakti Gawain, lists synonyms, such as God,

Spirit, Higher Power, the Universe, Higher Self, I Am, the Force, Source, Cosmic Intelligence, Inner Guidance, and Christ Consciousness, which she uses without making distinctions "to refer to the highest creative intelligence and power within us." Displaying what can be a fairly typical New Age antipathy to established religion, she seldom uses the word "God," because, she says, "it has confusing connotations. Frequently, people associate it with early religious training which is no longer useful to them."[68]

David Spangler, on the other hand, is anxious to articulate the distinction between God and the universe and to emphasize God's transcendence as well as the divine immanence. Even spiritual experiences, he cautions, which occur through contact with "higher realms of consciousness" are not to be equated with God, for "it is simply a connection with another part of the universe, important in giving us a sense of the vaster community of life of which we are a part but not to be confused with touching the inner heart of that community, which is God."[69]

In an effort to make the same point from within the Roman Catholic tradition—that God is within creation, but God and creation are not synonymous—Matthew Fox uses the term "panentheism" to interpret God's relationship to the creation, claiming that "theism" calls to mind deistic and dualistic understandings of the relationship between God and creation. "All theism," says Fox, "sets up a model or paradigm of people here and God out there. All theisms are about subject/object relationships to God." The answer to overcoming the "out-thereness" of God, according to Fox, lies with moving from theism to panentheism, which he defines as meaning "God is in everything and everything is in God." Like Spangler, Fox is concerned to distinguish his interpretation of divine immanence from pantheism. Fox promotes what the student of religion sees as a New Age understanding of divine immanence, and he does so by invoking the doctrines and sacraments of Roman Catholicism and without stepping outside the bounds of orthodoxy.

Unlike pantheism, says Fox, panentheism has need of sacraments, because the indwelling of the divine is not always apparent to us—the invisible must be revealed in the visible nature of the sacraments. For Fox "the primary sacrament is creation itself," but he invokes the doctrine of the incarnation as well as all of the seven sacraments of Roman Catholicism in order to reveal the divine within all that is. "The sacramental consciousness of panentheism," says Fox, "develops into a transparent and diaphanous consciousness wherein we can see events and beings as divine." For Fox, this way of understanding the divine presence has many consequences, among them a diminishing of the theistic inclination to relate to God as subject or object, a less compelling need "to invoke the actual name of God," and an impetus to express an understanding of God's embracing, inclusive, and cosmic nature in maternal images.[70]

Whether it emerges from esoteric Christianity, from an Eastern or occult orientation, or from Roman Catholicism's sacramental world view, it is the concept of immanence itself that is so pivotal in New Age thought. The interconnectedness of all things that is its root implication holds for New Agers the possibility of healing the fragmentation, the individualism, the purposelessness and the exploitation of the earth's resources which are described as typical of Western and particularly American culture. To understand the divine source as "with us"—"in the heart of every living form," as the Light of Christ Community Church puts it— rather than above us or away from us, or even against us, is to understand the divine as providing the foundation for a planetary culture.

New Age thinkers claim, further, that a doctrine of divine immanence may be the only interpretation of deity that can save us from the destruction of nuclear war. Scott Eastham, a religious studies scholar, writes in *Nucleus* that a doctrine of immanence compels us to accept that all of the world is sacred, that "secularization does not have to mean profanation." The process of secularization implies, rather, that "the secular world so long despised in many of the traditional spiritualities is also real, that God is not cut off from this world and, consequently, to seek God does not necessarily imply abandoning the world or one's fellow human beings. Today it means engagement with, commitment to, and responsiblity for the whole of reality."[71] As Eastham sees it, there is a transition occurring in Western culture from an emphasis on a static and alienating individual salvation to an understanding that all of reality is involved in any "authentic" attempt to achieve salvation. This transition is emerging from the growing understanding of God as separate from the world but as inextricably present in the world. Eastham speaks from within the Christian tradition, but he cites numerous examples from Eastern religions to make his points, as is characteristic of New Age thought. He calls on the disciplines of science and religion to proceed from the assumption of divine immanence and to contribute to averting the destruction that threatens the planet and humankind.

These few examples point to the fact that much of New Age thought is profoundly hopeful about what lies ahead for the planet and for humankind if the human consciousness of divine immanence continues to grow and bear fruit. In spite of a tone of urgency and sometimes detectable strains of apocalypticism, there is a strongly conveyed sense that ecological or nuclear destruction of the planet can be prevented. But what about evil in the New Age? If God dwells within, if all is in God and God is in all, what is the source of the obvious evil—both natural and moral— that is part of human lives on the earth? If God dwells within the world, why have we come to a point where we can carry out our own extinction?

First, and most obviously, say New Age thinkers, evil comes not from God, but arises from our very inability to acknowledge divine immanence and thus to see the connections of all things with each other. But evil comes also from human failure to acknowledge its own limitations. Spangler speaks of evil within the context of a discussion about the "shadows of Aquarius," as he describes what he considers to be the distortions of New Age thought. He recounts the "lure of limitlessness," which he interprets as "the desire not to be limited by anything, not by the past, by the future, by circumstances, or by others." In many ways Spangler's interpretation sounds like a traditional caution against *hubris*, pride, for he claims that the impossible desire for limitlessness causes us to forget that we are creatures, that we are limited and defined by our creatureliness. Not to acknowledge limitation is to give evil the opportunity to flourish. According to Spangler, "Evil . . . is a true imposition of limits. The limits that evil sets are always the wrong ones, the ones that disempower, that collapse one into a tiny ball of true powerlessness." Spangler does not speak of evil as a kind of cosmic force antagonistic to the divine but rather as the turning upside down of the constructive impulses of New Age thought, and thus he speaks in terms of "distortions" and "imbalances," lack of perspective, longings for power, and abuse of community. These are human failings out of which evil comes, not the result of divine punishment or of God's condoning of evil.

Brian Swimme, a physicist and associate director of the Institute in Culture and Creation Spirituality in Oakland, California, takes a different approach to the consideration of evil in the New Age, but with a somewhat similar result. Swimme absolves God, or the One, from responsibility for evil and places its origins within the human realm. Swimme echoes the Theosophical and New Age understanding that all of reality is one—that it emerges from the same source and exerts the power of what he calls "allurement" or love, an "attracting activity which is fundamental mystery." But, as Swimme sees it, this same power of allurement has within it the capacity for violence and suffering, and he finds the destructive powers of allurement reflected in all of the universe—among the stars and in the biological world as well.

The dangers of allurement, as Swimme understands it, are at their most intense in human nature because humankind has the power of self-reflection and the desire to know more and more. Even nuclear weapons emerged from human fascination with the cosmos and the desire of scientists to penetrate its mysteries. Swimme's plea for ridding the world of the destructive side of allurement is addressed not to God, but to men and women and it has its grounding in the interrelatedness of all creation: "Break out of egocentricity. Break out of ethnocentricity. Break out of anthropocentricity. Take the viewpoint of the Earth as a whole. In every fascination, in every allurement, include the vitality of the Earth. You are the Earth too."[72]

At the conclusion of this discussion about the alternative views of deity offered by the new religions, it is helpful to return to Gordon Kaufman's list of issues facing the contemporary person or religious movement that attempts to interpret the nature of the divine. It becomes obvious fairly quickly that the new religions are not concerned with matters of linguistic analysis, at least not in any sense that goes beyond the defining of terms. This is hardly surprising, since a new religious movement, even one as long-standing in the culture as Mormonism, needs to exert its energy chiefly in putting forth and interpreting its doctrines rather than analyzing their deep, underlying structures.

Epistemological concerns are important, on the other hand, since at a time in history when one choice regarding a divine being is unbelief, based on the assumption that human experience can detect no knowledge of God in the universe, it is urgent to talk about how God or ultimate reality can be known. Concerning this question, the new religions engage each other in debate and choose up sides in a manner that is familiar to Westerners. At issue is whether God or the ultimate can be known by human means alone, by inner knowledge, intuition, discovery, or enlightenment, or whether there are certain attributes of the divine being which we can only know if they are revealed to us. Mormonism and Unificationism insist that there are attributes of the divine nature, attributes that we need to know in order to be saved, that we cannot be aware of unless they are revealed to us. Christian Science reminds us that the terms of the debate cannot always be put in such an either-or fashion as knowledge or lack of knowledge, since in that movement the knowledge of God is more a matter of discovery than it is of revelation used in the way that Mormonism and Unificationism use the term. Scientology is not willing to deny that God can be known but to say that not much is known yet. Available sources indicate that this is not a question which intrigues the theological imagination as it is manifested in Scientology. Theosophy and New Age thought claim that because we are human we have access to knowledge of the divine reality that dwells within each man and woman and in every atom of the universe. Because all of these movements are concerned to put forth an interpretation of the knowledge of God which is coherent with human experience, their epistemological speculatations have as much to say about human nature as they do about the nature of the divine.

More pressing even than matters of epistemology among the new religions is the question, "What is God like?" Mormons and Unificationists hold to a personal God, one who is present in human history, both as a constant shaping force and as an occasional special presence. They mitigate the more terrifying and incomprehensible aspects of the biblical God—the judging sovereign who is "personal" and yet unpredictable because of "total otherness," by making the deity more accessible. They do so by drawing God to earth for the purpose of revealing what humankind needs to know and by intensifying certain of God's personal characteristics—empathy and suffering rather than anger and righteousness. God as envisioned by Christian Science offers another possibility here, for it vehemently denies the reality of God as "person" and at the same time maintains that God is not just Mind and Spirit but also Love.

Scientology, as has been the pattern in the chapter, does not have much to say in this conversation

For Theosophists and many New Age thinkers, the biblical concept of God as person has been too corrupted, too exploited by the established traditions as a source of fear, to be rehabilitated. Furthermore, they claim that the concept of an anthropomorphic God simply does not fit with the operation of the universe as we experience it in modern times. But these religious movements acknowledge that an ultimate reality understood as the One or the Absolute or the All, is so abstract a concept that it does not warm the heart. A concept of deity as ultimate reality requires, also, affective appeal that will speak to the whole human person, not just to our rational capacities. It is thus the emphasis on the immanence of the divine which connects all things, human and non-human, animate and inanimate, with each other—our oneness with the universe and with each other—that serves to stir the emotions in these movements.

Finally, and perhaps most pressing of all, there emerges from the issue of what God is like the question as to whether or not the divine has anything to do with the cause of evil in the world. The answer, on the part of all six religions (we can only infer a "no" on the part of Scientology) is negative. It would appear to be beyond the capacity of the theological imagination, at least as it finds expression in these six religious movements, to construct a concept of deity that holds the divine responsible for or even tolerant of suffering, evil, and sin. Whatever their various interpretations of the nature of evil and its origins, these religious movements also hold humankind responsible for much of the suffering that has befallen both us and the planet. Thus, it is in the next chapter, on human nature, that the causes of evil are elaborated in more detail. But the next chapter is not just about human sin; it is about human capabilities and responsibilities as well.

THREE

What Does It Mean
to Be Human?

Views of Human Nature in the
New Religions

The alternative concepts of deity and of ultimate reality set forth in the previous chapter give rise to another set of questions that stir the theological imagination to speculate about the possibilities, the limitations, and the obligations of men and women as we live out our lives on earth. How must we understand ourselves, according to these six religious movements, in relation to ultimate reality, however defined? What is the stuff of which we are made? Are we both spirit and matter? Spirit alone? Merely matter? What are our obligations as human beings? What are the aspects of our very nature that we must acknowledge in order to fulfill those obligations? What is at stake if we don't?

Mormonism, Unificationism, Christian Science, Scientology, Theosophy, and New Age thought offer views of human origins and responsibilities that differ substantially from each other in specific detail. But, as the discussion unfolds, it becomes apparent that overriding doctrinal differences and a century and a half of American cultural development are a set of common negations and affirmations that are directed by the new religions at both the established religions and the secular culture. This is not to say that the differences among the new religions really make no difference. That such is not the case will be demonstrated in chapter five. But the following areas of agreement emerge in spite of the differences.

We are not, the new religions say to the established traditions, particularly Christianity, totally sinful creatures, dependent for our being on a transcendent God who, however loving or merciful, could as likely terminate our existence as not. Neither, they say to the secular culture, are we merely biological entities, headed only toward our own deaths, helpless in the face of social and historical forces, biological urges, and psychological motivations of which we are for the most part unaware.

Out of these denials emerges a set of affirmations. First, no matter to what extent the importance of the physical body figures in a particular system, the new religions conclude that, ultimately, we are spiritual beings who have either within ourselves or available to us access to the divine. Second, we are necessary, not contingent beings; we cannot *not* exist. Third, our lives are purposeful, not meaningless. We have tasks to accomplish as human persons, and we are not on this earth by chance or for reasons that cannot be fathomed. Life may have its ambiguities, but it is not merely incomprehensible mystery. Even Scientology, which consistently describes life as a game, never suggests that the odds are so much against us that we cannot ever win the game. Fourth, the new religions see men and women as morally free agents. We are not coerced into nor are we obstructed from accomplishing the tasks that are ours.

These four characteristics add up to what theologians refer to as a very high doctrine of human nature. In fact, much of the theological critique of the new religions has been focused on an apparent inability to accept limitations in human nature and an attempt at deification of the human person. But, to conclude that these religions put forth unrealistic doctrines of human nature which fail to acknowledge life's great difficulties and tragedies as most people experience them is to miss a theme that is even more dominant than optimism about human potential in the new religions: namely, that we are the ones who are responsible for our own salvation or enlightenment. No matter what help is available or in what form it comes—new revelations, new scriptures, technologies, spirit guides—they go just so far. Finally, we must save ourselves and each other and even the planet.

The insistence on human responsibility ties in with the previous chapter's emphasis on the new religions' attempts to dissociate God or ultimate reality from any connection with the origins of evil. God is not the cause of evil in the new religions and God will not rescue humanity, in the traditional sense, from evil. As the new religions understand it, humankind is not saved by grace alone nor by scripture alone nor by prayers of petition but by our own efforts. There is help available to us, but the difference will be made by what we do and how we think.

MORMONS AND UNIFICATIONISTS: PARTICIPANTS IN A PLAN OF SALVATION

Mormons and Unificationists understand human life as purposeful because it is structured to coincide with the terms of a divinely ordained plan. In each of these movements, the plan involves humanity as a whole in the unfolding of a salvation history, and it involves, as well, the life span of each man and woman. Mormons call this the Plan of Salvation with its origins at the Council in Heaven, which preceded the creation of the earth. This plan "comprises all of the laws, ordinances, principles, and doctrines by conformity to which the spirit offspring of God have power to progress to the high state of exaltation enjoyed by the Father."[1] This is the divinely instituted plan—put in place by the Father not by Jesus or Adam—whereby human persons, the spirit children of the Heavenly Father, may take on human bodies and fulfill the opportunity to achieve divinity.

Unificationists, likewise, understand themselves as living their lives within the context of a divinely ordained plan, the outlines of which are provided in *Divine Principle*. For Unificationists, the purpose of life is concerned with achieving the Three Blessings promised by God to humankind at the creation and bestowed on Adam and Eve: "Be fruitful or unite with Him; multiply, or unite with each other; have dominion or unite with creation."[2] These blessings involve the reaching of spiritual maturity, dwelling in a loving, God-centered family, and living in a world of harmony centered on God rather than on Satan. For Unificationists, this is a crucial time in history, because it is again possible to achieve the Three Blessings which have not been known by humankind since the Fall.

Mormon theology understands the human person as having a threefold nature: the eternal intelligence, a spirit body, and a physical body. As David Yarn puts it: "Each man's original being, called an intelligence, was provided a tabernacle of substance called spirit. Spirit beings in turn are tabernacled in bodies of flesh. A mortal man, or soul, is thus a union of spirit and body."[3] In this brief description there is implicit the outline of the Plan of Salvation, sometimes called the Plan for Happiness, the beginnings of which reach back into eternity. First, we are possessed of original being. Our eternal intelligences have always existed; they were not created out of nothing by a God on whom we totally depend for our existence. Second, our spirit bodies were given to us by our celestial parents (God the Father and the Heavenly Mother) during a time, called pre-existence, in which we lived prior to our physical births. During pre-existence we received our spirit bodies and thus are literally the spirit children of the Heavenly Father. Finally, we have been given our physical bodies by our earthly parents in order that we might have a mortal existence and learn that which is necessary for us to achieve divinity and become in character like our celestial parents.

It is the earthly or mortal life that makes it possible to achieve divinity, because it is during this time that we have the opportunity to distinguish right from wrong and to choose freely between them. For Mormons the term "mortal" does not have negative connotations. The earthly life is not a time of unendurable temptation for human beings who are too depraved and weak to choose right over wrong. It is not a vale of tears. Rather it is a time of opportunity, a chance to educate persons in ways that can only be accomplished in a physical body. "Mormons," says Wallace Bennett, "see mortality as a blessing, an opportunity, and a step toward salvation—not as exile from God's presence because of Adam's sin."[4] Mormons understand themselves as having "been freed by their broader scriptures from accumulated errors about human nature—that man is essentially a mind and the body is an unimportant burden and human nature is depraved."[5]

If we are not depraved and contingent beings, then what is our condition during the earthly life? Yarn says that we call the human condition "mortal." "Simply," he says, "this means that we are subject to death,"[6] and to be subject to death is also to be subject to sin in Mormon theology. However, to say that we are subject to sin is not to say that we are helpless to choose against it, for Mormon theologians acknowledge that the world is in a bad state of affairs precisely because we are free to choose sin. But, they also claim that things would be even worse without God's "periodic restorations of the gospel in man's history." To say that we are sinful is not to say that we are the captives of original sin; the sins we commit are our own. "Man comes into the world innocent," says Yarn, "and even though the natural man may be 'carnal, sensual, and devilish,' . . . I must also say, and emphatically, this is not identical by any means with the apostate Christian doctrine of depravity."[7]

Even though Mormons do not use the term "depravity" to speak of human nature, they do describe humankind as "fallen." In Mormon theology this concept takes on positive rather than negative meaning and may suggest some affinity with the Christian concept of the "fortunate fall," an understanding that if we had not sinned we would not ever have known the blessings of God's mercy. But the Mormon understanding goes beyond that. "In contrast to the usual idea of the fall," says Bennett, "the Mormons believe that Adam had a full understanding of the Plan before his fall and the full authority of priesthood afterward."[8] In other words, Adam and Eve freely chose to fall, to make themselves susceptible to sin and death, so that they might also achieve divinity. Ken Miller, another contemporary Mormon interpreter, states this concept even more graphically in an introduction to Mormon theology: "Adam and Eve were very happy when they learned what would happen because of the fall." Miller quotes Eve (from *The Pearl of Great Price*): "Were it not for our transgression, we never should have had seed (children) and never should have known good and evil, and the joy of our redemption and the eternal life which God giveth unto all the obedient."[9]

The Mormon interpretation of the fall as a happy event rather than as a tragedy obviously requires a different understanding of the traditional Christian doctrine of the atonement. The atonement is not a minor part of Mormon theology, as one might suspect given its doctrine of the fall. Rather, as Bruce R. McConkie explains, "The doctrine of the *atonement* embraces, sustains, supports, and gives life and force to all other gospel doctrines. It is the foundation upon which all truth rests, and all things grow out of it and come because of it."[10] Mormons understand the atonement of Jesus, as enacted in the crucifixion, as a ransoming of humankind from the effects of the Fall: spiritual death, separation from God, and temporal death, defined as the separation of body and spirit body at the death of the physical body. "If there had been no atonement," says McConkie, "temporal death would have remained forever, and there never would have been a resurrection. The body would have remained forever in the grave, and the spirit would have stayed in a spirit prison to all eternity."[11]

To read about the atonement in Mormon writings is to encounter much of the language of traditional Christianity: Jesus died sacrificially on the cross to save us from sin and death, and, in order to benefit from the grace of the atonement, we need to repent of our sins. But, in Mormon theology, Jesus did not need to die to save us from original sin—he died, rather, to save us from our own sins[12] and to enable us to overcome death (the separation of body and spirit) so that we might one day experience the reunion of our physical and spirit bodies. Without such a coming together, we cannot be reunited with God nor can we become like God.

To learn more about the role that Jesus plays in Mormon theology is to get a better grasp on this movement's heavy emphasis on individual human responsibility. There is no doubt that Jesus as both God and human is central to Mormon theology and Mormon piety requires intense devotion to Jesus. But it is not Jesus's atonement that guarantees salvation. Wallace Bennett puts it this way: "To the Mormons, salvation is both a personal responsibility and a cooperative enterprise, to be achieved by what might be described as a partnership between Christ, our Elder Brother, and each of us as individuals." But Jesus's life and sacrifice do not guarantee salvation, for salvation is not a settled status in Mormonism. Bennett goes on: "Never at any point can we relax and say, 'Today I was saved.'"[13] Mormons agree that we are saved by "grace," but not by grace alone: "This measure of salvation, available to all, is only a common minimum and not the key to eternal progress and our ultimate destiny. Upon this minimum each of us must build for himself through his own efforts. . . ."[14]

Above all in Mormon theology, human beings are understood as free from any kind of natural or divine coercion. Men and women possess what Mormons call "agency," the ability to choose between good and evil and to act on that same ability. The concept of freedom is pervasive in Mormon teachings, and "agency" is considered one of the eternal principles which has always existed. The free agency of the human person in Mormonism has its beginnings in pre-existence. At the Council in Heaven when plans were made for creating the earth and its inhabitants, the spirit children of the Heavenly Father were given the opportunity to accept or reject God's plan of salvation. At the same council, when it came time to choose who would become the redeemer of humankind and release them from death, it was Jesus who was selected rather than Lucifer, because Jesus promised to honor the freedom of men and women to make their own moral choices, whereas Lucifer wanted to do away with human freedom in order to guarantee that not one soul would be lost. In the Garden of Eden, Adam and Eve chose freely to fall and to give all of humankind the opportunity to become like God, and we as human persons on earth are also free to choose between good and evil. "Agency," says Bruce McConkie, "is so fundamental a part of the great plan of creation and redemption that if it should cease, all other things would vanish away."[15]

With freedom, however, comes responsibility—finally, men and women must merit their own salvation. It is up to us to accept the teachings of God's restored church on earth and to act them out. It is up to us to make the right moral choices based on our faith in and knowledge of that church. A Mormon is admonished to recognize "what a tremendously grave responsibility rests upon him as one of the infinitesimally small number of God's children upon the earth who have made covenants with him."[16] If Mormonism's theology of human nature deifies the human person in promising individuals that someday godhood will be theirs, it also imposes on each person tremendous responsibility. Godhood is not easy to achieve; nor is it just around the corner. Mormons are advised not to get arrogant ideas about "catching up" with God. Yarn states that "God himself must be potentially capable of eternal growth, so we do not see ourselves as ever closing the gap and matching him."[17] Ultimate salvation and exaltation are finally earned through human merit. Only those who die in infancy are freed from this responsibility—for them Jesus's atonement is sufficient. The rest of us, by our own faith and works, must earn salvation.

This same strong emphasis on human responsibility is a central part of Unification theology, which articulates an intensely high doctrine of human potential and responsibility but does so in conjunction with a doctrine of the fall that is very different from that of Mormonism. In Unification theology we are not destined for godhood, but we are made in God's image and were originally created to hold a place in the universe higher than the angels. Because we have both a physical mind and body and a spiritual mind and body (which are replicas of each other), unlike the angels who are only spirit, we were to be rulers of both the physical and the spirit worlds and to be the center of harmony between the two.[18]

But the emphasis here is on what was "originally" intended, because Unification theology combines its high doctrine of human nature with an interpretation of the Fall that is drastically different from that doctrine as it is understood in Mormonism. Rather than a freely chosen opportunity, the fall is understood as an unnecessary tragedy that has distorted and diminished the give-and-take relationship among God, ourselves, and the creation. Had there been no fall, we would live in a world as harmonious and free from suffering as God originally intended it to be, but because we fell, we are at war with God, with each other, and with nature.

From the coming together of these two doctrines—that of a tremendous human potential and at the same time a fallen human nature—there has emerged an ethic of human responsibility in Unification theology that has a different quality to it from the theology of merit in Mormonism. In Mormonism we must follow God's plan for salvation as it has been revealed through Joseph Smith and the restored church of Jesus Christ, but there is no sense that the plan was put in place in order to combat a cosmic tragedy—instead it is to present a cosmic opportunity. In Unificationism we must live in accord with Divine Principle, but we must also pay indemnity, make reparation, to God for the suffering we have caused God and the creation since the time of the fall. "Who can know the yearning of His lonely broken heart?" says one Unification hymn. "Tears were falling as a river through His countless years alone."[19]

Therefore, in the Unification understanding, it is appropriate not only to experience suffering, but to seek it out, in order that we might make up for that which is our fault and also comfort the grieving heart of God. However heavy a burden such an interpretation of the fall places on human shoulders, Unificationists find it a more satisfactory explanation of the human condition and the state the world is in than that provided by other religious systems. "Historically," claims one source, "all religions have given some explanation of the separation of man from God and of man from his fellow man. Nevertheless, an explanation which both adequately explains the painful realities of our world and provides a vision for remedying them has been missing. For thousands around the world, this need has been met in the Divine Principle explanation of man's fall."[20]

The specific interpretation of the fall as given in *Divine Principle* emphasizes the fall not so much as resulting from a sin of disobedience but from a failure of love, the "misuse" of love, which ruptured the relationship of God with humanity and the creation. Unificationists interpret the eating of the fruit of the tree in Eden as a symbolic account of what was really a sexual, a relational, transgression. Adam and Eve, living in Eden as brother and sister, were tempted by Satan to engage in sexual intercourse before they were mature enough to do so, before they had achieved the First Blessing of spiritual maturity or union with God. This disruption in proper relationships brought about the fall of the physical world. But even before that event, Eve had already had intercourse with Satan which led to the fall of the spiritual world. *Divine Principle* explains the result for humankind: "Eve should have multiplied children of good lineage through her blood and flesh of goodness derived from the good 'fruit' she ate in her love centered on God. Instead, she produced a sinful world by multiplying children of bad lineage through her blood and flesh of evil derived from the evil 'fruit' she ate in her love centered on Satan" (p. 74).

This misuse of love brought about the consequences of the fall: humanity's formation of a four position foundation with Satan rather than with God. Unificationists understand the four position foundation as the basic unit by which God carries on the divine creative work, a reciprocal relationship among four entities that is present on the sub-atomic level as well on the level of international relationships. Because the source of this relationship since the fall has been Satan rather than God, distortions occur which have resulted in all the ills we see present in the world: wars, racial strife, economic and political unrest, troubles within families, and the egocentricity which makes us hate each other and compete with each other on an individual level.[21] Because of this distortion of relationships, we have lost the Three Great Blessings which God had originally intended for humankind, whom he created in the first place as an object of joy: to become one with God in heart; to become one with each other and to form ideal families; and to become one with the world—to have dominion over the whole of creation and live in oneness with God on the earth.[22]

As a consequence of the fall, humanity has had a history of struggle rather than of blessing. Unification theology does not go so far as to say that human history has been merely the acting out of Satan-centered rather than God-centered deeds, but instead it sees human history as "the providential history of restoration through which God has been working" (Divine Principle, p. 111). God's aim is to restore the broken relationship with humanity, a task which only God can accomplish. But the life task for men and women is to meet the conditions necessary for God to re-establish the loving relationship, to restore the earth to its original perfection. Unificationists speak of this process as "restoration through indemnity," and by it they mean "that God conducts a providence of restoration through indemnity [by choosing] to let humans participate in the process for reconciliation by participating in the establishment of certain conditions."[23]

So far humankind has been unable to meet these conditions, and human history is a record of the struggles and failures of men and women to do so. Adam and Eve failed, and even Jesus was not able to complete his mission as the Messiah, the second Adam, because, tragically, he was crucified before he was able to establish a perfect, God-centered family and thus bring about the kingdom of God on earth. In his death on the cross, Jesus effected a spiritual, but not a physical redemption. He did not live long enough to restore the creation due in great part to the disloyalty of his followers.[24]

Given the intensity of the Unification emphasis on our nature as fallen and estranged from God's love, we might expect an accompanying pronouncement of total inability on the part of humanity to accomplish anything at all without God's rescue and interference. In fact, we might expect a theology of human nature reminiscent of some of the great Reformers' insistence that our salvation has nothing to do with our own efforts. But, such is not the case. Unification theology speaks frequently of God's need for us as objects for him to love and even goes so far as to posit a theology of human necessity—not so unequivocal as that of Mormonism, but present nonetheless. In the Unification understanding, God needs us in order that God might experience reciprocal love. God could not have *not* created us because his own loving nature compelled him to do so. Thus, in spite of the insistence on human nature as fallen in Unification theology, there is not an accompanying sense of the utter contingency of human existence, no picture of the spider being dangled over the fiery pit.

Likewise, Unification theology insists on the reality of human freedom. The freedom to make moral choices is described in terms of God's "indirect dominion." Unificationists understand the time on earth as a period for the achievement of spiritual maturity, and they compare the "spiritual laws" by which humankind lives during this time to the growth of things in the natural world. God does not interfere with them.

Through this concept of "indirect dominion," Unificationists see themselves as resolving the "considerable tension for Christian believers between the faith that God rules man and the equally strong belief that man possesses free will."[25] This period of Indirect Dominion, however, is not one free from dangers. It is understood as a time of "difficulty and instability," and wrong choices, however freely made, bring suffering. The choice made by Adam and Eve is the primary example.

Nonetheless, this period, with all the risks that freedom brings, is necessary for our growth to the state of direct dominion which promises "living heart to heart with God as matured persons. In this union God governs by love, and law and commandments become unnecessary. Under the direct rule of God man is completely free—liberated to be who he was meant to be." Unificationists caution that this time of direct dominion does not involve a coercive relationship with God. Instead it must be understood as "a mutual loving companionship. It is the crowning jewel in one's interior life, opening immense new vistas of love, joy, and beauty."[26]

Above all in Unification theology, we as human beings are responsible for the condition of the world and its inhabitants and for restoring the creation to its original state of perfection. If Mormonism stresses human responsibility, it is nonetheless in a system in which nothing of cosmic significance has gone awry. The burden is a heavier one in Unification theology; and we cannot simply give it over to God. "There is a tendency in all of us," warns one Unification source, "not to take responsibility for our own lives. On occasion we would like to give that burden to God, to the church, or to any other figure representing strength and authority. Despite such tendencies, Divine Principle . . . affirms the critical role individuals must play in shaping their own destiny. We cannot pass off responsibility to someone else. Each of us is the captain of his own ship."[27]

So it is that we who were created to be above the angels, but are now fallen into a blood relationship with Satan, must bring about by our own efforts the conditions which existed before the fall. Such is our potential and responsibility. Unification theology sees us at present in the "last days" of human history, which makes the task even more urgent and specific. This is the time of the coming of the Lord of the Second Advent,[28] during which we once again have the opportunity to recognize a new messiah, a third Adam (the Reverend Sun Myung Moon), and follow him in establishing by means of perfect families the Kingdom of God on earth—to wipe out warfare, to unite people of different races and religions, to bring about the integration of science and religion in the search for absolute values, and to insure sufficient material goods for all. *Divine Principle* assures us that we are not alone in this task—God is with us—but, "God's efforts on our behalf become effective only when we do our part. In the course of growth, of achieving the direct dominion, of building the kingdom, God does His part and we must do ours. Until our portion is completed, God's efforts are futile. The Lord helps those who help themselves because He can *only* help those who help themselves."[29]

Both Mormons and Unificationists place a very high premium on the physical body. The work of humankind on earth is to be done, must be done, in fact, in the body—but without forgetting the reality of spirit—and in the world. In such systems it is not enough, then, to ask what it means to be human. We must also ask what it means to be a man or a woman—to inhabit a male or a female body. There will be an elaboration of differences in gender roles in chapter five, but suffice it to say for the moment that in Mormonism the priesthood which is available to all worthy males is not open to women. For women the arena for institutional religious work is to be found in the Relief Society and in a broader way through the role of motherhood. A *Relief Society Bulletin* for February 1914 indicated that "The Relief Society was firmly subordinated to the priesthood as an auxiliary."[30]

As is the case in other American religious groups that do not ordain women and in those that do as well, the issues of women's participation are of serious concern for many Mormons. In the introduction to a book of essays about Mormon women written by Mormon women scholars, the historian Jan Shipps suggests that there may be two reasons for the subordination of women's roles to men's roles in Mormonism as it has existed since the late nineteenth century. The first is developmental: Mormonism's change from a radical movement in its early history to a much more conservative movement which internalized Victorian values pushed women back into the domestic sphere from which they had emerged in the early years of the movement. The second is theological: Shipps speculates that the doctrine of atonement outlined above with its promises for humankind may have freed men from Adam's fall, but did not liberate women from the curse of Eve. Consequently, Mormon women do not experience in their lives the same degree of "agency" as do men, and they "are consigned to all the tasks connected with eternal motherhood."[31]

It is necessary to do more speculating about the role of women in the Unification Church. There are a number of characteristics in Unificationism that indicate a potential for the subordination of women. First, there is the tremendous emphasis on the role of the family in this movement and the very positive value placed on having children—factors which tend to circumscribe women's roles as wives and mothers. Further, men and women are described as being in a subject-object relationship to each other. Then, there is the understanding of God as incorporating both male and female principles (with the implication that these are eternally enduring entities in both God and nature) but nonetheless referred to as "Father." Finally, the origins of the movement are rooted in an Oriental culture that has relegated women to lesser positions in the family and in society. Add to these the emphasis in Unification theology on Eve's sin.

The reality for women seems, however, to be more complicated. Women hold positions of authority in the church. In fact, the major theologian of the movement in America (who returned to Korea in 1988), Young Oon Kim, is a woman. Various Unification publications, as will be indicated in chapter five, point to a feminist consciousness among women in the movement. Perhaps all it is possible to say at the moment is that the Unification Church is a newer movement than Mormonism. It came to prominence in American culture at a time when the newest wave of feminism was flowering, and it does not appear to have institutionalized the subordination of women to the extent that has been the case in Mormonism. Whatever the differences in the two systems, it is nevertheless necessary for the student of religion to ask, particularly in these two cases, what it means to be a man or a woman.

Ultimately, whether one is a man or a woman, the work of salvation within these two movements must be accomplished in the body and within the framework—the salvation history—of the church. It is through the teachings of these two religious movments that we learn who we are as human beings and what it is we need to accomplish. Not only are we free to fulfill the obligations of being human, we are also responsible for doing so. Although there is divine help for us, it is, as the Mormons say, "a common minimum." To become fully human, it is up to us to make what use we can of what has been revealed through the church and to achieve our own salvation.

CHRISTIAN SCIENCE AND SCIENTOLOGY: SEEKING FREEDOM FROM ERROR

Christian Science and Scientology offer interpretations of human nature that refute all systems of understanding, whether religious or secular, which affirm the necessity or the goodness of the physical body. Christian Science makes a more radical statement, because it denies the very reality of the body, whereas Scientology simply denies its usefulness for purposes of spiritual development and enlightenment. Christian Science and Scientology also deny an understanding of the human task as oriented toward this world, although both see the end of spiritual enlightenment as resulting in happier lives. Again, Christian Science makes the more radical statement in denying that the world of matter exists at all, but Scientology, too, sees the physical universe as fostering deceptions about the true nature of reality.

In Christian Science the task set for us is twofold. The first is to gain insight into and acknowledge our true nature: that we are not dual beings made up of both spirit and matter but spirit alone and that we are not fallen or sinful by nature. Rather we are the perfect creations of a perfect God. Our second task is to use this understanding to bring about the healing of sin and sickness in ourselves and in the world. These two tasks are interdependent. Just as an understanding of God's true nature makes healing possible in Christian Science, and, in turn, the healings serve to demonstrate God's nature, so too does knowledge of our true nature as God's perfect creation make healing possible in Christian Science. The healings confirm that what we have discerned about ourselves and about God is true.

In order truly to understand human nature, says Christian Science, it is necessary first to understand God. To begin an inquiry into human nature based on the premise that we are in any way material beings is to thwart insights into who we are. This, according to the critique by Christian Science, is exactly what the physical and biological sciences and the established religions have done. DeWitt John says, "so long as science or religion starts from the premise that matter is basic reality and that man is a physical organism living in a material world, can it ever explain the ultimate questions regarding man?"[32]

Christian Science supplies an emphatic negative answer: "Man is not made up of matter," says Eddy in *Science and Health*. "He is not made up of brain, blood, bones and other material elements. . . . Man is idea, the image, of Love; he is not physique" (p. 475). But, even more important, "man is incapable of sin, sickness, and death. The real man cannot depart from holiness, nor can God by whom man is evolved, engender the capacity or freedom to sin. A mortal sinner is not God's man" (pp. 475–76).

Eddy's use of the term "real man" is important in understanding what Christian Science means by human nature. Christian Science distinguishes between the "real man," who is the perfect reflection of a perfect creator, and "mortal man," the erroneous understanding of the human person as finite and fallen, corruptible and susceptible to sickness. It is mortal man who suffers and dies, and it is mortal man who is detected by the false evidence of the five senses. It is mortal man who, out of ignorance of true human nature, sins: ". . . the sinner is not sheltered from suffering from sin: he makes a great reality of evil, identifies himself with it, fancies he finds pleasure in it, and will reap what he sows; hence the sinner must endure the effects of his delusion until he wakes from it."[33] In other words, we will sin and suffer and die as long as we continue to believe that sin and suffering and death are real and that as mortal men and women we are at their mercy.

If we are to understand ourselves as perfect, then it is obvious that the confession of sin that Christian Science requires, the repentance it demands, differs radically from that imposed by most of the established religious traditions. We are admonished *not* to insist on ourselves as sinful and fallen by nature because by doing so we only perpetuate the error which has caused us so much pain, both physical and spiritual, in the first place. Instead we must come to understand that as God's idea, God's reflection, we are not sinful and flawed, but perfect and good as God is perfect and good.

Such a view of human nature has its confirmation for Christian Scientists in the first chapter of Genesis, in which we are told that we are made in the image of God. And further, rather than a description of the creation of matter, the first chapter is understood by Christian Scientists to be "a metaphorical description of the perfection, beauty, diversity, and completeness of God's wholly spiritual and good creation."[34] As part of that creation, as reflections of God, we too are "wholly spiritual and good." In fact, in the Christian Science view, to deny that we as human persons are a perfect creation is to come close to blasphemy. If we hold that men and women are created in the image and likeness of God, then to understand humanity as by nature sinful reduces "the image of the Most High to the status of a worm."[35]

Does not this view of human nature lead to a deification of humankind that is really just another kind of blasphemy? When Christian Science says, "The spiritual man is that perfect and unfallen likeness, coexistent and coeternal with God,"[36] is that another way of saying that we ourselves are God? To such a question Eddy answers that "man is not God and God is not man" (*Science and Health*, p. 480).

If we are not God, neither are we helpless creatures at the mercy of a God who could as well let us slip from existence as not. We are, rather, necessary beings, just as is the case in Mormonism and Unificationism. We must exist, for Christian Science maintains that as reflections of God we make it possible for the divine to know itself: "God, without the image and likeness of Himself, would be a nonentity, or Mind unexpressed. He would be without a witness or proof of His own nature. Spiritual man is the image or idea of God, an idea which cannot be lost nor separated from its divine Principle" (*Science and Health*, p. 303). It is not possible in Christian Science theology to speak of ourselves as contingent beings or as alienated from God—as God's idea, we are necessary to and inseparable from Divine Mind.

If such is the case, if we are perfect and inseparable from God, why do we suffer from sin and sickness? Why is there any need for healing? Healing from what? From false belief and false ways of thinking, Christian Science answers—from the false belief that sin and sickness are real. This, in fact, is the salvation, the deliverance, that Jesus came to offer: "Our Master understood that Life, Truth, Love are the triune Principle of all pure theology; also that the divine trinity is one infinite remedy for the opposite triad, sickness, sin, and death."[37]

To heal and to be healed in Christian Science requires that we be liberated from the false belief that the sufferings of the world have any basis in reality. To believe in the reality of cancer, for example, and the pain it brings is to imprison ourselves within a cosmic framework based on error and which ascribes to God—who is all-in-all—the creation of that which would harm us. To continue to believe that God created cancer and that it is real is to perpetuate the power of cancer over us—to give it the ability to harm us.

To accept the spiritual fact that as reflections of God we cannot by our very nature participate in sin or sickness is to free ourselves from their power over us. Jesus came to heal us by way of demonstrating this spiritual fact. He neither came to save us from our fallen nature nor to perform miracles of healing that required his suspending of the material laws of nature. He came, instead, to demonstrate by his own healings that sin and sickness have no power if we afford them no reality.

It follows from this that the essential insight in Christian Science about human freedom is not concerned with our freedom from coercion or our freedom to make moral choices based on our ability to discern right from wrong. It involves, instead, freedom from misunderstanding of a cosmic nature, the freedom to recognize that we have never been anything less than free from the tyranny of sin and sickness. We do not need Jesus to atone vicariously for our fallen natures. We need Jesus as the unique exemplar who has sacrificed and demonstrated to us our own nature and potential.[38]

What is our own responsibility as individual persons in Christian Science? What obligations do we have if we are already the perfect creations of a perfect God? What effort, if any, must we exert? The answers to these questions depend upon an understanding of what Christian Science means by "perfection." Christian Science insists on the perfection of humankind, but it does not promise perfection of an instantaneous, unchanging sort; it is more developmental, more process-oriented than that. "The perfection of which Mrs. Eddy speaks," says John, ". . . is not to be understood as a static condition of abstract bliss in which development has forever ceased. Perfection for her was the standpoint from which man acted, not the cessation of action."[39] Gottschalk explains it a little differently: "Man's perfection must be demonstrated step by step and human patterns can be dissolved only as they are superseded by actual demonstration. To the extent that this demand is taken seriously it places a responsibility on all Christian Scientists to work to their utmost to achieve the highest spiritual good in every area of their experience."[40]

To be perfect in Christian Science, then, is not to be relieved of the responsibility for demonstrating this perfection. The first step is to acknowledge the true nature of God, of reality, and of humanity. The second step, or—more accurately—the series of life-long steps, requires that we apply this understanding to every inharmonious, apparently evil, situation in which we find ourselves from matters of personal relationships to sickness to concerns about war and peace.

This step-by-step process is illustrated by a specific incident in a recent issue of *The Christian Science Journal*, in which a daughter, mother, and father related an account of the healing of the daughter's injured wrist and later an injured vertebra. "What does God know?" the mother asked herself as she drove to pick up her daughter after the first injury had occurred. "The answer came," she said, "that God knows perfection and completeness—not separation." Such knowledge, the mother testified, preceded the healing of the wrist. The father, too, added his testimony about the later healing of his daughter, in which the daughter asked the father whether she could do Christian Science as well as he. "I answered 'yes,' and I will always remember that awareness of her own capacity to understand and demonstrate His power dawning on Stephanie's young face."[41]

Christian Science would see this series of events as the step-by-step process to which Gottschalk refers. Understanding—our own—precedes healing and healing demonstrates understanding. But the process is a gradual one, for the most part, a dawning realization of the spiritual nature of reality. Eddy herself did not expect instant change to result in the world from her discovery of Christian Science, but she did envision a growing unfolding of healing consequences as we become more and more aware of God's perfection, of the spiritual nature of reality, and of our own perfection. She equated human progress with an increasing realization of our spiritual nature: "Every step of progress is a step more spiritual. The great element of reform is not born of human wisdom; it draws not its life from human organizations; rather it is the crumbling away of material elements from reason, the translation of law back to its original language—Mind, and the final unity between man and God."[42]

Such a claim—that individual and social change for the better will come not from human actions, as such, but from understanding the nature of reality—has brought accusations that Christian Science is not concerned with efforts to make the world a better place in which to live. Interpreters of Christian Science describe this judgment as coming from an inaccurate reading of the obligations Christian Science places on its members. Gottschalk responds that "the specific purpose of the church Eddy founded is to be an effective agency for the spiritual awakening upon which, as Christian Scientists see it, the solution of humanity's manifold problems ultimately rests. Christian Scientists generally would agree that bringing prayer to bear on human tragedy and suffering does not preclude taking practical steps to alleviate them."[43]

For the Christian Scientist, then, the human task must combine two elements—insight into the nature of reality and the practical application of that insight for the living of a good life and the bettering of the world. In this world view, life is not a journey from birth to death according to a divinely ordained plan, as is the case for Mormons and Unificationists.

It is a kind of journey, nonetheless, a progression toward greater and greater understanding. Agnes Hedenbergh sums up the path of human life in Christian Science: "Through a clear vision of perfect, spiritual ideals, we progress heavenward. We see God as Spirit and man as His spiritual idea; we hence enjoy in our daily experience health, happiness, and harmony, which manifest God, good."[44]

In contrast with Mormonism, Unificationism, and Christian Science, Scientology does not base its understanding of human nature on a detailed doctrine of deity, since, as may be recalled from the previous chapter, it understands the knowledge of God's nature as not yet discovered. Nonetheless, Scientology shares with these three other movements a conviction that there is an eternally existing aspect of human nature that is spirit rather than matter. The spirit of the person in Scientology, the real person, is the thetan, which inhabits a body. The body is controlled, up to a point, by the mind. Scientology understands these parts of the human person as arranged hierarchically, with the thetan not only predominating, but constituting the essential identity of the person.

It is the journey of the thetan in its attempt to survive across the Eight Dynamics, those concentric circles that organize the chaos of Scientology's universe, which is the focus of what it means to be human in Scientology. The thetan seeks enlightenment about its own nature at all the levels of the Dynamics: freedom from the restraints imposed by the body and mind, and liberation from forgetfulness about its own past lives and true nature. The thetan seeks to be "at cause," rather than to be affected by the restrictions of the physical universe, other people's expectations and manipulations, and its own undisclosed memories which make it act in an irrational manner.

The thetan is hindered by the physical body in its efforts to be truly itself and to fulfill its potential. Scientology does not deny the very existence of the body, but sees it as a fairly negligible entity. "The body," says Hubbard, "can best be studied in such books as Grey's Anatomy and other anatomical texts. This is the province of the medical doctor and, usually, the old-time psychiatrist or psychologist who were involved in the main in body worship."[45] The mind is higher on the scale, for it is "a communication and control system between the thetan and his environment."

But the mind, also, has its limitations, for it is divided into three parts distinguished by degrees of awareness of motivation. The analytical mind knows what it is doing, and The Basic Dictionary of Dianetics and Scientology indicates that because of this it can be equated with consciousness rather than the unconscious. The reactive mind is primarily a stimulus-response mechanism with little ability to conclude rationally, and the somatic mind is even lower than the reactive mind, because "it contains no thinkingness and contains only actingness."[46] The thetan and the analytical and reactive minds all have control over the somatic mind.

Scientologists would remind people who get too caught up in the metaphysical aspects of the movement that it is an "applied religious philosophy," whose purpose is to make life better. *In Scientology: The Fundamentals of Thought*, Hubbard specifies that the goal of Scientology is not "the making into nothing of all existence or the freeing of the individual of any and all traps everywhere." It is intended, rather, to help the individual live a better life and play a better game.[47]

Scientology uses the metaphor "game" to refer to life itself, but this understanding arises out of a hopeful interpretation of what "game" means rather than a cynical assessment that we are enmeshed in a trap that makes our efforts to seek knowledge of our true selves pitiable foolishness. Through its technology[48] Scientology offers the opportunity for everyone to win and in so doing make possible better lives for individuals and a safer world.

To speak of Scientology as offering universal salvation is pushing traditional language onto a movement that does not use it, but Scientology itself occasionally refers to theological concepts in speaking of human nature; however, it uses its own language to describe what is the matter with human nature. According to "The Scientology Catechism," humankind is not evil but good by nature. But to be basically good does not mean that we do not commit sinful acts: "Man is basically good but aberrated; he does harm or sin certainly—and reduces his awareness further by so doing." Sin is defined in Scientology as composed of "lies and hidden actions and therefore untruth."[49]

In the game of life as Scientology understands it, sin does not call for repentance as much as it does for the eradication of error, and that must come through the technology, the auditing process, sometimes referred to as pastoral counseling. In fact, in regard to getting rid of sin, Scientology sees parallels between the goals of its technology and Jesus's saving action. "Jesus Christ," says "The Scientology Catechism," "was the Savior of Mankind, the Son of God, and instructed his disciples to bring wisdom and good health to Man, and promised mankind immortality. In Scientology we believe in these three things Christ intended for Man. It is our mission as Scientologists, as it was for Christ's disciples, to bring wisdom, good health and immortality to mankind."[50] At the same time, Scientology does not claim that its own founder, Hubbard, is a divine savior: "L. Ron Hubbard personally states that he is a man as others are men. He is a much loved friend and teacher."[51]

Scientology uses graded levels to chart the human pathway to freedom from aberration. The first goal toward which the Scientologist works is that of "Clear," a term and status that emerged from Dianetics, the earlier phase of Scientology's development. Those who have achieved Clear through the auditing process of Scientology are described as having come to an awareness of themselves as free from the unremembered traumas of this life and past lives that have kept them from acting rationally, and, as a result, from being happy and successful. To be Clear is to have one's engrams washed away.

The *Basic Dictionary of Dianetics and Scientology* defines Clear in several ways: "A being who is unrepressed and self-determined. . . . beings who have been cleared of wrong awareness or useless answers which keep them from living or thinking. . . . One who has become the basic individual through auditing." As a verb "to clear" means "to release all the physical pain and painful emotion from the life of an individual."[52] In the early days of Dianetics and Scientology, the claims made for the powers of Clear status were considered extravagant by critics of the movement. They included mental powers as well as healing capacities.

Now Scientology offers cautionary advice as to what may be expected from Clear and also from the E-Meter, the device that Scientologists use in the auditing process. In the front of *Dianetics* there is this statement: "The Hubbard Electrometer, or E-Meter, is a device which is sometimes used in Dianetics. In itself, the E-Meter does nothing. It is not intended or effective in the diagnosis, treatment or prevention of any disease, or for the improvement of health or any bodily function" (n.p.). On the other hand, Scientology continues to tie Clear status to health in a qualified manner. For example in "The Scientology Catechism," the answer to the question, "Do Clears get colds and get sick?" the answer is as follows: "A Clear is very rarely ill. This doesn't say that a Clear in a body won't get sick, for the body is susceptible at times to various things."[53]

Clear was the highest status one could achieve in Dianetics, but Scientology has developed a status above that of Clear called Operating Thetan, described as "an individual who could operate totally independently of his body whether he had one or didn't have one. He's now himself, he's not dependent on the universe around him."[54] One of the capabilities of the Operating Thetan is to "go exterior," to leave the body without causing death and to return to it. The status of Operating Thetan is laid out by hierarchical gradations. The "ability gained" in the higher states is still marked "confidential" on the "New Streamlined Classification, Gradation, and Awareness Chart of Levels and Certificates."

One might expect that such a means to enlightenment would impose few burdens other than the sacrifice of time and auditing fees on the part of individuals who wish to undertake the full process—and that success would be assured. But it is at this point that the recurring theme of individual responsibility for salvation or enlightenment, so characteristic of the new religions, emerges once again. Scientology has its own way of indicating that each person is responsible for enlightenment and, particularly, for his or her own identification of themselves as enlightened. The title page of *Dianetics* is preceded by an admonition that "the benefits and goals of Dianetics can be attained only by the dedicated efforts of the reader." Further, "The Scientology Catechism" indicates in several places that, whereas

Scientology places its learnings and its technology at the disposal of the individual, it is up to that person to apply them: "That which is real to the person himself is all one is asked to accept of Scientology. No beliefs are forced upon him. By training and processing he finds out for himself."[55]

In answer to the question, "Can't God be the only one to help Man?" "The Scientology Catechism" gives an answer that has already been articulated in this chapter as one of the assumptions of Unificationism: "We take the maxim to heart that God helps those who help themselves. You have the answers to the mysteries of life; all you require is awareness and this Scientology can and routinely does teach you. Man asks for pat answers, he is used to doing this. Scientology requires that the person thinks for himself and thus learns wisdom."[56] In reinforcement of this emphasis on individual responsibility, recent studies by sociologists William Sims Bainbridge and Rodney Stark indicate that individuals must claim the status of Clear for themselves. They are not tested but must identify themselves as having achieved Clear."[57]

Finally, since there is no detailed doctrine of deity in Scientology, no measure against which all else is measured, it is very much up to the individual to define what will operate as criteria of ultimate value and how he or she will define the meaning of success, happiness, and "survival." Many Scientologists describe their "wins" or "gains" in Scientology in specific terms related to improved relationships, better self-esteem, and job success. But in a column called "Spectacular Wins" in a Scientology publication, *Source: Magazine of the Flag Land Base*, there are also many testimonials by Scientologists—with their levels indicated (OT I, OT III, etc.)—to the success of the technology and a specific auditing process. For example, "in addition to all the incredible spiritual gains of OT III, I have the win of having done it very easily and faster than I thought. . . . With standard tech, nothing bad can happen."[58]

In sum, it is its technology that Scientology offers to its members, providing the means to becoming as fully human as possible, to ascend not to heaven but to all the circles of the Eight Dynamics and to the highest level possible of Operating Thetan. The technology in combination with Scientology's definition of the thetan, the spirit, as constituting the real person, offers the individual freedom from the tyranny of matter, but, more important, the chance to live a better life. For Scientologists the technology, as it has come through Hubbard and the Church of Scientology, presents not just one among many ways to achieve this better life but the only proven way to fulfill our potential as human persons.

Both Christian Science and Scientology espouse the common notion that to be human is to live within the parameters of a particularly acute paradox: that our individual dwelling places, our bodies, and the dwelling place of the whole human species, the physical world, are not truly our homes. In fact, they confine us and mislead us and, through the illusion of reality which they present, can keep us from knowing our true identity—that by nature we are spirit. To put this another way, both of these religious movements suggest that in order to live well in the world we must acknowledge that the world is not real. In order to have minds free from fear and bodies free from pain, we must recognize that spirit is the only reality.

In regard to the reality of the body, Christian Science makes a more radical statement than Scientology in claiming that as human persons we are spirit alone. Scientology grants a measure of reality to the body, but places it at the bottom of a hierarchy of spirit or thetan, mind, and body. These two movements also offer different means of recognizing the reality of who we are. For Christian Scientists the appropriate response to our false thinking is prayer and study. For Scientologists it is use of the technology developed by L. Ron Hubbard.

THEOSOPHY AND NEW AGE:
HUMAN BEINGS ROOTED IN THE COSMOS

The insight that both Theosophy and New Age thought wish to convey about human nature is threefold: that we are complex entities made up of interpenetrating planes of matter and consciousness; that, since we are all manifestations of the divine, we are interconnected with every aspect of the universe; and that in us as human persons consciousness is most highly developed, a reality which makes us the most responsible beings in the universe.

For Theosophy this triple insight provides the foundation for the outline of a cosmic history in which we as men and women participate during many lifetimes over billions of years on our journey out from the Absolute and back to it. We work out our destinies and our spiritual development through the process of evolution as it is guided by the laws of karma and reincarnation. And when we engage in that which is wrong, that which retards our progress and that of the entire universe back to the One, we do so not because we are sinful by nature, but because we are egocentric. We have forgotten our interconnectedness with all the rest of the universe, and we are acting on a perverse and ignorant insistence on the reality of the personal ego rather than what Blavatsky calls the Higher Personal Ego.

Theosophy depicts the human person as a highly complex being related both to the material and spiritual realms. We are made up of seven bodies or sheaths, it says, which are divided into "higher" and "lower" or "outside" and "inside" sheaths. Theosophists caution that these terms are to be used metaphorically. In *The Key to Theosophy*, Blavatsky speaks of the "Lower Quaternary," which includes the physical body, the etheric double, the astral body, which is the medium of feelings, and the mental or manasic sheath which has two levels—one for ordinary problem solving and the other for metaphysical thought. She describes, also, the Upper Imperishable Triad, comprised of Mind, or Intelligence (*Manas*), the Spiritual

Soul (*Buddhi*), and Spirit (*Atma*), which is one with the Absolute "as its radiation."[59]

These latter three make up what Theosophy calls the causal body, that which persists through various incarnations and which during a resting time after the death of the physical body assimilates the learnings acquired during each incarnation. The four lower sheaths disappear during the process of death. It is the causal body which carries the true identity of the individual, an identity not associated with "personality" or with any particular "I" through the various incarnations that comprise the cosmic journey.

If such a complex description of what makes up the human person seems to outsiders to invite an understanding of human nature that is even more susceptible to destructive body-spirit dualisms and fragmentation than the traditional interpretation of the human person as body and soul, the Theosophist sees it as a way to remind us that we are not autonomous beings on separate journeys through one physical lifetime. Instead we are what Robert Ellwood calls "cosmic pilgrims who have become human beings fully clothed with flesh of dense matter on planet Earth."[60] These seven sheaths signify our identities as temporal and eternal, material and spiritual, individual and communal beings. We are the stuff of ancient, primordial civilizations and of profound developments in human nature yet to come. The history of one individual or even of the planet we inhabit can come nowhere near conveying the immensity of the cosmic drama in which we—individuals, the human race, all sentient beings, and the planet—are participants.

Ellwood pinpoints this time in history, the late twentieth century, as being the middle of the cycle of the fifth of seven "root races," all with different composites of matter and consciousness and with particular tasks to perform. It is our obligation at this time in the working out of cosmic history to "become fully at home in the material realm, learn how it works, how to use it as a vehicle for expression, how through it to know and love Ultimate Reality as the ideal of knowledge and beauty."[61]

Our obligation to learn the lessons which must be learned through the vehicle of matter also presents us with the temptations and dangers that could keep us from accomplishing them, for we may forget that we are more than matter. It is not inevitable that this failure occur because Theosophy does not understand human nature as fallen in the biblical sense. Instead, the danger is present because we might remain ignorant of and alienated from the knowledge of our true nature as spiritual beings. Theosophy speaks of this condition as marked by egocentricity—Blavatsky calls it "ferocious selfishness." It is the conviction that our true selves are totally identified with the desires of the particular body we inhabit during one incarnation.

How do we become aware of our egocentricity, and how do we exorcise it from our understanding of self? We do not pray or petition the Absolute to "take away" sin or egocentricity in the Theosophical view, because prayer, according to Blavatsky, only kills self-reliance and refutes the Theosophical understanding of divine immanence. Instead, "we try to replace fruitless and useless prayer by meritorious and good-producing action."[62] We must also turn inward to that source of wisdom, that manifestation of the Absolute which is always with us and always accessible. But, "the Spiritual Ego can act only when the personal Ego is paralyzed,"[63] says Blavatsky, and so we must seek what help is available in order to bring about that paralysis. Whereas Theosophy does not offer a technology as does Scientology, it does offer techniques for fostering spiritual awareness, among them meditation, study, and fasting, as well as the searching of our own experiences for those incidents in our lives which speak to us of different realms of consciousness and go beyond what we perceive by sensory means.

We may look for assistance, also, to those Masters or Mahatmas who have found and followed the path to enlightenment and who have chosen to return to the earthly plane to guide those who are still struggling. They have already rendered selfless service to the universe and have developed fully the virtues of wisdom and compassion. This help from the Masters does not always come in obvious ways, and the relationship between a Master and a student may be inward rather than outward. Often, Robert Ellwood points out, "such things are expressed in dreams, mystical experiences, and subtle communications."[64] Jesus is one of the Masters in Theosophy, but as such he does not offer help that is different in kind from that of other Masters. Rather, the classifying of Jesus with other Masters such as the Buddha and Blavatsky's Koothumi and Morya serves to confirm Theosophy's identity as a religious movement which derives its teachings from many different sources.

Theosophy's understanding of the inevitable journey across the aeons prompts a question concerning human freedom. Where is there room for it in Theosophy if, as Ellwood claims, "human life is impelled to move in the direction of fuller being and greater wisdom and joy"?[65] Theosophists would answer this question by saying that we do indeed have the freedom to make moral choices. We are free to ignore any evidence that we are other than material beings. We can revel in our identity as individual, non-connected beings who have no responsibility for anyone other than ourselves. We are free to retard the evolutionary process of all creation by failing to assume that we have anything to do with it, and, in that process of ignoring, we can cause unnecessary suffering for ourselves and for the entire universe.

We are free from coercion, according to Theosophy, but, finally, it would appear that however much we resist, we will be swept into the movement of life back to the One. It is our responsibility as human persons to speed up that movement rather than to hold it back. We participate in the power afforded us by the divine within, but it is up to us to discover both the reality of the divine immanence and of the divine Trinity—the causal body—which constitutes the essence of our being. By our recognition or lack of it we are able to affect the rate of our return and that of all reality to the Absolute. If we can speed the process, we can at the same time eliminate much of the suffering that goes on all around us. According to Ellwood, "nothing prevents our avoiding another decline and cataclysm if we so choose, or transmuting it into an inner initiation to a higher moral level rather than projecting it outwardly as natural or nuclear holocaust. Nothing prevents our accelerating past rates of evolution many, many times to make earth a paradise in one generation."[66]

Shirley Nicholson makes this same point about human responsibility a little differently when she speaks of the process of "self-induced evolution." She sees humankind at a turning point in its history because we have experienced the birth of self-consciousness: "Because we can choose our inner feelings and thoughts, we have the ability of self-control and self-direction. This gives us some control over our environment and over our world. Our evolution is now self-induced through our own decisions and efforts [and] we can begin consciously to direct our own evolution, both as a species and individually."[67]

Nicholson goes on to speak further of the "immense potential" of human nature. Given the tremendous responsibility that the human person is asked to assume in Theosophy—a cosmic responsibility for oneself, for the good of the human race, the welfare of the universe, and, perhaps, even the good of the One—a doctrine of human nature that stresses potential rather than helplessness in the face of sin seems to be very much in order. As Theosophists see it, the very capacity for access to the divine within may be warped by self-centeredness, but Theosophy never goes so far as to say that we are fallen creatures, for the divine is always present to us waiting to be acknowledged.

The understanding of human nature and its tasks which emerges from New Age thought maintains the same conviction as Theosophy, that we are at a turning point in human development and in the history of the planet, a time when the recognition of ourselves as beings of higher consciousness connected with all other forms of life can—and must, if we are to save ourselves from extinction—have positive consequences for the human race and for the whole earth. And like Theosophy, New Age thought fosters the concept of divine immanence in order to speak not only of the accessibility of the divine but of the interrelatedness of all things. "We believe that in the heart of every living form is found a spark of that Almighty Power," says one of the tenets of the Light of Christ Community Church. "We believe that all humanity is becoming One Family. We love all religions, traditions, nations and races without discrimination of color, creed or sex."[68]

But, it is not enough, say New Age theorists, simply to assert our oneness with all members of the human family. We must likewise recognize our connection to and identification with our planet, the earth. We must

learn to understand ourselves as citizens of the entire planet who are responsible for its well-being and for each other. Much of the foundation for
what New Agers call a "planetary perspective," is the Gaia hypothesis, developed in part by the British scientist, James Lovelock, which affirms that
the Earth is a living being. David Spangler asserts that both science and
many religious traditions lay claim to this hypothesis, and, if there is any
truth to it, we must re-vision the way we as human persons view ourselves
as a species: "If Gaia exists, then we are part of her, part of a larger life,
a greater body of existence, a wholeness to which we are accountable in
our actions."[69]

What part do we play in Gaia and how does that influence the ways
in which we need to understand ourselves as human beings? According
to New Age theorists, we are the planet's nervous system, its means of
achieving self-awareness. "In humanity," says Matthew Fox, "for the first
time in twenty billion years, the cosmos can reflect on itself. Here the awe-
some doctrine of our being royal persons finds a beautiful expression, one
that moved Teilhard de Chardin to exclaim, 'Being in the forefront of the
cosmic wave of advance, the energy of humanity assumes an importance
disproportionate to its apparently small size.'"[70]

Fox, like many other New Age writers—although most of them, unlike
Fox, outside the Roman Catholic tradition—claims that the fall-redemption
theology of original sin and its need for a rescuing and redeeming God
has sapped us of our confidence that we can do very much about our own
suffering or the state of the world. To counteract that sense of helplessness
we must think of ourselves as "royal persons" who see ourselves acting
out of "our dignity and responsibility for building the kingdom/queendom
of God."[71] Brian Swimme maintains that we have contributed to our sense
of helplessness because we have given ourselves too narrow an identity:
"We have performed mightily in our role as Americans, and we have suc-
ceeded in our role as scientific Westerners. Even as humans—in the role
of subduing, conquering, and controlling the environment—we have accomplished wonders. But we have failed as yet to evolve into our role as
human Earthlings, and this failure lies behind our present pathological im-
passe."[72]

To think of ourselves as sinful, as helpless, as estranged from creation
and from God or the Light or the One—in short to espouse traditional fall-
redemption theologies of the Protestant or Catholic varieties—is to keep
ourselves from realizing our true identities as participants in the unfolding
creation of the universe. We fail, as a consequence, to develop the compassion and the confidence we need in order to take on the responsibility that
is ours—the development of a planetary culture that can preserve and save
the human species and the planet.

From a source very different from that of the Roman Catholic Fox comes
another admonition that we must build human confidence by the way in
which we understand human nature. In *Five Great Mantrams of the New-Age,*

H. Saraydarian speaks of the "Affirmation of a Disciple," which he sees as "an awakening in one's true Self to the reality of his essence. . . . Affirmation acts as a reminder to the conscious man of what his true Self is and as a great magnetic vision which reestablishes his confidence in himself."[73]

One begins to see the need for confidence when New Age thinkers elaborate on the implications of the New Age emphasis on human responsibility. Fox speaks of our "divinization as images of God who are also co-creators," and he quotes from the Jesuit scientist Thomas Berry and from Albert Einstein as to what is required of us. "Contemporary creativity," says Berry, "consists in activating, expressing, and fulfilling the universe process, the earth process, the life process, and the human process within the possibilities of our historical moment." Einstein sums up this responsibility a little differently: "The greatest formal talent is worthless if it does not serve a creativity which is capable of shaping a cosmos."[74] For Fox, the acts of "fulfilling the universe process" and "shaping the cosmos" are also tied tightly to the more specific task of fostering a just society: "On the part of the poor, this means being actively involved in asserting one's dignity, which means one's rights, and of letting go of oppressive self-images that others have handed to one. On the part of those who are comfortable, this means letting go and siding with the afflicted."[75]

Emphasis on human responsibility in New Age thought also takes the form of ecological concerns that have to do not just with living a good life but with survival—of the human race and of the planet. George Trevelyan, a New Age thinker who has influenced Americans such as David Spangler and who is referred to as "England's Father of the New Age," speaks of the human obligation to "cleanse" the planet, a term which he uses both literally and figuratively. In doing so, he invokes the Gaia hypothesis: "If we as a race are to survive, there is no choice but to turn about and begin living again with Gaia, consciously planning our life-style to avoid the entropy which is bleeding energy out of the body of the earth."[76] In confirmation of the eclectic sources of New Age thinkers, Trevelyan describes himself as indebted to Rudolf Steiner's anthroposophy, to Esoteric Christianity, and to eastern religions, particularly Buddhism, for his conviction that we will do two things: "recognize our true humanity," and "lift our thinking and see that we have a major role to play in the transformation and redemption of the planet."[77]

Over and over again New Agers articulate that same double theme: that we are the epitome of creation or of the evolutionary process and that as such we have responsibility for the salvation of the planet and of each other. If we are indeed royal persons, if we are the nervous-system of the planet, if we are the product of twenty billion years of cosmic development, then what keeps us from changing our perspective and bringing about exactly those changes in human consciousness which are needed for us to make the connections between our own individual selves and destinies and that of the whole universe? What stands in our way? New Agers claim along with Theosophists that it is egocentricity, that "ferocious selfishness," that paralyzes our ability to see our true natures and our interconnectedness with all creation.

As human persons, according to Brian Swimme, we have the capacity and the responsibility to cleanse the earth and to transform evil into good, even past evils: "Each individual person has the power of participating in the transformation of the whole Earth. The evil that reaches you after so many millions of years of existence can be absolved and transformed. You have the power to pass it on to another, to forgive, to end the needless torment, and, most of all, to transmute evil into energy for the vitality of the whole."[78]

If the list of responsibilities that New Age thought puts together for humankind seems overwhelming in the face of the problems of the world, New Age spokespersons are quick to point out that help is available. There are the ancient teachings long lost to human civilization and now emerging again in contemporary culture. Spirit guides make themselves known to human persons in order to impart the wisdom they have acquired as "older souls." Spangler, for example, speaks in *Emergence* of "John," a spiritual presence he describes as a "friend and co-worker."[79] Spiritual practices such as meditation, yoga, and "visualizing" exercises are a part of life in many New Age communities. They are designed to help develop greater consciousness of God within as well as to pool psychic energy in order to see things as they could be and to foster encouragement for individals and communities.[80] New Age groups also invoke Jesus as one of the "way-showers" of humanity. All of these aids, New Agers are cautioned, must be used not just for individual spiritual development, but for the good of the species and the planet. Otherwise the individual has refused to assume the responsibility that in the New Age understanding is an essential part of being human.

By emphasizing the interior of the human psyche as the dwelling place of the divine, both Theosophy and New Age thought convey that the primal spiritual journey is the journey inward in order to recognize and then to acknowledge and finally to cultivate the divine within. In both movements this pilgrimage involves "body work": massage, meditation, fasting, yoga, imaging, even dancing, at least on the part of many New Age groups. This body work is not intended to "mortify the flesh" so that it will cease the distractions that keep the human person from achieving spiritual development; it is intended, rather, to help the body to furnish its own kind of wisdom and to supplant the body-spirit dualism that New Agers, particularly, see as standing in the way of an understanding of our true selves.

In addition, however, to their emphasis on the need for individual spiritual development, Theosophy and New Age thought foster ways in which to move beyond the individual self to a more cosmic arena. For Theosophy, this involves the journey which Ellwood characterizes as across the aeons back to subsumation in the One. For New Agers the broader arena is the life of the planet. In each movement, "sin," or that which puts up barriers both to individual transformation and to cosmic identity, comes from the refusal to acknowledge this interconnectedness with the divine, with the universe and with each other. Neither movement is willing to claim that any one religious tradition can furnish the individual with sufficient wisdom or with adequate techniques for such a journey, and thus there is a kind of obligatory eclecticism, even for those—Roman Catholics, for example—who claim identity within a particular tradition. Thus the longing for a planetary religion as well as a planetary culture.

In constructing their theologies of human nature, the new religions have needed to address certain dual realities of human experience and to bring the theological imagination to bear in order to offer coherent responses to these experiences. We are acutely aware as human persons that we are finite creatures with bodies that will eventually die; and at the same time we intuit that there is "more," that there is something about us which is eternal. We encounter the concreteness of both good and evil. We cannot deny that the world is filled with terrible tragedies and needless suffering occasioned by both moral and natural causes; nor can we say that there is no good in the world, that the beauties of natural world do not exist or that there are no heroic deeds or kind acts or occasional lessenings of personal and corporate hatreds. We wonder what we as men and women have to do with any or all of it, and we are led to ask to what extent we are helpless in the face of that which seems simply visited upon us and to which we must be resigned, or to what extent we can exert effort or make choices.

As the new religions confront these realities, they acknowledge implicitly, and sometimes very explicitly, that they offer theological responses which are different from those put forth by the established traditions and by the secular culture and the disciplines of the social sciences that offer their own interpretations of what motivates and what limits men and women.

If we turn again to those general affirmations and negations of the new religions outlined at the beginning of the chapter, they are a reminder that these six religious movements offer interpretations of human nature that insist on great potential and at the same time tremendous responsiblity. In spite of a variety of ways of valuing or de-valuing the physical body, the new religions claim that the most essential aspect of the human person is spirit, which is eternally ongoing in some manner. For Mormonism and Unificationism the individual human body figures into the story as well. In Mormonism, the moral choices that can lead eventually to divinity can only be made in a physical body during the mortal life, and that same body, glorified, will be reunited with the spirit body in the celestial regions. But even more prominent in Mormonism is the eternal intelligence that will not only exist into endless future time but has existed from all time and is not dependent for existence on God's sustaining power in the same sense that is the case, for example, in Christianity. Among Unificationists, too, the body is the necessary vehicle for that which must be accomplished during the earthly life. But, as will become apparent in the next chapter, it is the spirit body, the exact replica of the physical body, which will persist into eternity; the physical body will decompose and will not rise again.

In Christian Science, the physical body has no basis in reality; it is, in fact, the false belief that the body exists which accounts for both sin and suffering. In the Christian Science understanding we are spirit not body, mind, not matter, necessary reflections of Mind and Spirit or God. For Scientologists the body is real, but an encumbrance, a low-level stimulus-response mechanism which responds to past traumas called engrams and impedes the search of the thetan, the eternally existing aspect of the individual, for its true identity and power.

Theosophists and at least some New Age thinkers posit a very complex interpretation of the make-up of the human person. It is the four lower bodies in Theosophy that gradually fall away and disappear upon the death of the physical body. The causal body, the three higher bodies, which survive through as many incarnations as are necessary to achieve reunion with the One, persists. Because New Age thinkers derive their understanding of human nature from occult, eastern, and Christian sources, there are differences in interpretation as to the actual make-up of the human person. Mention of the "ethereal body" is frequent, for example, in the Light of Christ Community Church and in the Aquarian Light Church but would not be a likely topic of conversation at the Institute of Culture and Creation Spirituality or Common Ground. Nonetheless, for New Age thinkers in general, the human person is more than the physical—there is that which transcends the body and endures, whether it be called spirit or higher consciousness or soul.

Among groups that put forth such optimistic interpretations of the spiritual destiny of humankind, it is instructive to note in all but one (Scientology) warnings against equating human nature with divine nature. There is no doubt at all that Mormons are promised the opportunity to be as God is now (just as God was once human), but it may be recalled that Mormons are also warned not to assume that one who is human now can ever catch up with God the Father. We have the opportunity to be as gods—that is what it means to be human—but we should not confuse ourselves with God. In Unification theology, there is no danger that humankind will confuse itself with God. Because of its heavy emphasis on the fall, there is nothing in this theological system that invites such confusion.

In Christian Science, even if we are invited and admonished to seek communion with God, who is Mind, Spirit, Love, Truth, Principle, Wisdom, and Being, there is the careful description of the human person as the reflection of God, not as God. Scientology, with its emphasis on the Eighth Dynamic as the Supreme Being, about which we know little, does not seem to encourage identification of the person with the Supreme Being. However, talk of "hidden splendor" housed unaware within the individual seems to point to a gnostic understanding of the individual harboring a spark of the divine light, and it is hard to say what might develop along these lines in Scientology in the future.

Finally, for all their insistence on the divine within, neither Theosophy nor New Age, at least in its more serious manifestations, is willing to let go of the concept of the Absolute as transcendent—or at least as not totally immanent. Interpreters of both movements speak of the absolute or the One as that which remains in part unmanifested in the many. Although they may say, "We are God," or "God dwells within every atom of the universe," the many are discouraged from confusing themselves with the One.

If we are not to confuse ourselves with God, according to the new religions, that does not mean that we are not expected to take on many of what might be called God's responsiblities as they have been interpreted by the established religions. This theme of responsiblity becomes apparent when the new religions confront the realities of evil and suffering and as they speculate about where evil comes from and what is to be our response to it. The second chapter enumerates the ways in which the new religions dissociate God or the Absolute from responsiblity for evil. In this chapter, the new religions demonstrate an awareness that humankind is accountable for much of the evil that befalls the world as well as individual persons. But these religious movements do not want to go so far as to say that we do wrong because we are sinful by nature—that there is something about us so skewed that it can only be righted by God. For, in the face of what must be undertaken by men and women in their earthly lives, both as individuals and as members of the human species, we cannot see ourselves as helpless creatures and still accomplish what must be accomplished—the eradication of evil and suffering, the preservation of the planet, and the fulfillment of human spiritual development. There are certain things that God cannot, will not, or should not have to do. Even in Mormonism and Unificationism, two religions in which God is perceived as a deity who is personal and loving and who takes an interest in the daily lives of individuals, the ethic is one of self-help.

These concepts—a high doctrine of human nature and a heavy burden of responsibility—are not new in Western civilization, nor are they confined to the teachings of new religions. For thousands of years, Psalm Eight has told us that we are made just a little less than the angels, and the theme of human responsibility is becoming more and more prevalent in contemporary theologies. In an article entitled "Reconceiving God for a Nuclear Age," Gordon Kaufman claims that in regard to nuclear warfare and the possibility of total nuclear disaster, ". . . our fate today is very much in our own hands, and we must take full responsibility for it." If we bring nuclear disaster on ourselves, "It will be . . . a disaster for God. And we humans in this generation will have been responsible."[81]

But, aside from the novelty or lack thereof of their individual teachings, it is the combination of concepts that is so striking in the doctrines of human nature in the new religions. Whatever the differences in doctrines or in the specific tasks they set before their followers or in what they claim is at stake in the accomplishment of these tasks, all of them profess a conviction that what we must acknowledge about ourselves as humans is that we are not depraved. None of the six denies that we are sinners, however they may define sin—as resulting from wrong choices, ignorance, or egocentricity. But, to go so far as to see ourselves as evil in our very natures is to render us incapable of discerning our true identities. We can only accomplish the tasks that belong to human persons if we become aware of the power, the freedom, and the responsibilities—for achieving divinity, for restoring the world to perfection, for seeing the error of material reality, for speeding the process of evolution, for saving the planet—that belong to the human species. We must acknowledge that we are strong rather than weak, powerful rather than helpless, capable of ascertaining knowledge of divine reality and of making use of what the Mormons call "the common minimum" that has been given to us. And then we must make our own best effort in accordance with what has been laid out as our obligations by each of these new religions.

If there is an exception to this general statement, it is Unificationism's theology of human nature that insists we can understand the present condition of the world and what to do about it only if we know the true story and far-reaching consequences of the Fall. But even in this case, Unificationism contends that in the original creation we were higher than the angels, the only creatures, in fact, able to mediate between God and creation. Its insistence that it is within human power to restore the world would seem to indicate that, even if Unification theology sees us as fallen, it does not see us as helpless and contingent beings.

In the following chapter this theme of responsibility receives even more attention, for in none of these six religions does the obligation to continue growing and learning and developing as spiritual beings end with the death of the body. All of them insist in one way or another that there is more work to be done after death.

FOUR

The Dead Learn Forever:

Death and Afterlife in the New Religions

In his book *Eternal Life?*, the Roman Catholic theologian Hans Kung quotes an excerpt from a play, *Triptych*, by German playwright Max Frisch. In his play Frisch suggests that there may be an even worse alternative to the secular interpretation of death as simply the cessation of life—an eternity of boredom. "Nothing is happening," says one of the characters, "that hasn't happened before, and I'm now in my early thirties. There's nothing more to come. I sit rocking in this chair. Nothing more to come that I haven't already been through. . . . How awful! The dead never learn. . . . "[1]

To survey the beliefs about death and afterlife in Mormonism, Unificationism, Christian Science, Scientology, Theosophy, and New Age thought is to encounter a common refutation of an apprehension that the dead never learn, that the afterlife is boring and unchanging. Such a survey comes up also with a denial of traditional Christianity's understanding that death is a kind of culmination of human spiritual striving, the end of which affords us a place in either heaven or hell.[2] It also comes upon at least the implication of a rejection of some of the more subtle religious interpretations of death and afterlife, such as immortality promised through the memories of those left behind or process theology's offer not of individual survival after death but of a return to a more generalized way of being a participant in ultimate reality.

If, as has been indicated in chapter two, the new religions reconceptualize God or ultimate reality in order to challenge the mistakes of classical theism and construct an idea of deity that is more coherent with human experience, they do not take on what Charles Hartshorne refers to as the mistake of assuming that immortality is to be a career after death.[3] In fact, the new religions all argue to one extent or another that death is indeed the pathway to another career or period of individual learning in the afterlife. In the belief systems under consideration, the dead not only learn, they change, develop and grow, and, in some cases, return to another life span.

What questions do the new religions seek to answer about the nature of death and the afterlife, and how do the answers they give relate to their understandings of God and human nature? The questions are the same ones that have intrigued and terrified humankind for millennia, to say nothing of the last one hundred fifty years. What is the meaning and purpose of death, or more poignantly, why do we have to die? What happens, if anything, after the death of the body? Will we survive as individual entities with consciousness intact? Will justice be meted out in the afterlife? Will the good be rewarded and the bad punished? If so, does that mean there are differing degrees of reward and punishment? Do we live more than one life? The new religions provide different specific beliefs in response to these questions, but, in their various ways, they all insist that one human life span, even at its most prolonged, does not furnish sufficient time to develop to our full potential as human beings. We have destinies and responsibilities that reach far beyond the time allotted to one human life, and we must be given the opportunity to fulfill them.

MORMONISM AND UNIFICATIONISM:
MISSIONARY WORK IN THE AFTERLIFE

It is helpful to begin an analysis of Mormonism's and Unificationism's views of death and afterlife by pointing out three very basic differences between them in their interpretations of death, resurrection, and heaven and hell. These differences make even more compelling the catalogue of similarities to follow. It is in their differences that we see, perhaps more than even in the doctrines of God and of human nature, the effects of Mormonism's materialistic or finitist metaphysics, its literal-mindedness, working in contrast with Unificationism's more spiritually and relationally oriented metaphysics.

Mormon scriptures acknowledge several kinds of death, among them absence from the presence of God and death as the wages of sin. Truman Madsen speaks of death metaphorically as the absence of God and the wages of sin, as "darkness of mind, hardness of heart, and numbness of conscience,"[4] but the more common meaning of death to which Mormons subscribe is physical death. "When the scriptures speak of death," says Bruce McConkie, "they ordinarily mean the *natural* or *temporal* death."[5] This means the separation of the physical body from the eternal spirit for a period of time during which the physical body is returned to the earth and the spirit waits in the spirit world for the day of resurrection, the reuniting of the body and spirit.

This is the death—the separation of body and spirit—that was brought about by the fall as it is understood in Mormon theology, and this is the death that Jesus suffered to overcome. Because of the essential role that the body plays in Mormon theology—one must have a body like the Father and the Son in order to achieve divinity—the separation of body and spirit and their eventual reunion become focal points of the Mormon doctrines of death and resurrection. "To become like our Heavenly Father," says Ken Miller, "we must be resurrected. *Resurrected* means to have our spiritual body and our physical body come together again, never to be separated."[6]

In Mormon theology resurrection is the gift that was given to all of humanity (not just Mormons) by Jesus's death—redemption from annihilation of the body, the expectation that the physical body will be reunited with the spirit. It is in this sense, also, that Mormons understand the meaning of the Atonement: not as redemption from the sin of Adam and Eve, for which we are not held liable, but from the death of the body. "With the atoning sacrifice of Jesus Christ," as Boyd Packer explains it, "the terrible spectre of the eternal death of the body no longer hovers over us. We are redeemed from temporal death, which death is the grave. Jesus Christ offered resurrection without condition and without cost. This restoration comes to all, the just and the unjust. Otherwise man would be punished for Adam's transgression and injustice would prevail."[7]

Unificationism, by contrast, denies emphatically that physical death is the death caused by the fall. According to *Divine Principle*, death is part of the natural order, and it is not a tragedy from which we need to be redeemed. It is not the "terrible spectre" of which Mormonism speaks. As *Divine Principle* states, "God created man to grow old and turn to dust; this would occur even if man had not fallen. Therefore, when Adam died at the Biblical age of 930 and turned to dust, this was not caused by the fall" (p. 168). For Unificationists, the death caused by the spiritual fall, the death with which their theology is concerned, is a spiritual death—the separation from God's direct dominion. In the Unification interpretation, Adam and Eve "died" on the day of the fall, even though their physical lives continued. "From this fact," says *Divine Principle*, "we can clearly understand that the death caused by the fall does not mean the expiration of physical life, but the state of having fallen from the good dominion of God, to the evil dominion of Satan" (p. 169).

Such an interpretation of death obviously requires a very different concept of resurrection from that put forth by Mormonism. In Unification theology the Resurrection does not refer to one event brought about by Jesus Christ for the sake of all, and it is not the reunion of the raised and glorified body, an occurrence that Unificationists see as not only impossible but unnecessary. In fact, in Unification theology the resurrection of Jesus Christ is itself considered to be spiritual in nature rather than physical: "Divine Principle assumes that since resurrection does not involve bringing corpses back to life, there were in fact no physical bodies that arose from the grave at the time of the crucifixion."[8]

In Unification theology the concept of resurrection refers to a process rather than to an event. It is an on-going process of the restoration of humankind to the direct dominion of God and out from under the dominion of Satan. Further, it has not only individual dimensions but historical implications as well, for resurrection is a cumulative process that involves the entire world. For Unificationists resurrection is, in fact, not only a life-long process but one that continues in the spirit world, which the individual enters at a level dependent on the kind of life he or she has lived on earth.

Mormon and Unificationist disagreement on the meaning of death and after-life extends to their concepts of heaven and hell, although both movements concur that the traditional Christian interpretations of heaven and hell are not sufficiently complex to account for the ambiguities of human experience. Mormonism not only retains but embellishes the traditional Christian understanding of heaven and hell as actual places, and Mormon literature is filled with complicated teachings about them. Mormon writings describe existence in the afterlife, particularly in paradise,[9] as one of great activity and as being filled with "organized, industrious people" engaged in gaining knowledge and performing such services as ministering to spirits of a higher level, making preparations for future earth events, gathering genealogical data, doing missionary work, checking temple records, watching over mortals as guardian angels, preparing clothing for anticipated spirit world entrants, guiding newcomers, serving as messengers to earth and to other spheres, constructing buildings, and engaging in kitchen labors.[10]

Mormons also speak in detail about hell, that place where the unrighteous await the Resurrection. McConkie describes hell in a way that sounds very familiar to a traditional Christian: "There they [the spirits of the unrighteous] suffer the torments of the damned; there they welter in the vengeance of eternal fire; there is found weeping and wailing and gnashing of teeth; there the fiery indignation of the wrath of God is poured out upon the wicked."[11] But hell, like paradise, will come to an end after the resurrection. Most of the souls will end up in the telestial kingdom, the lowest of the three kingdoms of glory, although some terrible sinners will be cast with the devil and his angels.[12]

Unificationism rejects the traditional doctrines of heaven and hell and calls adherence to them "the product of an incomplete religious awareness."[13] At the same time, this theological system speaks of the spirit world as filled with many levels. It is not God who determines our place in the spirit world or who imposes a punishment or reward, but we ourselves according to the life we lived on earth. Life in the spirit world, in keeping with the Unification understanding of resurrection, is a continued working out of one's spiritual status. The process proceeds hierarchically along three levels very roughly equivalent to Mormonism's telestial, terrestrial, and celestial kingdoms.[14]

Such different interpretations of death, resurrection, heaven, and hell do not prevent Mormons and Unificationists from coming together at a number of other points. Both movements promote hopeful understandings of the meaning of death. For Mormons death is the third stage in the Plan of Salvation, one which follows pre-existence and the mortal life. McConkie describes this experience as "one of the most important and desirable events that can transpire. . . . It is just as important to die as to be born, for the spirit to leave the body as it is to enter that same body. . . . without death there would be no resurrection, and hence no immortality or eternal life. Thus to do away with death frustrates the whole plan of redemption."[15]

Unificationists likewise do not see death as a tragedy. Their cosmological understanding of the material and the spiritual worlds as overlapping circles may, in fact, contribute to a more sanguine attitude about death as a transition from the material world to the spiritual, because Unificationists understand themselves as always having contact with the spirit world even in this life.[16] For Unificationists the spirit world is not a strange land: "Even during our physical lifetimes we are existing in two realms at once—a material one and a spiritual one."[17]

Mormons and Unificationists share the further conviction that moral striving and moral decision making do not cease with the death of the body. Nor does it make sense to interpreters of either movement that there be no opportunity for progress in the afterlife. Both movements, however, connect such progress with their own particular revelations, and the level of perfection that the dead eventually attain, whether in Mormonism or in Unificationism, depends on their acceptance of the teachings of the church even if that be accomplished in the afterlife.

In Mormonism this conviction finds shape and elaboration in what Latter-day Saints describe as one of the three missions of the church: the redeeming of the dead (the others being the perfecting of the saints and the proclaiming of the gospel to those who have not accepted it). It is understood by Mormons that those who have died without awareness of the Restoration, or who were aware but rejected the church, must have access to it in the spirit world as well as the opportunity to embrace the church and its ordinances. This means that missionary activity must persist in the spirit world, and such is the work of the Mormons who go there after death. This belief also has implications for those still living, because certain ordinances, like baptism, can only be performed on earth. "The Ordinances of the gospel," says Duane Crowther, "must be performed on earth. The living who understand the gospel and have the opportunity to do so must receive these ordinances. Otherwise ordinances may be performed vicariously for the dead."[18]

Mormons do not perform vicarious work for the dead simply to benefit individual persons who did not have the chance to accept the gospel on earth. They do so, also, in order to bind families together for all eternity. As Truman Madsen explains it, "our individual immortality is in no way contingent on that of others. On the other hand, the highest immortality is a family affair. In that sense we are either exalted together or not at all. Thus, others are crucial to the quality and intensity of our own eternal lives."[19] Crowther elaborates: "The major objective of missionary work and vicarious work for the dead is to bind the righteous of all eras into an unbroken chain of family relationships, under the patriarchal order of the priesthood. The righteous who are thus united are to dwell in this family relationship following the resurrection."[20]

Unificationists do not speak in the same way that Mormons do of missionary work in the spirit world. They assume, nonetheless, that knowledge of the true church is made available to those who have died and that part of the on-going resurrection requires that they accept its teachings even if they did not do so on earth. However, since the actual "work" of resurrection must take place on earth in conjunction with a physical body, the spirit person (who has both a spirit mind and a spirit body) must return to earth and cooperate with someone still living in leading them to the Lord of the Second Advent and the Unification Church: "They do so by helping and guiding people who are still on earth. As the spirit person assists the growth and achievement of such people on earth, he himself is spiritually benefited and progressively resurrected."[21]

The spirits return to guide those of their own faith, whether or not it is Christianity, or even no faith at all. The spirits of former Muslims, for example, who have accepted Unificationism in the spirit world will return to guide other Muslims still on earth. It is through this process that the unification of all religions in Unificationism will occur. According to *Outline of the Principle Level 4*, even though believers in the various religions have had no contact with each other up to now, through the influence of spirit people all of the faithful of various religions are destined to unite centered on the Lord of the Second Advent, the Reverend Moon. In a sense this is the reverse of the Mormon process—the spirits return to earth to do missionary work.

According to *Divine Principle*, the spirit who returns to earth may set up give-and-take action with an individual whose own spiritual development makes spirit communication possible. The spirit person contributes to the growth of the other by helping him or her to "receive revelations or to have deep experiences of truth, and sometimes . . . to experience other spiritual phenomena such as the power to cure diseases, the ability to prophesy, or spiritual fire."[22] Like the time of Jesus, our own time in history, that of the Second Advent, is particularly conducive to spiritual development; thus, we may expect relationships between the material world and the spirit world to be more common. Unificationists do not want their belief in the return of spirits to the world or their insistence that spiritual maturity must take place in conjunction with a physical body to be interpreted as in any way supportive of the doctrine of reincarnation.

Unificationism rejects the possibility of reincarnation on four grounds. First, it refutes God's original plan that the human person was to become spiritually mature in one lifetime. Second, in the Unification understanding, reincarnation denies the possibility that spiritual progress can be made in heaven. Third, Unificationists deny that reincarnation explains worldly injustices: "Such states cannot be simplistically attributed to one's prior goodness or evil. As most people would agree, material wealth, physical comfort, prestige and power are not true blessings of ultimate spiritual value." Fourth, the doctrine of reincarnation seems to defy common sense. If the world were full of "perfected souls," say the Unificationists, wouldn't there be more evidence of such perfection among "the wealthy, the beautiful, and the powerful on earth? On the contrary, in many instances such people seem to be just as immature and imperfect as the rest of mankind, if not more so!"[23]

Mormons and Unificationists share a final area of agreement about death and the afterlife, at least in general terms, in their understanding of the eschaton, the end of history and of the world. These religious movements are concerned not just with the life cycle of individual persons but with the life cycle of the earth as well. Both of these historically oriented religions look to the time when the earth itself will become the kingdom of God.

Mormons, in fact, speak of the earth as a living being (one is reminded of the Gaia hypothesis). "This earth," according to McConkie, "was created as a living thing, and the Lord ordained that it should live a celestial law. It was baptized in water and will receive the baptism of fire; it will die, be resurrected and attain unto a state of celestial exaltation."[24] Unificationists agree that the end of human history does not mean the death or annihilation of the earth, for in Unification theology it is the earth where God will establish the kingdom. The earth in Unification theology is eternal, and *Divine Principle* refutes a literal understanding of the Biblical notion that heaven and earth will pass away. Instead, Unificationists interpret this concept as referring to the destruction of Satan's reign.[25] In both Mormonism and Unificationism, when human history has ended and the dead are assembled, the righteous will be together on an earth that has been transformed to be the heavenly kingdom.

It is not surprising that two religious movements which hold that the heavens are in close proximity to the earth, that God is made known not only by special revelation but also in creation, and that much of what is essential to eternal salvation must be carried out on earth in a human body would fashion doctrines of death in which "earthly" activity persists in the afterlife and in which there is constant traffic of several sorts between earth and the spirit world. These doctrines keep the dead close to the living, and, in fact, make the dead and the living responsible for each other in carrying out the processes of exaltation and resurrection. That families are exalted or resurrected together and that marriage persists in the afterlife in both movements are not startling revelations, either, given the salvific role the family plays in both Unificationism and Mormonism.

Mormons and Unificationists see their doctrines of death as allaying fears of what lies beyond the grave. Mormons have the assurance that they will meet their loved ones again, and Latter-day Saints see their interpretation of death as contributing to the relative ease with which they meet death. Truman Madsen reports that the closest analogy to a Mormon funeral at graveside is a missionary farewell: "Here is a group of loved ones, not hard-faced and stoical, not blank and numb, but sensitized. There is apparent grief, but not despair." Madsen cites his impressions of Mormons meeting death: the old woman who "cheerfully sews her own white burial clothes," the well-known speaker who tapes his own funeral sermon and "sparks it with his verve for life," and the requests that are typical of the deathbed scene in which others ask the dying person to greet for them those who are already in the spirit world.[26]

For Unificationists death is seen merely as the transition from the material world to the spiritual world, and, given the Unification cosmology, it is not a very drastic transition. Even though Unificationists have what might be called a high doctrine of the human body, they see no need to lament the death and decay of the physical body, first, because physical death has always been a part of God's plan. Whereas traditional Christianity has taught that physical death is a punishment that we must suffer because of the Fall, Unificationism claims that Adam and Eve's physical bodies would have died whether they had sinned in Eden or not. And, since the human person has a spirit body that is a replica of the physical body, individuals will retain their identities in the spirit world and will be comforted by the recognition of each other.

CHRISTIAN SCIENCE AND SCIENTOLOGY: DEATH AS ILLUSION

However optimistic Mormon and Unification theologies might be about death and however inviting their descriptions of the spirit world, neither of these religious movements cultivates a sense of death as a longed-for and desirable cessation to the cares of the world. Both condemn suicide[27] and short circuit any inclinations in that direction by connecting salvation to work that must be done during the earthly life and through the vehicle of a physical body. Because Christian Science and Scientology are not body oriented and because in neither of these movements is the world considered revelatory of saving knowledge, one might predict that these two religions would advocate, perhaps even cultivate, an acceptance of or a longing for death as release from the body and from earthly life. Such is not at all the case. Neither movement advocates death as freedom from the fetters of the flesh and the world, but, as we have come to expect by now, they interpret death in very different ways.

Christian Science contends that we have nothing to fear from death, not because death is part of the plan of salvation or the gateway to a better life or to spiritual perfection but because this movement refutes the very reality of death. For Christian Scientists, belief in the reality of death and fear of its inevitability is another part of the overall belief in the reality of matter that keeps men and women from realizing their own identities as spiritual beings who cannot die.

If Christian Science does not grant the reality of death, it acknowledges that people do indeed die. But they die because they believe in the reality of death and therefore give this false idea power over them. "Is it unchristian to believe there is no death?" asks Mary Baker Eddy in *Unity of Good*. "Not unless it is a sin to believe that God is Life and All-in-all. . . . To God alone belongs the indisputable reality of being. Death is a contradiction of Life, or God; therefore it is not in accordance with His law, but antagonistic thereto."[28]

While the contention that there is no reality in physical death is a thoroughly radical statement, it is nonetheless a coherent statement within the framework of the Christian Science world view. If death is defined, whether medically or theologically, as the separation or the departure of the life force from the physical body, then that definition does not fit with Christian Science's understanding that the human person is totally spirit and not at all body. Birth in Christian Science does not involve the infusion of life or spirit into a physical body, and death does not mean the departure of life from that same body.

If death is not the departure of life from the body, then how does Christian Science define it? In the Glossary of *Science and Health*, Eddy describes death as "An illusion, the lie of life in matter; the unreal and untrue; the opposite of Life" (p. 584). She also frequently refers to death not just as an illusion but as a kind of dream. Thomas Linton Leishman speculates that she was recalling Jesus's description of death as sleep: "Mrs. Eddy writes of it in numerous passages in terms of illusion or delusion and describes it as a dream, indicating further her assurance that sooner or later man must awaken from the nightmare of death to the realization of its unreality and of the permanence and indestructibility of life, God-given and consequently God-sustained."[29]

Why is it, Christian Scientists ask, that millions of people cling so tightly to the belief that death is real and thereby experience the illusion of death? Christian Scientists attribute this to the pervasive materialism first of the nineteenth and now of the twentieth century. To believe in the reality of matter is to be compelled to believe, also, in its temporality and thus in death. According to Eddy, "Holding a material sense of Life and lacking the spiritual sense of it, mortals die, in belief, and regard all things as temporal."[30]

As Christian Scientists see it, it is not just belief in matter that causes men and women to die; it is also fear of death. Leishman points out that many decades before doctors and psychiatrists began to realize that fear contributes greatly to physical and mental illness, Eddy was aware of this phenomenon. "In its extreme form," says Leishman, "fear has been known to be so acute as to result in death itself. . . . Christian Science banishes fear on the basis of an ever increasing recognition of the nature of God as the source and support of all His creation—as Love, in which fear cannot subsist, as the apostle John reminds us."[31] In *Science and Health* Eddy repeated frequently that Christian Science properly understood could take away the fear of life's sufferings and the belief that death could put an end to them. "When it is learned that death cannot destroy life," she said, "and that mortals are not saved from sin or sickness by death, this understanding will quicken into newness of life. It will master either a desire to die or a dread of the grave, and thus destroy the great fear that besets mortal existence" (p. 426).

Christian Scientists are well aware that to claim there is no death and to mean it in any other than a metaphorical way is to invite ridicule and outrage. Even the insistence that sickness is an illusion is not quite so startling, since the modern person is familiar with the concept of psychosomatic illness. To insist, however, that there is no death would seem to refute in an entirely futile way both biblical passages that refer to Jesus's raising of the dead and human experience as it is recorded on the daily obituary page.

In response to others' citing of biblical passages that refer to the raising of the dead, Christian Science approaches them with an exegetical perspective that emerges from its own world view. Leishman acknowledges that "all who accept the accuracy of the Biblical records are aware that the Master restores the dead to life, and further, that prophets in the Old Testament period and apostles in the New, did likewise; and it is clear that Jesus expected such wonderful works of his followers."[32]

Leishman, however, interprets Jesus's ability to raise the dead, as in the case of Lazarus, as stemming from his knowledge that they were not dead, but asleep. Jesus's oneness with God enabled him to understand totally that death does not exist. He did not understand himself as bringing back to life a person who had died. Instead his power came from the knowledge that Lazarus had never died at all.

For Christian Scientists, then, those passages from the Bible that refer to raising the dead do not call into question their understanding that death is an illusion; instead, they reinforce it. The ability to raise the dead belonged to Jesus not because he was a supernatural being with powers that set him apart from the rest of humankind but precisely because he had achieved the fulfillment of his humanness—total unity with divine Mind, "an inevitable sense of his oneness with God." That sense of oneness with God and together with it the ability to recognize that the dead are only sleeping is within the capacity of all human persons, but not until we abandon belief in the reality of matter. Christian Science promises that "when you can waken yourself or others out of the belief that all must die, you can then exercise Jesus's spiritual power to reproduce the presence of those who thought they died—but not otherwise" (*Science and Health*, p. 75).

The exegesis of biblical passages on raising the dead is in many ways not so challenging a task in Christian Science as coming to terms with the constant reality of death in human experience. Although Christian Science may explain that death is the result of materialism or fear, that does not seem to deal sufficiently with the fact that Christian Scientists themselves die, including Eddy. For Christian Science this objection to its teaching about death—that it flies in the face of empirical evidence—is interpreted within the context of Eddy's understanding that a culture-wide acceptance of death as illusion was not possible at her time in history.

In *Science and Health*, Eddy stated her case against death plainly: "It is a sin to believe that aught can overpower omnipotent and eternal Life, and this Life must be brought to light by the understanding that there is no death, as well as by other graces of Spirit." If a demonstration of the unreality of death was not yet possible, nonetheless Eddy insisted that "we must begin . . . with the more simple demonstrations of control, and the sooner we begin the better. The final demonstration takes time for its accomplishment. When walking, we are guided by the eye. We look before our feet, and if we are wise, we look beyond a single step in the line of spiritual advancement" (pp. 428–29).

In a more contemporary account, Leishman repeats the confidence that death can be overcome, for in the Christian Science understanding there is not the admonition that this overcoming must await the Second Coming or the end of human history. He is more optimistic that death can be overcome soon: "Triumph over death," says Leishman, "if we were only aware of it, is to be had now. My own feeling as a Christian Scientist is that so far from being impossible, the overcoming of death is capable of accomplishment in this age, as in earlier ages, on the basis of sufficient consecration, humility and understanding of the permanency of God and of man as His image and likeness."[33]

As concerns an afterlife, Christian Science makes use of the terms "heaven" and "hell," but interprets them as "states of mind" rather than as places. In the Glossary of *Science and Health*, hell is described as "Mortal belief; error; lust; remorse; hatred; revenge; sin; sickness; death; suffering and self-destruction; self-imposed agony; effects of sin; that which 'worketh abomination or maketh a lie.'" The "Kingdom of Heaven" is defined as "The reign of harmony in divine Science, the realm of unerring, eternal, and omnipotent Mind; the atmosphere of Spirit, where Soul is supreme" (pp. 587–88). DeWitt John maintains that definitions such as these have the capacity to survive the skepticism about heaven and hell as "places" occasioned by contemporary science's discoveries about the vastness of the cosmos. Because Christian Science has never thought in terms of heaven and hell as actual locations, it is spared having to redefine or reinterpret its understanding of these traditional concepts.[34]

As to whether there is the possibility of communication with those who have died, Eddy and Christian Science answer this question in terms of the over-all framework of Christian Science. As is obvious from the chapter in *Science and Health* on Spiritualism and Theosophy, Christian Science wants nothing to do with spirits who return to earth and produce physical manifestations or with returning Masters or Mahatmas. But Eddy answers a question about the afterlife in *Miscellaneous Writings*: "After the change called death takes place do we meet those gone before—or does life continue in thought only as in a dream?" Eddy's response indicates that although there is no communication between those who are living and those who appear to have died, all those who have achieved the same level of consciousness in God, who "have come upon the same plane of existence" and know that death is not real will be able to recognize each other. We do persist as individuals after "the change called death," says Christian Science: "Man is not annihilated, nor does he lose his identity by passing through the belief called death."[35]

Another part of the answer to the question above reveals what it is that the dead must learn in Christian Science, and that is the reality that there is no death. Learning this is an on-going process. It is not enough simply to die in order to learn the lesson that there is no death. Enlightenment is not automatically granted on the other side of the grave as a kind of reward for dying, since "after the momentary belief of dying passes from mortal mind, this mind is still in a conscious state of existence; and the individual has but passed through a moment of extreme mortal fear, to awaken with thoughts, and being, as material as before." The knowledge that there is no death can only be achieved by "conscious union with God," and the learning must continue until the individual consciousness understands that "life, God, being everywhere, it must follow that death can be nowhere, because there is no place left for it."[36]

After Christian Science's vehement denial of the reality of death, Scientology's attitude toward it comes as a contrast. Unlike any of the other religious movements under consideration, Scientology's treatment of death is characterized by a kind of matter-of-factness, and the movement lacks a theological interpretation of what death means or why it is necessary. Death, in fact, does not figure very prominently in Scientology's written materials, except for the volume by Hubbard, *Have You Lived Before This Life? A Study of Death and Evidence of Past Lives* in which the author maintains that "the first thing one learns about death is that it is not anything of which to be very frightened. If you're frightened of losing your pocketbook, if you're frightened of losing your girl or your boyfriend—well that's how frightened you ought to be of dying, because it's all the same order of magnitude."[37] In *Dianetics* there are very few references to death, although early in the volume there is a "descriptive graph of survival" that designates "potential immortality" as "ultimate pleasure" and death as "ultimate pain." "The thrust of survival," says *Dianetics*, "is away from death and toward immortality."[38]

In *Have You Lived Before This Life?*, Hubbard responds to the question, "What happens to Man when he dies?" by saying that what occurs is a separation of the thetan from the physical body. In Scientology (in great contrast with Mormonism, for example) this phenomenon is referred to as a kind of mechanical process. In describing what it is that Scientology has come to know about death, Hubbard maintains that in Scientology the "mechanics" of death have become thoroughly understood and Scientologists are the first people who do know a great deal about death: "It is one of the larger wins of Scientology."[39] At another point Hubbard speaks of death as a "technical" subject.[40]

Hubbard makes use of what he calls a "cycle of action" to explain death, which he refers to as "create-survive-destroy." For Hubbard this cycle is applicable to a variety of things, including buildings or trees. "When we apply this cycle to the parts of Man," he says, "we get a death of the body, a partial death of the mind, and a forgettingness on the part of the spiritual being which is, in itself, again, a type of death."[41]

It is the issue of "forgettingness" in death that brings Scientology to an interpretation of "past lives." And it is the concept of "past lives" that is the focus of *Have You Lived Before This Life?* more than the actual phenomenon of death.[42] The concept of "past lives" in Scientology is concerned with the understanding that the individual has lived many lives previous to the present life and will live many more in the future. According to *What Is Scientology?*, "past lives are not a dogma" in the movement, but many Scientologists have described experiencing their reality in the auditing process: "With Scientology you are the judge of your own certainty in your past experiences, because you will know for yourself without reservation what they are. After all, only you were there!"[43]

"Past lives" in Scientology are not to be considered as the foundation for a belief in reincarnation, which Scientology describes as a system requiring that individuals be born again and again into many life forms. Nor does the concept of past lives have anything to do in Scientology with a larger religious system such as Hinduism or Buddhism, which see reincarnation as a means to dealing with issues of justice. "Past lives," says Hubbard, "are not 'reincarnation.' That is a complex theory compared to simply living time after time, getting a new body, eventually losing it and getting a new one."[44]

If past lives do not serve the same systematic function in Scientology as does reincarnation in many religions, then what is their purpose? For Scientologists, looking into past lives is a matter of extending the search for engrams beyond one lifetime on the theory that one cannot make satisfactory progress in the Scientology auditing process without taking into account traumas incurred in previous lifetimes (according to Scientology, "past lives" were discovered by auditors during the 1950's). In the first chapter of *Have You Lived Before This Life?*, Scientologists give testimonials reminiscent of the "Fruitage" chapter in *Science and Health* to explain how the recovery of information about past lives has been helpful to the present life. A "sculptor and poet" discovered in the auditing process that, although he had never studied either sculpture or poetry, he was very talented in both these areas. He states that "I discovered the truth about past lives without any hocus-pocus, candles, strange rituals or secrecy." One woman who suffered from chronic unhappiness in spite of obvious success concluded that "I could not have possibly gotten so mixed up in one lifetime." What she discovered about past lives helped her to resolve longstanding personal issues. For an artist the knowledge of past lives makes this life more fruitful: "Since I now know that I will 'go on' after this life, I am much saner about my decisions. Time has become more available, needless to say, so I do all those things I wish to do, properly, and I do not have compulsions to hurry or grab at life as others find themselves doing." Finally, a tennis professional "saw how the unpleasant occurrences from past lifetimes caused me trouble in *this* lifetime."[45]

The obvious pattern here is that a knowledge of what happened in past lives makes the living of this life more successful and happy. Another pattern emerges, however, as one surveys the forty-one cases included in *Have You Lived Before This Life?* and that is that all the past lives included terrible traumas and violent deaths. This is not surprising since the auditing process in Scientology is designed to bring to awareness past experiences of pain, whether psychic or physical, so that they lose their power to cause destructive reactions in individuals that are beyond their comprehension.

The predominance of terrible experiences in the past life accounts also helps to explain why it is that the process of recovering past lives is described as an arduous one in Scientology. In the process of dying, the thetan has lost all memory of a previous life, and in finding a new body manages to suppress the pain of death. Thus death brings on a kind of amnesia in the thetan, even though it has taken along into death and into the next life "old tin cans, rattling chains, bric a brac and other energy phenomena that he feels he cannot do without and stashes this in the next body that he picks up."[46] It is the auditing process that uncovers and renders harmless the old tin cans and rattling chains.

What is to be learned, then, in conjunction with death in Scientology is not information or wisdom that can only be acquired in the spirit world after the death of the body, for the sojourn of the thetan in the afterlife seems to be as brief as is possible. Instead, the vital information is about past existences and must be gleaned through the auditing process in the present life.

Because auditing is carried on in the present life, the recovery of past lives is an end in itself for the sake of this life, and it does not point to a kind of culmination in an afterlife or in any equivalent of a heaven or hell. The thetan approaches that which might be called transformation in other religious traditions not by undergoing a purging or learning process in another more celestial realm but rather by ascending the various gradations available to thetans in the Scientology system. Death, then, seems to be merely a very brief interlude with little to recommend it in Scientology other than the opportunity to take on a new body. It is difficult to tell from Scientology writings exactly how the seventh dynamic—the urge to survival as spirit—fits into the over-all understanding of death in the movement when there is so much emphasis on the thetan's securing another body as quickly as possible after the death of the previous body. Perhaps there is nothing to be discerned here, since Scientology sees itself in regard to death as the first religion "to enable an individual to be released from the very narrow limitation of having just one lifetime. This is a tremendous release for the individual because the significance and terrible consequences of death fall away. Death has lost its sting."[47]

In two very different ways Christian Science and Scientology understand themselves as doing away with the terrors of death, Christian Science by denying its reality and Scientology by denying that it has any grave significance in the existence of the thetan. Christian Science undergirds its interpretation of death as unreal by incorporating it into its doctrine of deity, a God who is all-in-all and leaves no room in the universe for the illusion that is death. Scientology ties its disarming of death to the effectiveness of its auditing process and the technology which has revealed in its uncovering of past lives that death is a temporary, if inconvenient, condition. Neither movement seems to be eschatologically oriented in its view of death, although that seems to be less true of Christian Science than of Scientology, since Christian Science anticipates a growing recognition of the spiritual reality of all things and along with it the disappearance of death. Scientology sees death solely in individual terms.

THEOSOPHY AND NEW AGE THOUGHT: DEATH AS BIRTH AND REBIRTH

Theosophy and some aspects of New Age thought posit a belief in reincarnation as one of their foundational concepts, and, thus, the many lives with intervening periods of rest on more ethereal planes of reality that Mormonism, Unificationism, Christian Science, and Scientology all deny become the focus of much of the discussion about death and afterlife for these two movements.

Like Scientology, Theosophy incorporates into its interpretation of death an emphasis on past lives, but Theosophy integrates its understanding of past lives into a system that embraces reincarnation as one of its most basic concepts for understanding what it means to live and what it means to die. Theosophy perceives death and successive rebirths as related to the natural cycle of the entire universe, and because this system assumes that humankind also participates in these cycles, along with every other aspect of the universe, death is not only inevitable but necessary for spiritual growth. But so too is rebirth. As one Theosophist puts it, " . . . when we find periodicity, cycles of activity followed by rest, rhythmic alteration, everywhere else in the universe, why should human life be the one exception?"[48]

Tightly tied to reincarnation in Theosophy's interpretation of the meaning of death is the accompanying concept of karma, the cosmic law of cause and effect. In *The Key to Theosophy*, Blavatsky defines karma as "the unerring law which adjusts effect to cause on the physical, mental, and spiritual planes of being."[49] Theosophists are very clear in their understanding that the system of karma and reincarnation is a much more satisfying interpretation of human experience than is the traditional Christian doctrine which grants to the individual one lifetime of moral striving upon which the soul's disposition depends for all eternity. As Theosophists see it, such a system fails to make sense for many reasons, one of which is the immense variety in the human situation. Anna Kennedy Winner contends that "the utter absurdity and senselessness of a procedure which would find one earth life, and only one, necessary for spiritual development, and yet give different people such entirely different samplings of earth life, seems so obvious that it is hard to understand how the Christian church ever managed to retain its hold upon the Western mind for so many centuries, without any more sensible explanation of the purpose of life."[50]

At the same time there is acknowledgment that karma, with its claim that "justice rules the world" is not a simple doctrine but very complex. Diana Dunningham Chapotin, a faculty member at the Krotona Institute of Theosophy in Ojai, California, claims that as soon as one goes beyond the basic idea—"that everything we think, say, or do has an effect whether we see it or not and will rebound on us inevitably in this life or another"— the concept of karma can be confusing. In an article entitled, "Do We Ever Suffer Undeservedly?" Chapotin distinguishes three levels in which karma operates: as cause and effect in an individual life; as the expression of character traits that are carried on through many incarnations; and at the monadic level that has to do with "a sharing of humanity's karma." Karmic activity at all three levels gives rise to questions of interpretation.[51]

Theosophy goes further in its interpretation of death and the afterlife than to articulate general principles. It provides a very detailed account of what happens to the various parts of the human person during the period of time between the death of the physical body and the next incarnation. The human person, it may be remembered from the previous chapter, is understood in Theosophy as comprised of seven interpenetrating sheaths which progress from the densest, the physical body, to the least dense, that which participates in the Absolute. In the process of death, the physical body is left behind. As Ellwood explains, " . . . that is *all* that happens at death—the remaining components continue as before but more vividly, no longer constrained in their astral, mental, and higher life by the weight of dense matter, though also unable to experience reality directly through the medium of matter."[52]

What takes place on the less dense planes of consciousness? It is the assimilation of experiences acquired in the incarnation just previous. This learning—and rest—is in preparation for the next life. As Ellwood interprets the process, the etheric double separates from the physical body (the silver cord that occult lore tells us holds the astral body to the physical body snaps) at the moment of death and after a few hours the etheric double dissolves. The astral body, which carries with it the higher forms, remains on the astral plane until all the desires associated with earthly life are exhausted, and then it also dissolves. Whether this interval is a time of rest and pleasure or of extremely painful purgation depends on how attached the person was to the material world.[53]

At the moment the astral body dissolves, the forms that are left experience what Blavatsky calls the "second death" and awake to life in what Theosophists call Devachan, or "heaven." Theosophists define Devachan as a place of pleasure, of "mental life on a very high level," but also as a place where effort must be exerted in order to learn what must be learned for the next incarnation. We can learn no more than what can be gleaned from the experiences of the previous incarnation, so there is no sense of enlightenment freely given; it must be achieved. According to Ellwood, "we can and do . . . create our own Heaven. But it will be no better than what we bring to it. . . . "[54]

In the Theosophical system, then, there is no joy or sorrow imposed on us as reward or punishment which seems grossly out of proportion either to what we have done or what we have failed to do during our earthly lives. Once the lessons of Devachan are learned, "the stream of karma . . . lifts the Pilgrim back into the course of this (or another) world, where it will find a womb prepared."[55] The person who emerges into a new life from this process will not bring with him or her specific memories or bits of information from Devachan, but what Ellwood calls images or "seeds," perhaps a way of thinking or an inclination to a particular kind of character.

When inquirers asked Blavatsky why the reincarnated person retained no memories of previous lives or of the time in Devachan, memories which might offer proof of the reality of reincarnation, she found the answer within Theosophy's understanding of what transpires at death: "Reincarnation means that this Ego will be furnished with a *new* body, a *new* brain, and a *new* memory. Therefore it would be as absurd to expect this *memory* to remember that which it has never recorded as it would be idle to examine under a microscope a shirt never worn by a murderer for the stains of blood which are to be found only on the clothes he wore."[56] To the objection that it is hard to believe in that which one cannot remember, Blavatsky appeals both to "circumstantial evidence" and to the need to "put oneself in *rapport* with one's real permanent Ego, not one's evanescent memory." She compares the law of reincarnation to those of the forces and abstractions of science that people believe in without being able to touch, see, hear, or smell them.[57]

As far as reward and punishment in an afterlife are concerned, Theoso-phists are willing to talk in terms of such traditional concepts as heaven and hell, if only to point out the limitations of those same terms as they have been interpreted by traditional Christianity. Blavatsky objects to the Christian interpretations in part because they are described as eternal. "Nothing is eternal and unchangeable," she says, "except the concealed Deity." Further, she says, "we believe in no hell or paradise as localities; in no objective hell-fires and worms that never die, nor in any Jerusa-lems with streets paved with sapphires and diamonds."[58] For Blavatsky and for Theosophists in general, karma, the "unerring law of Retribu-tion," deals out a system of punishment "as stern as that of the most rigid Calvinist, only far more philosophical and consistent with absolute justice."[59]

Like Mormonism and Christian Science, Theosophy is vigorous in its denunciation of suicide as a way of shortening the earthly life span. To cut off the experiences that karma dictates must be undertaken in a particular incarnation insures only that the lessons to be learned must be learned in another lifetime. Blavatsky ascribes suicide to "morbid brain disease" and an attempt to escape the duties which karma imposes. To shirk these duties is to impose "the creation of new Karma." "Duty," she says, "is that which is *due* to humanity. . . . This is a debt which, if left unpaid during life, leaves us spiritually insolvent and moral bankrupts in our next incarna-tion."[60] In other words, there is no short-cut to spiritual maturity in the Theosophical system. By devotion to duty, to the development of wisdom and compassion, and to the finding of our own particular paths to the One, we can speed up the cycle of death and re-birth, but we cannot circumvent its demands by means of suicide. Is there nothing resembling the biblical assurance of mercy in this system, inquirers have asked? Theosophists re-spond by saying that mercy lies in the opportunity provided by many life-times to discharge all debts.

In its interpretation of death and afterlife, Theosophy argues for affirm-ative responses to some of the most urgent questions humankind asks. Yes, we are right, says Theosophy, in our intuition that individual con-sciousness persists beyond the grave. We are correct, also, in asking for an answer to questions of justice, of reward and punishment, that make sense in light of what we observe in our experiences—that drastically vary-ing human circumstances demand more than one lifetime to be adjusted. Finally, we are on the right track, according to Theosophy, if we prefer jus-tice over mercy, if we ask for the opportunity to come to terms with our own failings over a series of lifetimes rather than to take the chance that we may or may not be forgiven for our sins. The heart of Theosophy's mes-sage about death and even most of the details have not changed since the early days of the movement: that the human individual, the Self, the Ego, the "real man," as Blavatsky calls it, survives the death of the physical body and undergoes purgative and integrative experiences on a variety of planes of consciousness. Eventually, though, the individual, the Ego, the product of many lifetimes, will be subsumed into the One.[61]

Like Theosophy, New Age thought interprets death as participating in the natural and orderly principles that undergird the universe, but the emphasis in New Age literature is on a different aspect of the dying experience. If Theosophy pays a great deal of attention to the unfolding of events in the afterlife in its interpretation of the meaning of death, much of New Age thought is concerned with the process of death itself, the actual experience of death and what it means. If Theosophy concentrates on the learning that must take place during the intervals between incarnations, New Age thinkers seem more interested in what the individual and all of humankind must learn about death itself. New Age writings on death are filled with references to Raymond Moody's *Life After Life*, a famous study of near-death experiences, Elizabeth Kubler Ross's *Death: The Final Stage of Growth*,[62] and Kenneth Ring's *Life at Death*.[63] For many, a near-death experience is what prompts interest in New Age thinking in the first place. Marilyn Ferguson cites such experiences as highly influential in motivating a serious inquiry into New Age thought. In *The Aquarian Conspiracy*, she states that many of those who filled out her Aquarian Conspiracy questionnaire commented that they gave up their conviction that consciousness ended with the death of the body because of near-death experiences: "The strongest believers were those who recounted brushes with death."[64]

The near-death experience has become a well-known phenomenon in American culture over the last fifteen years, and its characteristics are described in similar terms by people with particular religious orientations as well as by those with no interest in organized religion at all. These include an out-of-body experience occasioned by a trauma such as surgery, childbirth, or an accident; sometimes the sense of a buzzing noise and a journey through a long tunnel; the felt presence of supportive friends and relatives who have already died; the presence of a beckoning light; and an overwhelming sense of well-being. The widespread reporting of these experiences has involved not just theologians, but medical doctors and psychologists, in speculating about their significance for proving that human consciousness survives bodily death. Critics point out that the experiences may prove something about the process of death itself, but nothing about life after death.[65] Nonetheless the near-death experiences provide something of the scientific validation—reminiscent of nineteenth-century spirit apparitions—deemed necessary in contemporary culture for pursuing the survival question, and they give impetus to the New Age understanding that consciousness pervades the universe and does not cease at death.

The physical sciences are also seen as allies in learning more about what happens to the human individual after the death of the body. An exhibit originally titled "Continuum—Immortality Principle," which traveled around the country (a reproduction has ended up on permanent display in the Minnesota Technology Center), cites as many scientists as theologians and psychologists to undergird its several theses about survival of consciousness, among them, "that matter is not limited to the perception of the five senses . . . that consciousness can exist independent of the physical body . . . " and "that there is no proof that consciousness ends at death . . . and much evidence that it continues."[66]

The Continuum Exhibit displays on huge panels photographs and excerpts from sources both ancient, such as *The Egyptian Book of the Dead*, and contemporary, mostly from the works of scientists and psychologists. For example, William A. Tiller, identified as Professor of Natural Science and Engineering at Stanford University, is quoted on his speculations about a multi-dimensional universe and its implications for survival of consciousness after death. "New energy fields exist," according to Tiller, "completely different from those known to us through conventional science. These energies function in different dimensions from the physical space-time frame." The existence of a multi-dimensional universe suggests to Tiller that over-arching premise of New Age thought: "At some level of the universe we are all interconnected . . . to each other and to all other things." For the future Tiller suggests that "experimental devices must be generated to carefully study different levels of substances and show their connection to physical substance."[67]

Because they tend to be somewhat more concerned with dying itself and survival in general than with the details of an afterlife, New Age thinkers for the most part have not developed a consistent approach to life after death. There is frequent mention of reincarnation in New Age writings, however, along with obvious debts to Theosophy. In *Bridges*, a compendium of occult, Theosophical, and New Age thought, Aart Jurriaanse refers to life after death in terms of reincarnation. He speaks of death as "a change in consciousness" and as the process of "discarding a temporary garment which has been cramping the inner life's activities and restricting its expression! It involves entry into familiar activity from which the soul has been absent while gaining experience in an assumed body in the world of phenomena." Jurriaanse describes the after-death process of shedding the etheric double, the astral body, and the other sheaths, much as does Theosophy, but there is an anti-matter bias in his interpretation that most Theosophists and New Agers would refute. "If there is a stage to be 'feared,' he says, in the soul's cyclic existence, it is much rather the time of birth into the physical world . . . for it will then be temporarily smothered in darkness." For Jurriaanse, the most appealing aspect of his understanding of death is that it provides even "the worst sinner" with sufficient lifetimes to bring about rehabilitation and redemption."[68]

Carol Parrish-Harra, another New Age thinker and founder of The Light of Christ Community Church, is not so concerned with the specifics of life in the hereafter as she is with supporting the contention that human consciousness survives death. In *A New Age Handbook of Death and Dying* she maintains that the worst part of death results from fear over lack of knowledge about it: "As consciously awake life participants, we know, we live, we think, we anticipate. And it's terrifying to think about not knowing or not planning, or even worse, not hoping." For Parrish-Harra it is most important to know that life and death are part of a continuum. While she is obviously sympathetic to occult and Eastern understandings of the after-life, she does not see her task as providing a detailed account of what transpires after death. "Whether or not one accepts reincarnation," she says, "I want to deal here with the idea of life continuing in *some* form, with which we are not yet familiar." She echoes excerpts from the Continuum Exhibit in her conviction that "energy only changes form; it cannot be destroyed. I believe emphatically in life here and there, onward and upward, linking together a chain of humanity, our lives and souls intertwined. Whether we know or hope or care, humanity moves forward, made in the image and likeness of the intelligence of the All."[69]

In *A New Age Handbook of Death and Dying*, which in many ways is just as much a pastoral counseling resource as a treatise on the nature of death, Parrish-Harra does not display much confidence in the doctrines of death in specific religious traditions as a means to ease the pain of death. "True enough," she says, "the spiritual and philosophical undergirding of our lives is our great, built-in strength. But do not expect these strengths to prevent or protect us from the searing pain of loss. . . . Faith is structure; pain is pain." Thus as a New Age interpreter of death and as a counselor to both the dying and the bereaved, Parrish-Harra feels that it is much more appropriate to aid "in constructing a theoretical framework that will give comfort and support as the death experience occurs." For her that involves sharing her convictions, which she articulates as "New Age" in nature, that the process of death is the reverse of the process of birth and no more mysterious—that "life continues . . . not in the clear-cut heaven-hell, Judaeo-Christian concepts."[70]

Parrish-Harra attributes her own career as New Age teacher to a near-death incident that she experienced during childbirth at the age of twenty-four. It is her understanding that during this time she became a "Walk-in," one whose original spirit had left the body during the near-death experience. The soul who returned was an older soul. "Walk-ins," says Parrish-Harra, "are incarnating souls who take a short-cut into physical life. Instead of the usual route, fetus to adult, a Walk-in figuratively 'walks in' to an already grown human body. The original occupant gives its body as a gift to an incoming soul so that it can save the time and energy usually required in the human maturing experience."[71]

Parrish-Harra does not contend that all near-death experiences result in walk-ins, but she interprets the walk-in phenomenon as indicative of the coming of the New Age, during which spiritual messengers come both to warn and to instruct humankind about what they must to do save the planet and themselves. For her the near-death experience and the walk-in phenomenon give us information not about what we must do after death but what we must do on earth, for it is the duty of the "incoming soul" to "convert this life into a meaningful experience for the good of all."[72]

We must die, say most Theosophists and New Age thinkers, because dying is an inevitable part of the endless cycle of earthly and spirit lives experienced by individuals in their movement back to reunion with the source of all that is. In a sense, it is our duty to die. Brian Swimme reinforces this sense of death as duty and in doing so emphasizes that theme of New Age thinking which is usually more obvious in New Age treatments of life than of death. In *The Universe Is a Green Dragon*, he maintains that death is actually a fairly recent development in the history of the universe and is, in fact, an invention of evolutionary creativity: "For billions of years death was not a biological necessity. Nothing died 'naturally.' The earliest creatures might be killed, crushed, or starved to death, but death as we know it was not inevitable." Swimme posits death as a necessity that evolved in response to the limitations of the planet's resources. To eliminate natural death, then, would be to require the elimination of reproduction as well: "Once the continents were jammed, we couldn't allow for any newcomers."[73]

This much established, Swimme goes on to ask a different kind of question: "What is gained for the unfolding cosmos to include particular creatures—humans—who are aware of their own deaths?" His answer hearkens back to the New Age contention that it is the obligation of humankind to serve as the nervous system, the consciousness of the planet—to embody its capacity for self-reflection. And so, Swimme responds to the question above: " . . . How else could the universe feel *its* own staggering value? How else but through a human space aware of its own individual end? Within human self-reflexion can be felt a glimmer of the supreme preciousness of being, and we would certainly not be able to feel this were it not for our awareness of death." This obligation carries with it, of course, the suffering and anguish that comes with the knowledge of the preciousness of life and of the inevitability of our own death, but, says Swimme, "our reverence is our gift to the universe."[74]

For New Age thinkers and Theosophists death is not to be feared, it is not unnatural, it is not a punishment for sin, it is not a catapulting into an eternity of either heaven or hell, and it is not, finally, nothingness. Neither is it a cessation of labors. Something must be learned or accomplished through death and after death—whether it is the wisdom needed for entry into another life or whether it is simply the conviction that death is not a tragedy.

In presenting their alternative views of death, it is apparent that, with the exception of Scientology, the new religions are concerned with more than mere survival, more even than with the survival of the individual, which is guaranteed one way or another by all of these movements. If there is a longing here stronger than survival, it is for alternatives to the one-life, one-chance for eternal salvation that the new religions see offered by Christianity. More than that, there is the overwhelming sense of much work to be done, more than can be accomplished in a single human life-time. If there is not much said about suffering in the after-life in these movements, neither is there much intimation of untold riches or glory. What there will be of exaltation or enlightenment must be earned, whether on earth, in the afterlife itself, or in a succession of lives. That is true even of Mormonism, which promises eventual divinity.

The various doctrines of death of these six groups produce the generalizations mentioned at the beginning of the chapter. But, looked at individually, they also reinforce some of the particular features of each religion. It is possible, for example, to describe Mormon and Unification doctrines of human nature without needing to mention that both of these movements are intensely active in proselytizing. To gain some familiarity, however, with their common understandings that missionary work must go on in the afterlife is to gain some insights into this part of their world view, as well as their understanding that the church itself prevails in the afterlife. To encounter Christian Science's insistence that there is no death is to become even more acutely aware of the radical premise on which Christian Science is founded. And to comprehend that Scientology denies that its concept of "past lives" has anything to do with reincarnation, that thetans return to human bodies as quickly as they can, is an aid in understanding the intensity with which Scientology uses the term, "survive." Theosophy's detailed description of what happens to the seven sheaths that make up the human person after the death of the body reinforces its understanding of the human person as an immensely complex being whose cosmic pilgrimage worked out through many lifetimes cannot be adequately described in terms of only two components: body and spirit. Finally, New Age thought uses death-rebirth imagery to emphasize its contention that death is not different from life but connected with it; it is not the extinction of life but the renewal of it.

The next chapter moves in a different direction. Rather than a laying out of beliefs, its focus is on some of the ways in which the new religions apply their beliefs to specific moral situations—how the members of the new religions see themselves as ethicists and how it is that they see their beliefs providing insights into the moral dilemmas that confront everyone in the culture. The chapter on ethics and morality follows the chapter on death and afterlife, because, as is apparent from this chapter, moral striving does not necessarily end at death in the new religions. Thus it is important to know the whole life/death spectrum in order to understand the significance of the ethical reflections and moral prescriptions of these six religions.

FIVE

How Shall We Live Our Lives?

Ethical Reflection and Moral Issues
in the New Religions

Generally, when the topics of ethics and morality and the new religions come together, the concern is about such matters as proselytizing, fundraising, and the integrity of the founder. In this chapter, I am not interested in looking at those issues but at the ways in which the six alternative religious movements in this study apply their insights to various moral questions. How do the interpreters of these groups engage in ethical reflection? How do they think about moral action—what is the right or the good or the fitting response to situations and dilemmas that face not just the members of new religious movements but are of concern to the whole culture?[1] In other words, how do the various movements' understanding of God or ultimate reality, their interpretations of human nature and the human task, and their speculations about death and afterlife provide a framework from which to make decisions about how we are to live our lives—in matters ranging from issues of personal morality to global concerns. How do these movements respond when their members ask, "How do we think about these things?"

It is in this chapter that the implications of different cosmologies and specific beliefs become more obvious, because they affect the issues that will be of most concern to a particular group, for example family issues in Mormonism and Unificationism or ecology and world peace in the New Age groups. Here, also, it is possible to see that the issues that arise around matters of morality in the groups which are legalistic in their ethical orientation are different from those faced by the groups which are less prescriptive. In the former there is often need to find room to maneuver within regulated moral codes; whereas in the latter, efforts must be made to demonstrate how broad metaphysical insights can provide guidance about specific issues.[2]

MORMONISM AND UNIFICATIONISM:
REGULATING FAMILY MATTERS

With their beliefs in a personal God, a divinely ordained, earth-oriented salvation history, and a single life span for each individual, Mormonism and Unificationism are prescriptive about particular aspects of their members' lives. Both these movements are hierarchical and authoritarian in their governing structures. They interpret themselves as defenders of traditional American values and capitalism and as foes of communism. Thus, political leanings in both movements are generally conservative.[3]

A defense of the family structure in Mormonism and Unificationism is part of the general conservative orientation, but both movements have very specific theological reasons for wanting to see the family strengthened in American culture. In each movement, the family is not just a contractual, social unit, but an institution which is essential for salvation. Bruce R. McConkie describes the family as "the basic unit of the Church and of society, and its needs and preservation in righteousness take precedence over all other things."[4] Unificationists use the same phrase, "basic unit," to describe the family and see it as the essential vehicle "for the restoring of God's love and the ideal state of being which was lost in the fall."[5] It follows, then, that in each movement there is much attention in the moral value system to issues involving sexuality and gender roles.

Mormonism is understood in American culture as a religious movement that is highly prescriptive, but it is important to note that "prescriptive" in Mormonism often means something different from what it does in Roman Catholicism, for example. Scholars have noted particularly over the last fifteen years that there is a great deal of flexibility within Mormonism in spite of its authoritarian nature.[6] Nonetheless, there are multiple expectations for members that emerge from what Lester E. Bush calls "consensus": "What most often passes for 'doctrine' within Mormon society is, in reality, a widely held consensus, perhaps espoused in sermon or print by Mormon General Authorities, but ultimately without sanction by the First Presidency. In practice, it is not unlikely to change."[7]

Birth control is an especially interesting issue to trace in Mormon development with regard to flexibility precisely because it requires the Mormon system to respond to the claims of competing goods. The value of the large family competes against the economic and psychological realities of raising many children in an industrial culture. The pressure of the church's predilection for large families competes against the situations of particular families and of the equally strong emphasis on "agency," freedom of choice, in Mormonism.[8]

The basis for encouraging large families in Mormonism is theological and derives from the Mormon understanding that reproduction is one of the great powers and privileges of the mortal life. It is also one of the primary responsibilities, because only those with human bodies can provide other bodies for God's spirit children. Thus, within Mormonism, sexuality is considered sacred. It is sacred, explains Ernest Eberhard, Jr. in a book on that subject, because it is the means by which God's spirit children receive bodies and thereby obtain the opportunity to achieve exaltation (divinity). It is so sacred, in fact, that its use must be governed within the institution of marriage. According to Eberhard, "the functions connected with the creation of a mortal body have been declared to be sacred next to power to take another person's life. No other human power has effects which are more inclusive and far-reaching. . . . The emotions of love are at once so deep and so exalting that they cannot and should not be shared with any other person than husband or wife."[9]

Such a stance toward marriage and reproduction has dictated much of Mormonism's attitude toward what it considers appropriate expressions of sexuality, and it has had broad implications for both men and women about how Mormon life should be lived. It has resulted in great reverence for the family itself, a strong preference for married life over singleness, expectations for large numbers of children, affirmation of traditional gender roles, and prohibitions against premarital sex, birth control, abortion, homosexuality, and divorce. It has also influenced Mormonism's political inclinations in a variety of ways, including church opposition to the passing of the ERA.[10]

Recent scholarship indicates that Mormons have done two things in response to consensus favoring large families and generally disapproving of birth control: they have had larger than average families in terms of American culture, and they have also practiced birth control. The church itself has generally discouraged birth control, particularly by artificial means and for reasons other than health. At the same time, it has strongly upheld the right of individual parents to make the decision as to how many children they will have.

In an article in *Dialogue: A Journal of Mormon Thought* entitled "Birth Control Among the Mormons: Introduction to an Insistent Question," Lester E. Bush reviews historical patterns in official Mormon attitudes toward birth control from the end of the nineteenth century to 1976. The pattern moved from treating birth control as synonymous with abortion to limitation through abstinence when the health of the mother was in danger to the use of rhythm in the 1940's to the use of contraceptives for medical reasons (the latter position has remained in effect until the present). Bush cites a statement from 1969 by President David O. McKay, which he describes as "ambiguous" on the subject of whether or not birth control was permissible. According to Bush, the ambiguity was in aid of McKay's judgment "that the final decisions rested solely with the family." Bush mentions also that, "notwithstanding an occasional zealot," questions about birth control are not part of periodic moral evaluations that Mormons undergo for such matters as "temple recommends" and advancement in the priesthood.[11] Bush concludes that high birth rates among Mormons have more to do with the value that Mormons place on large families than on the fact of official church disapproval of birth control.

A study of contraceptive use among Mormons published also in *Dialogue* in 1983 seems to substantiate Bush's interpretation. Tim B. Heaton and Sandra Calkins indicate that the birth rate in Utah prior to 1965 paralleled that of the rest of the nation. After that, "the Utah birth rate has risen, diverging sharply from the U. S. rate which has generally stabilized. . . . " Nonetheless, according to Calkins and Heaton, the use of birth control by Mormons exactly paralleled that of white, married Protestants in 1965 and was slightly higher in 1970.[12]

In a second article, published in 1985, Bush addresses the broader subject of ethics and "reproductive issues" in Mormonism and again speaks to the subject of birth control. In an interpretive summary statement about changes in the LDS position on birth control, Bush refers again to McKay's statement of 1969 on birth control, in which he repeated the Mormon preference for large families for theological reasons and at the same time "placed specific behaviors above ecclesiastical review." Bush mentions that the success of the statement "is indicated by the fact that Mormons across the entire spectrum of possible attitudes toward birth control cite it in defense of their beliefs."[13] While Bush describes the evolving attitude of the LDS church as "accommodationist" in regard to birth control, he does not use that term pejoratively. "The point to be made," he says, "is not that the Church capitulated on the issue of birth control, but rather that a change in societal perspective was accompanied, eventually, by a similar change within the Church. In fact, the Church did not really capitulate on its more fundamental concern—that procreation and family life lie at the heart of human beings' reason for being."[14]

Bush speaks to other reproductive issues from the Mormon perspective, among them abortion,[15] sterilization, *in vitro* fertilization, eugenics, and sex change operations. He speculates about future scenarios in regard to these matters but also cites seven patterns from the past that he sees as illuminating. He maintains, for example, that the church and "the uniquely authoritative First Presidency" often choose not to address issues "with obvious ethical or theological overtones." When the First Presidency does comment, it is generally done privately at first with public statements made late in the discussions. Most pertinent from the theological perspective is Bush's contention that out of these discussions within Mormonism there emerges over and over again what he calls the "core of ethical concern," which is tied to the central tenets of the faith: "the centrality of marriage and children; the overriding importance of maintaining family harmony and stability, and protecting the health and well-being of mother, children, and 'tabernacles-to-be;' the preservation of free agency and personal accountability; and the total unacceptability of decisions based on 'selfish' rationales."[16]

Bush's articles are highly illuminating about the ways in which Mormonism attempts to engage in ethical reflection in such a way as to do two things: to reaffirm its theological understanding of the human task and at the same time to accommodate itself to changing demands in the culture. There are Mormons, however, who have begun to say that ethical reflection in Mormonism has placed too much emphasis on internal considerations—that Mormon ethics must begin to interpret the implications of its ethical stances in broader ways. In an article in *Sunstone*, L. Jackson Newell, an editor of *Dialogue*, in fact, calls for "enlarging the Mormon vision of Christian ethics." Newell maintains that because Mormonism attaches so much importance to "specifics of personal behavior," it has remained provincial in the matter of ethical reflection, particularly in regard to such issues as ecology, the arms race, human rights, and population growth. Newell addresses the subject of birth control as an issue that must be interpreted more broadly by a church that is expanding in Asia, South America, and Africa, claiming that "what is believed and taught regarding birth control is much more than a personal matter. Our doctrines and how we interpret them may have a direct bearing upon the health and welfare of literally billions around the globe."[17]

Whereas Bush cited Mormon doctrine concerning the human obligation to create bodies for spirit children in his interpretation of reproductive issues, Newell focuses on another theological concept—the nature of divinity—and asks the question "how does God act in human affairs?" Mormons may agree, he says, on belief in a personal Father God who loves and cares for his children, but there is still room for disagreement as to how God is known in the world and on how God expects us to respond to questions of morality: "Are we given basic principles and expected to govern ourselves, as Joseph Smith so explicitly encouraged us to do, or are we rewarded and punished regularly as a means of correcting our course?"[18] Newell's sympathy is with the former interpretation, and he is of the opinion that such an emphasis will move Mormonism away from ethical reflection that is confined to personal and very specifically church-related concerns and provide the opportunity for consideration of global concerns.

In another call for the broadening of ethical concerns, this time specifically related to sexual issues, Marybeth Ranes comments on the double bind in which Mormons find themselves on matters of sexuality: "On the one hand there is the positive goal of happy people in happy marriages based on a positive theological stance toward eternal sexuality. . . . On the other hand is a negative approach to teaching that goal."[19] Ranes sees a solution to what she considers Mormon narrowness on matters of sexuality in the fostering of positive messages about sexuality, as well as attention to how single people can increase self-esteem in a system so devoted to marriage: better sex education and a system of ethics that would "frame sexual behavior in terms of internally governed principles of behavior rather than labeling specific acts right or wrong according to an external standard."[20]

Certainly Mormonism's ethical concerns extend far beyond matters of sexuality and reproduction, but for this religious movement, sexuality is so tightly tied to basic doctrines of the nature of the divine and what it means to be human that it is a particularly apt arena in which to understand how Mormon doctrine, Mormon culture, and the broader American culture's attitude toward sexuality and reproduction contribute to the process of ethical reflection in Mormonism. While it appears that in reality there is much more flexibility within the Mormon system in a specific instance, such as birth control, than the popular concept of Mormonism assumes (and more than many Mormons are aware of), the doctrine that upholds the centrality of marriage and of having children in Mormonism is unlikely to diminish in importance and thus will always need to be both reaffirmed and reinterpreted in light of new understandings about the nature of the family.[21]

In the Unification Church, marriage and the family are likewise central to understanding the nature of God and of the human task in the world. For Unificationists, the family is the saving social unit, an "eschatological type," as one scholar calls it, rather than simply a social contract. Marriage is a sacrament in the Unification Church. In fact, it is really the only sacrament, and the engagement and wedding ceremonies, called the Blessing, do not just join a couple in matrimony—they also signal re-birth or entry into a "true family." Frederick Sontag speaks of the newly married couple as being "grafted into the bloodline of the True Parents" (the Reverend and Mrs. Moon). In Unification theology, those who live within a married relationship participate in the very nature of God. Male and female joined together in a God-centered marriage reflect God's androgynous and creative being, and the children who are born to blessed couples are understood to be born without sin—not incapable of sinning themselves but born without sin.

The centrality of marriage and family in Unification theology dictates a strong concern for the regulation of sexuality, just as is the case in Mormonism. Among Unificationists the term "morality" is frequently shorthand for "sexual morality," and ethical reflection among Unificationists centers on the interpretation of such practices as pre-marital celibacy, the matching of couples in marriage, which is the custom of the Church,[22] and fidelity within the marriage. Also, similar to Mormonism, singleness is not a state to be sought or cultivated, and Unificationists look upon the single life not as a permanent state but as preparation for marriage. Unificationists are encouraged by the Reverend Moon to have large families, and as far as birth control is concerned, there seems to be a widespread disinclination to use it. On the other hand, as one woman member explained, birth control is not considered sinful. She is convinced that "the majority of couples would say we have to take responsibility for what we do."[23] And, as one member explained to me, parents should have no more children than they have the "heart" to love and raise well.

If Unificationists share with Mormons a preference for large families and a commitment to pre-marital celibacy, both for theological reasons, one nonetheless senses from reading sources dealing with sexual ethics in Unificationism a different emphasis than is found in Mormon sources. In Mormonism there are strong connotations of duty connected with repro-duction and with sexuality, but there is not the same connection between sexuality and "sacrifice" that is found in Unificationism. The overtone of sacrifice undergirds the Unification interpretation of pre-marital celibacy, of the period of abstinence after marriage (usually forty days, sometimes longer), and the periodic separations of spouses who are doing mis-sion work. Such a focus makes sense within the overall theology of Unificationism, because it is the human obligation to suffer, to sacrifice, to pay indemnity for sin in order to restore the world to its pre-fall state of perfection. Thus, it is a feature of ethical reflection in Unification theol-ogy to assume that action which is "good" is also likely to be action which requires suffering and sacrifice from the moral agent.

Pre-marital celibacy is a case in point, and its practice within Uni-ficationism is a good illustration of the emphasis in this system on waiting—on "waiting" that is disciplinary in nature. Adam and Eve failed to establish a true family on earth because they didn't wait— they engaged in sexual intercourse before they were mature enough to do so. Contempo-rary Unificationists, involved in the attempt to establish a true family on earth, are admonished that part of their task involves waiting until after marriage to initiate the God-centered sexual relationship that will be the foundation of the marriage.

Unificationist Tom Walsh speaks of the period of celibacy prior to mar-riage as a time during which the individual cultivates virtue and seeks to perfect his or her character—a reference to the First Blessing—spiritual maturity—which Adam and Eve failed to fulfill. Walsh sees the process as one of sublimation of what he calls "natural urges" rather than repression. This sublimation takes the form of a spiritual quest and "is designed to prevent any lapse into sexual fixations or preoccupations, actions which would represent a detour from the path to spiritual maturity."[24] Foregoing a sexual relationship in the time prior to marriage enables the individual to cultivate exactly those virtues that will be essential for marriage itself, which Walsh lists as "the acquired moral virtues, pertaining to the manage-ment of the passions, the familial virtues of loyalty, filial piety, and obedi-ence, and finally the theological virtues, namely, faith, attendance (service to God) and heart."[25] Most important, in Walsh's estimation, is the practice of celibacy as an aid in controlling the passions, since it was this very lack of control that led to the human fall in the first place. Always present in interpretations of celibacy is the emphasis on a higher good. Another male member of the church claims that " . . . it's not so difficult to live a celibate lifestyle if there is some sort of transcendent vision for which one is living rather than for self-gratification."[26]

If Unificationists practice celibacy in order to gain a greater human good than the immediate satisfaction of sexual passions, they also specifically tie it to God's suffering heart. Walsh speaks of this as the "heartistic" (this is a very frequently used Unification term) dimension of celibacy, for its sacrificial nature "functions as an experience which opens the way for an understanding of what *Divine Principle* views as the broken-heartedness of God."[27] As the Unificationist longs for marriage and for inclusion in a true family, so, too, can he or she have some sense of the loneliness of God in longing for his lost children.

The same note of suffering and sacrifice occasioned by sexual absti-nence is struck in the interpretation of the Unification insistence that mar-ried couples wait at least forty days after the Blessing to consummate their marriages. Nora Spurgin, frequently a spokesperson along with her hus-band, Hugh, on family matters, describes this time of abstinence as "a time to offer to God one's marriage, first making a spiritual foundation for a God-centered marriage. We liken it to Jesus fasting in the wilderness for forty days prior to beginning his public ministry."[28] The period of time can be longer depending on the kind of mission work to which couples are as-signed, since the suffering required is related to the difficulty of the task.

Nora Spurgin recounts a time in 1975 when the Reverend Moon asked that couples remain separate for three years. This lengthy time period was required because these couples were given "special providential work," and their marriages were to provide the foundation for worldwide spiritual work rather than national work which had been the case with previously married couples. The theme of providential work, in fact, comes up again and again in Unification discussions of celibacy, whether before or after marriage. "We talk a lot about pain," explained Diana Muxworthy, "and it often seems that Moonies are very sadistic and possibly masochistic. . . . The fact is that we believe that . . . each one of us is in a providential situa-tion. . . . There is a certain mission, there is a certain responsibility that we are carrying."[29]

Finally, Unification couples explain their frequent separations from spouses and children after marriage in terms of sacrifice and suffering. Many critics of the movement have noticed that, while Unificationism sees the family unit as salvific for the individual as well as for the world, spouses are separated for long periods of time. Unificationists themselves make it very clear that such separations are not easy, and the pull between family obligations and church assignments causes great suffering. One is reminded by this Unification custom of the growing feminist critique of Mormonism that the church requirements for priesthood duties for the men keeps them from active involvement with their wives and children. But in the case of Unificationism the women, too, are asked to leave their families for periods of mission work. Nora Spurgin speaks of "the times when I cried myself to sleep just thinking about my children and husband and wishing I could be with them, yet wanting to make this sacrifice at the same time for providential reasons." Spurgin goes on to say that "even though we feel a certain joy in being able to offer ourselves to God and our church in this way, it is always with a deep sense of internal suffering and pain."[30]

In the foregoing examples, Unificationists would be more likely to talk about "family ethics" than sexual ethics, for, as they see it, the family is at the heart of the restoration process and family ethics is concerned not just with individual family units and with individual actions, whether of a sexual nature or not, but with the salvation of the world. Nora Spurgin speaks of her sacrifices as having future efficacy both for her own life and that of her family and far beyond that small unit. "We in the Unification Church," she says, "feel we are leaving our families now for the sake of protecting our nation and ultimately ourselves from the lack of God-centered values."[31]

Unificationism's family-centered system gives rise to many of the issues that characterize Mormonism in regard to the role of women, homosexuality, and singleness. Although women are not excluded from doing church work even when they are pregnant and also hold prominent places in the church's hierarchy of Blessed couples, American women, particularly, have felt oppressed by traditional Oriental attitudes toward women. Unificationists see themselves in the same struggle for equality of women within the church as is characteristic currently in the larger culture, and Unificationists do not seem hesitant about articulating conflicts as far as female roles are concerned.[32] The *Unification News*, reporting on a Blessing Workshop (designed to support Unificationists in their commitments to marriage) held at the Unification Seminary in Barrytown, New York, published comments made by women at a sisters' lunch to the effect that in spite of expectations that women are to be "bottomless pools of love," there is a bottom to the pool for most women.[33]

Other sources indicate that Unificationists are discussing the role of single persons in a church for which marriage is normative, as well as the reality that many of those attracted to the movement, particularly in America, have been single.[34] As far as homosexuality is concerned, the Unification Church is opposed to it on the grounds that God's androgynous nature as it is reflected in males and in females dictates that the ideal relationship for bringing these aspects of God's nature together is heterosexual marriage (the second of the Three Blessings). Nonetheless, there is discussion in Unification circles of that issue, also.[35]

A further very important area of exploration into Unificationism's moral stances is that of conservative politics. Unificationist theology depicts political battles in terms of the battle between God and Satan, and for Unificationists the dominion of Satan is embodied in world communism. Dr. Bo Hi Pak, a Korean church leader who is chief executive of the Washington *Times* Corporation and president of CAUSA International, a Unification organization dedicated to educating people about the dangers of communism, interprets the fight against communism as a fight against godlessness. "Every true Christian," he maintains, "every decent person believing in God—should understand that international Communism not only threatens us personally but is an enemy of God and of all humanity."[36] Unification's antagonism to communism helps to explain why conservative churches are attracted to dialogue with this new movement in spite of what they would consider Unificationism's unorthodox christology.

In matters requiring ethical reflection and the need to make moral choices, Unificationists operate within the same general framework as Mormons. Their task is not to try to figure out what the church demands of them but rather how best to meet those demands that are already articulated and how to adjudicate their priorities. Unificationists as well as outside students of the movement speculate that with the growing numbers of families with small children in the American church, members may need more and more to engage in the kind of ethical reflection that has been characteristic of Mormonism in an area such as birth control: how to build the kingdom of God and at the same time tend to the needs of the individual person and the particular family.

CHRISTIAN SCIENCE AND SCIENTOLOGY: OBLIGATIONS IMPOSED BY SPIRIT

Even more than has been the case in regard to their doctrines of God, human nature, and death, Christian Science and Scientology part ways immediately on the subject of ethical reflection. Christian Science interprets its moral stance on matters such as sexual morality, racial harmony, and world peace in light of its chief metaphysical claim—that there is no reality in matter. In Christian Science, the struggle between good and evil is interpreted as one between matter and spirit, and contemporary moral issues are reflected on from that perspective. Scientology is at a place in its history, and has been almost since the beginning of the movement, where its chief concern is with preserving the technology of Scientology as Hubbard has discovered and expanded on it. Aside from its battle against mental health professionals and the Internal Revenue Service, the ethics of Scientology are concerned chiefly with internal regulation.

Christian Science has long experienced the criticism that because of its spiritual orientation it is not interested in making the world a better place in which to live, that it is not concerned with doing good works "in the world." Christian Scientists refute this claim, for they see themselves as dedicated to a spiritual awakening that will solve the many problems of humankind. But, says Stephen Gottschalk, "bringing prayer to bear on human tragedy and suffering does not preclude taking other practical steps to alleviate them." In this context, he mentions the substantial sums that the mother church has sent to earthquake and war victims, and he cites the answer of a Christian Scientist to a medical nursing class when asked "how would you deal with the starving children in Africa?" The Christian Scientist responded, "I would cradle as many as I could and feed them with all the food I could lay my hands on. . . . " At the same time, this particular Christian Scientist hopes to remember to seek a Christian Science understanding of the nature of reality in "healing the fears, hates, misunderstandings, and cruelties that bring suffering to humanity."[37] For the Christian Scientist, the task of ethical reflection is always twofold: not just to discern what action to take in a particular situation, but to understand how the insights of Christian Science apply to that situation and thus demand a response.

If this description of the ethical task seems to call for a contextualist stance—to attempt to discern what's going on in a particular situation— in regard to moral matters, Christian Science reflection on an issue such as sexuality conveys a somewhat different sense. Christian Scientists contend that moral behavior, particularly in regard to sexuality, does not change over time. Moral behavior has its origin in perfect God and in perfect humanity as a reflection of God. To accept what Dewitt John calls "the counterfeit or opposite of this real man . . . the concept of man as physical, weak, corrupt, a prey to appetites, fundamentally material and amoral, a sinner from the start and doomed to death," is to render impossible the kind of ethical reflection in which Christian Science engages. Ethical reflection in Christian Science begins with the premise that we are sinless rather than sinful and that all moral guidance must issue from this assumption. Christian Science also understands the human person as spiritual rather than physical in nature, and this premise has led to an affirmation of conservative cultural mores regarding sexuality rather than to a disregarding of rules that govern what might be called bodily behavior.

In an article in the *Christian Science Sentinel*, Beulah M. Roegge describes sexuality as "strictly a human condition" and not a spiritual state. She understands the value of morality, then, as emerging from the impetus "to lift human experience out of depraved physicality and into closer accord with spiritual reality—man's natural state." For Roegge, the area of sexuality is one that particularly invites the false understanding that we are physical rather than spiritual beings and thus it is an area particularly in need of ethical reflection. "There are few who have not shed sexually related tears," she says. "These may be caused by failure to fill a stereotyped sex role, discrimination encountered because of gender, grief over sexual activity engendering guilt, remorse for failure to fulfill a legitimate marital role, or the torment of perversion."[38]

All of these sufferings of a sexual nature Christian Scientists would attribute to the perception of the human person as a physical organism. On the other hand, Christian Science is not willing to deny that sexual activity is necessary for the perpetuation of humankind, even though Mary Baker Eddy intimated on occasion that as the spiritualization of humankind progressed there might be less physical ways to produce children.[39] One answer, then, to unbridled sexuality is the confining of sexual activity within marriage. Roegge cites Old Testament condemnations of such practices as bestiality and prostitution as evidence that such regulation is necessary in so natural an activity as the conception of children: "Sexual relations," she says, "are placed within marriage to provide the care of progeny and to protect those relationships from exploitation." Roegge does not want to say, though, that sexuality in marriage is "just a matter of physical adjustments. Like all things in human experience, sexuality needs spirituality to guard, purify, and uplift it." She calls for celibacy before marriage and "sexual intercourse only within monogamous marriage between members of the opposite sex. . . . "[40] Overall, Christian Science sees increasing spirituality as the means to sexual morality, and, although the church does not produce multiple volumes with detailed admonitions about sexuality, it seems nonetheless to take a conservative stance.

Christian Science applies to reflection about issues of global concern, such as world peace, the same reiteration of its understanding that matter and sin, evil, discord, hatred, and war are the fabrications of mortal mind. Thus, the primary obligation of the Christian Scientist is to engage in prayer regarding these matters. It may be recalled from previous chapters that for the Christian Scientist the nature of prayer is not petitionary in nature; the Christian Scientist does not ask God to end or to take away suffering and evil which are illusory and which God has not created in the first place. Instead, the Christian Scientist's task in prayer is to understand the nature of reality as God understands it, and prayer must begin with the individual consciousness. "In Christian Science," according to William E. Moody, "we learn that when we correct our thinking about the nature of reality—when our thought comes into conformity with Christ, Truth—there are direct changes in our lives. . . . not excluding the wider sphere of world affairs in which we all have a stake."[41]

Christian Scientists acknowledge that their efforts and admonitions to pray for peace are likely to be met with either scorn or indifference. To pray seems to many to involve taking no action—doing nothing. But the Christian Scientist understands the process of prayer differently—it is not petition, it is not begging, it is the process of understanding what is already the case—it is knowing that war and hatred do not exist. Prayer is the process of thinking not about the terrible turmoil in which the world finds itself but of thinking about the way the world really is, the spiritual fact that God did not create war, has nothing to do with war, is not willing to tolerate war for some mysterious purposes out of which will emerge a greater good. The Christian Scientist does not advocate that there should be only prayer and no participation in anti-war demonstrations, no financial contributions or volunteering of time, but insists that, " . . . our heartfelt prayers are our greatest contribution." Not only that, but "our prayers do improve world conditions. We find increasing evidence of this through spiritual sense and through more courageous initiatives taken by individuals and nations to solve the world's problems. We *can* pray for peace!"[42]

Some of contemporary Christian Science's ethical reflection hearkens back to Eddy's contention that thinking thoughts about the reality of war and hatred is not only erroneous but dangerous. There is danger in thinking negative thoughts, for in dwelling on mental images of war we run the risk of being overwhelmed and harmed by them. This is a danger that goes beyond retarding our progress in understanding the spiritual nature of reality. Whereas the contemporary interpreters do not speak of "malicious animal magnetism," the phrase that Eddy used to speak of mental images that could act from a distance and inflict harm, there is a sense in what they say that is reminiscent of Eddy's warnings to her followers during her lifetime.

"With so much naked aggression and not-so-latent hostilities on the international scene, it is tempting for the good citizen to become mentally embroiled,"[43] says Cynthia Howland. We need to be watchful, claims another source, about the thoughts we cultivate. "Christ Jesus," she says "instructed his followers to watch. Unlike military watching, Christian watching takes place in thought. It is a spiritual activity. Still, much as a sentry would demand that a prearranged watchword be correctly given to identify those eligible to pass his post, one challenges the thoughts coming to one's consciousness for admittance according to the standard of Jesus' teachings."[44]

In its approach to ethical reflection, Christian Science does not say that "thinking makes it so," whether it is a matter of what Christian Science considers appropriate sexual behavior or whether it is world peace. It is already so, the Christian Scientist maintains, and our task as moral persons is to understand, to know, that we are not captives of physical needs beyond our control, that the world is not so embroiled in hatred that nuclear war is inevitable. To believe the worst, to acknowledge its false reality, is, in fact, to postpone the coming of peace, whether it be in personal or in world relations.

Sexuality and world peace are matters of concern to anyone who lives in American culture, but there is a specific area of activity that is central to ethical reflection in Christian Science—when to seek medical help. The Christian Scientist who lives in a culture in which traditional medical practice is the norm is likely to be faced at sometime or another with the prospect of turning to the help of medical doctors (it is already the case that in certain contexts such as childbirth and the need for bone-setting it is appropriate to call upon mainstream medicine). This may occur because of the persistence of a particular illness,[45] because of pressure from friends or family, or even because of legal considerations.[46] For the Christian Scientist such a situation poses a dilemma. How does the tradition help him or her to reflect upon the most authentic course of action?

In *Spiritual Healing in a Scientific Age*, Robert Peel makes it known that to seek traditional medical help or not is understood as completely voluntary in Christian Science. Peel quotes Eddy in *Miscellaneous Writings* to the effect that "wisdom in human actions begins with what is nearest right under the circumstances and thence achieves the absolute."[47] Sometimes what is "nearest right" appears to the individual to be the help of medical doctors. In such cases, other Christian Scientists are admonished not to be punitive or judging. In *Science and Health*, Eddy suggests that those who turn to medical help will most likely be disappointed, but she also says that "while a course of medical study is at times severely condemned by some Scientists, she [Eddy] feels, as she always has felt, that all are privileged to work out their own salvation according to their own light, and that our motto should be the Master's counsel, 'Judge not, that ye be not judged'" (p. 443).

But, in keeping with Christian Science teaching, Peel insists that Christian Science must not be understood as merely a supplement to medical teaching—nor should the reverse be considered true—as is the case with some kinds of faith healing. The two systems, he says, are radically incompatible as to their assumptions about the nature of reality. Christian Science understands illness as unreal, although not to be ignored. Medical practice treats illness as real, an assumption which, Christian Science contends, only reinforces a false understanding about the nature of illness. "Experience has shown," says Peel, "that any attempt to combine Christian Science with medical treatment is likely to lessen the efficacy of each, since they start from exactly opposite premises. So a practitioner would normally withdraw from the case at that point, but with Christian love rather than doctrinaire censure."[48]

Eddy stated in *Science and Health* that "if Christian Scientists ever fail to receive aid from other Scientists,—their brethren upon whom they may call,—God will still guide them into the right use of temporary and eternal means" (p. 444). But, as Peel points out, "there is no definitive official interpretation of what this may or may not mean in practical terms." It is up to the individual to choose a course of action, "but the individual is encouraged to consider it in the light of all that Mrs. Eddy has written on the subject."[49] There is only one case in which action is taken if a Christian Scientist seeks medical help. If it is a Christian Science teacher or practitioner who is listed in the monthly directory of *The Christian Science Journal*, that person may be asked to remove his or her name "for a year or two until further spiritual progress has brought or restored the full assurance necessary for spiritual healing."[50] Such a situation might, perhaps, be considered the Christian Science equivalent of "giving public scandal."

It is apparent that Christian Science provides a framework within which one can reflect about a choice to consider medical help. There is little doubt that to remain with Christian Science is considered the better course, although there is acknowledgment that this will not always be the case. It becomes necessary to talk about appropriate responses—on the part of the individual seeking medical help, the practitioner who may have been involved in the case, and other Christian Scientists as well.

Christian Scientists focus their ethical reflections around the understanding that matter is not real. The implications of such a focus can be extended to shed light on a great variety of issues. The focus of ethics in Scientology is very different, and it proceeds on the assumption that ethics is concerned not so much with moral behavior in a general way but much more specifically with Scientology's concern for maintaining the integrity of its technology. Scientology does publish materials that can be looked upon as a listing of general moral principles in the popular sense. One such publication, *The Way to Happiness*, contains twenty-one precepts that advocate such virtues as the practice of temperance, honoring one's parents, safeguarding the environment, being competent, and respecting the religious beliefs of others. These admonitions are easily comprehensible without a knowledge of Scientology. The terms defined in footnotes are not peculiar to Scientology, nor do the definitions use Scientology's terminology. The back cover describes the list as what "may be the first non-religious moral code based solely on common sense." [51] There is nothing controversial about the precepts, nor do they provide an opportunity to discern the pivotal insights on which ethical reflection in Scientology is based.

Another booklet, *The Marriage Hats*, written by Mary Sue Hubbard, the wife of L. Ron Hubbard, offers advice to husbands and wives that is so firmly based on traditional gender roles that it is startling to read at this point in history. One Scientologist explained to me that the booklet emerged from the Hubbards' own experience of marriage. Among the main duties listed as those of the wife are keeping the home neat and tidy, doing the shopping, raising and looking after the children, doing the washing and ironing, and being responsible for birth control. The husband's role is described as that of leader of the family, in charge of providing food and shelter for the family and of making the major decisions in the relationship. Some of the advice about communication between husband and wife makes use of Scientology terminology, for example, not to commit "overts," or hostile actions, or to practice "withholds," the deliberate keeping back of information about one's actions. [52] But, again, this is not a source that provides information about the foundation for ethical reflection in Scientology.

It is in the *Introduction to Scientology Ethics* that one begins to get a good sense of what constitutes the primary focus for ethical reflection in Scientology. This volume by Hubbard defines the purpose of ethics to be the additional and essential tool for the application of Scientology's technology. Hubbard dissociates the ethics of Scientology from what he sees as the popular conception of ethics as related to the meting out of justice by means of punishment. Such disciplinary systems, he claims, make the individual worse rather than better, and he cites as evidence of this contention the increase in crime around the world. By contrast, Scientology ethics is meant to insure that the technology of the movement is administered accurately and as it has been developed by Hubbard.

Hubbard begins his book on ethics in a fairly general way by identifying two different kinds of people: social personalities, who make up eighty percent of the human population, and antisocial personalities, who make up twenty percent (2 1/2 % of whom are considered dangerous). Antisocial personalities are destructive persons who fear the talents and successes of others. They are not amenable to therapy or reform, and Scientologists are advised to recognize them and stay away from them or restrain them (Hubbard is not specific about what he means by restraint). It is even more important, says Hubbard, to recognize social personalities and keep them from "undue restraint" in society. In defining the antisocial personality more specifically as one who is opposed to individual and social betterment, Hubbard makes the connection between antisocial personalities and anti-Scientologists, since Scientology is defined as dedicated to the betterment of human civilization.

Scientology is not a perfect system, says Hubbard, but it is a workable system. To say, however, that Scientology is a workable system is not a modest claim, for Hubbard sees it as the *only* workable system of justice available to humankind. Thus, the need to make sure that the technology is administered exactly as developed becomes the burden of ethics in Scientology: "Ethics policies are leveled primarily at making auditing and training honest and flawless."[53]

Scientology has its own terminology for reflecting on ethical matters, and it is compiled in a code of offenses. These offenses are categorized as errors, misdemeanors, crimes, and high crimes, also called "suppressive acts." The latter are concerned primarily with engaging in "actions or omissions undertaken to knowingly suppress, reduce, or impede Scientology or Scientologists"[54] and includes what might be called giving Scientology a bad name in the broader community, for example by writing anti-Scientology letters to the newspapers or testifying against Scientology in a public setting. This list also includes first-degree murder, mentioned, one assumes, in order to convey the degree of gravity of the offenses against Scientology.

The vocabulary of ethical reflection in Scientology refers not only to offenses of varying degrees of seriousness, but to two types of people: suppressive persons (or groups) and potential trouble sources. Although the glossary defines "suppressive person" broadly as one who "covertly" stands in the way of able and successful persons who, because of their talents, appear dangerous to the suppressive person, the text itself is more specific in referring to someone who "actively seeks to suppress or damage Scientology or a Scientologist by Suppressive Acts." A "potential trouble source" is a person active in Scientology who maintains a connection with a suppressive person.[55]

Hubbard describes Scientology as the means by which humankind can find its way out of the labyrinth of human suffering. Without it, "man would just go on wandering around and around the way he has for eons, darting off on wrong roads, going in circles, ending up in the sticky dark alone."[56] Thus, from Scientology's point of view, to endanger the integrity of its technology, or to hold it up to public ridicule and scandal, whether through small and unintentional instructional mistakes (defined as "errors") or by damaging testimony against it in a public forum (defined as a "high crime" or suppressive act) is unethical behavior.

Scientology confines its use of the term "ethics" to matters of internal regulation and to efforts to maintain the technology and the organization system intact as Hubbard devised them. But, as a religious movement, Scientology also interprets itself as concerned with social issues. In the booklet called "Scientology: What Is It?" distributed several years ago with a number of metropolitan Sunday newspapers, Scientology defines itself as helpful both to the individual and to society. In answer to the question "what role does the Church of Scientology play in social reform?" it describes its codes as dictating that the movement be concerned with social injustice and with human suffering. "In that role," says the booklet, "the Church has for nearly twenty years investigated and exposed 'dirty tricks,' crime, psychiatric abuses and other forms of oppression and violation of individuals' civil rights. Whenever possible, the Church has also helped to handle the abuses found through Congressional testimony and legislative reform."[57] The booklet goes on to list some of the issues with which it has been involved: the harmful effects of psychiatric treatments such as drugs and shock therapy; the enslavement of Blacks in South African mental hospitals that were really labor farms; FBI-Nazi connections; the Nazi background of Interpol; illicit CIA activities; army experiments with bacteria; and abuse of the Internal Revenue Service.[58]

Scientologists describe themselves, further, as working to create a world where abuses of freedom do not occur, as well as a world where "men of goodwill work together to expose and stall the efforts of the few who abuse their rights and powers against the well-being of mankind." Even though the booklet does not make references to or connections with the Scientology code of ethics or with terminology such as "antisocial personality," familiarity with Scientology ethics enables one to see how the Scientology ethical system, which seems at first to be almost totally related to internal matters and regulation of technology, might be applied to broader issues. On the whole, though, it is apparent that Scientology does not engage in ethical reflection in the way that the other religions under consideration do, or at least it does not use the term "ethics" in a way that is consonant with most other religious movements. It has at present a different focus—the preservation of its auditing technology. Depending on future developments, Scientology may broaden the way it thinks and talks about ethics or at least articulate some specific connections between its own ethical system and broader social issues.

THEOSOPHY AND NEW AGE THOUGHT: COSMIC OBLIGATIONS

The focus of ethical reflection in Theosophy and New Age thought is directly related to the doctrine of divine immanence and the interconnectedness of all aspects of reality. Theosophists reflecting on ethical issues are particularly interested in the development of ethics as an evolutionary process, but they are also committed to tying the ancient wisdom, or perennial philosophy as some call it, to the illumination of contemporary ethical issues, both personal and political. New Age ethical thought, as might be expected, concentrates its efforts toward articulating ways of living that reflect its general concern with ecology and with planetary culture. Neither movement is inclined toward prescriptive ethics of a personal nature. On the other hand, and in spite of the constant theme of interrelatedness, both Theosophy and New Age thought are very much concerned with individual transformation. "In transforming ourselves, we transform the world," says Joy Mills.[59]

Contemporary interpreters of Theosophy are agreed that any ethical system that emerges from this movement must be non-prescriptive in order to honor the very high value Theosophy places on human freedom. It needs to acknowledge, also, Theosophy's assumption that all of the cosmos is evolving toward the only Absolute that exists. "It is futile," says John Algeo in an article in *The American Theosophist*, to look for a 'Ten Commandments' of the ancient wisdom—some list of specific things that one should or should not do."[60] In his history of the Theosophical movement, Bruce Campbell speaks of Theosophy as having doctrine but no dogma. It is a movement with a set of ideas that can be identified as Theosophical but without broadly accepted criteria for determining the validity of Theosophical ideas. The result has been, at least in the eyes of some critics, ethical reflection which produces ambiguity rather than certainty about moral dilemmas.[61]

For most Theosophists ambiguity is preferable to prescription. From a Theosophical perspective, ethical reflection serves to provide followers with insights into moral issues rather than with resolutions to dilemmas. Unlike Mormonism and Unificationism, Theosophy does not have at stake specific dogmas which undergird social structures. Nor is Theosophy like Christian Science in needing to illuminate a radical ontological statement or like Scientology in its desire to safeguard a technology by means of an ethical system.

Contemporary interpreters of Theosophy are relieved that their own ethical reflection does not have to bear the burdens mentioned above. At the same time they acknowledge that their open system can bring charges of moral relativism or a too philosophical attitude toward evil in the world. Thus, they are concerned to articulate and to interpret major values in the process of ethical reflection and to elaborate on the implications these values have for both ethical reflection and for living a worthy life. They do so while maintaining that Theosophical ethics cannot dictate rules for living; it can only imply a way of behaving. "Through the doctrine of karma," says John Algeo, "the tradition's emphasis on personal responsibility for one's decisions and actions creates an ethics that is individual, situational, and relative, rather than categorical and absolute."[62]

Theosophists are not totally on their own in deciding what is appropriate action in a particular situation, since the values of freedom and, particularly, of wisdom and compassion provide a guide. In "Theosophical Living," the final chapter of Robert Ellwood's book on Theosophy, he elaborates on the meaning of five principles that shape the foundation of daily life for Theosophists: duty, service, expression, naturalness, and fellowship. Right living, he claims, cannot be a matter of legalistic prescription but must emerge from wisdom, insight into the way things truly are, and compassion, the capacity to "feel with" all the rest of the cosmos and to put one's own desires no higher than anyone else's. The cultivation of wisdom and compassion—an ongoing effort over many lifetimes—has prompted Theosophists to concentrate their efforts at moral living in some particular directions, among them human rights, animal welfare, and concern for children, prisoners, and the blind.[63]

According to Ellwood, the desire to live "naturally," that is, in tune with the universe as it really is, grows out of spiritual maturity. "As a part of living naturally," he says, "many theosophists are vegetarians and do not use tobacco, alcohol, and nonmedicinal drugs. Meat and the latter substances are not necessary to a complete human life, nor are they grounded in any biological need." Naturalness (Ellwood chose this term rather than "disciplined") also inspires Theosophy's attitude toward sexuality. Ellwood quotes George S. Arundale, an international president of the Theosophical Society, in his assessment that "the urge of sex . . . though it has been so degraded everywhere, means in fact the Creative Spirit of God. . . . To draw nearer to our essential Godliness or to create like a God, or to do both, that is the purpose, the objective of the sexual urge."[64] Because of its connections with divine creativity, Ellwood defines sexuality as having a special potential, likewise, for evil and exploitation, which must be kept in check by the disciplining of egocentricity.

In aid of more specificity about the values which undergird Theosophical ethics in addition to wisdom and compassion, Algeo interprets a brief writing by Blavatsky called "The Golden Stairs," originally published in 1890 as a single paragraph. Algeo picks up, as did Ellwood, on the importance of naturalness and he sees the "prefatory injunction"—"behold the truth before you"—as a statement "about the naturalness of moral law and its public availability." Algeo sees it "as a call also for us to respond consciously to it."[65] Algeo claims that a superficial reading of the thirteen steps of the Golden Stairs may reveal a collection of "pious banalities," but he himself interprets them as "a tightly structured guide to moral action." The first five—"a clean life, an open mind, a pure heart, an eager intellect, an unveiled spiritual perception"—are general precepts, and the latter eight, among them "a loyal sense of duty to the Teacher" and "a valiant defence of those who are unjustly attacked," are more specific.

Algeo sees the steps of the Golden Stairs as more useful than "simple moral codes" that tell us not to lie or kill, because these precepts do not necessarily apply to many of the situations in which we find ourselves and do not provide us with insights with which to make moral distinctions— sometimes lying or killing are necessary from a moral perspective which is non-absolutist. Instead, our moral actions must be guided by the last of the steps, which is keeping "a constant eye to the ideal of human progression and perfection which the secret science depicts." To follow the steps of the Golden Stairs, according to Algeo, is to climb to the Temple of Divine Wisdom," which can be approached only by those who lead an ethical life. But we will still not have answers to specific questions about moral dilemmas which tell "the world what it should think about capital punishment, abortion, homosexuality, draft resistance, vivisection, or any of the other social issues of our time." Algeo sees it as the "inescapable burden" of each person to make his or her own judgments about such matters.[66]

What are the questions that the individual must ask if he or she is going to engage in ethical reflection from a Theosophical perspective and make those judgments of which Algeo speaks? Geddes MacGregor, writing in *The American Theosophist*, addresses one such issue, that of homosexuality, in the context of describing ethical systems as evolutionary in nature. He begins with three major assumptions. First, any ethical system has at its foundation an understanding of human nature and of how the universe operates. Second, a change in world view means a change in ethics, just as it does in other disciplines. Astronomers, he says, no longer operate out of pre-Copernican concepts of the universe. Third, because evolution is at present understood as our prevailing paradigm of reality, we must accept that fact that ethical precepts, like everything else, are subject to change.

The first thing to acknowledge about homosexuality, says MacGregor, is that we don't yet know enough about it to make major, absolutist statements. Further we need to look at it within the broader context of marriage and the family. When we do so, "it is difficult . . . to avoid the conclusion that whatever homosexuality is and however many the variety of forms it takes, it cannot but be accounted deviant from the norm that sustains and perpetuates life."[67] MacGregor says that we cannot simply end there, however, because such a conclusion only raises more questions about whether or not homosexuality is unchangeable and whether it is a danger to the individual or to society. And finally, what for MacGregor is a "poignant central question: Who are you and who am I to decide what is right and what is wrong for the growth of any particular individual? No bird soars too high who soars on his own wings."[68] MacGregor ends his assessment of the ethical issues associated with homosexuality with questions rather than with answers. But his final reference, which we may take, I think, as normative for the Theosophist, is concerned with the spiritual growth of the "particular individual."

It is this emphasis on the individual in ethical reflection that is guided by a Theosophical perspective that brings us back to Joy Mills's statement that, "In transforming ourselves we transform the world." Finally, for the Theosophist, the universe itself can be transformed and the process of evolution can be forwarded, only as individuals recognize their duty to themselves, to each other, and to the universe. Theosophists assume that the need for systemic change—in political structures, in families, in economic systems—will be met by the growing spiritual maturity of individuals.

If this sounds contradictory, Theosophists would point out that the interrelatedness of all things dictates that the individual doing his or her duty contributes to the good of the whole. Ellwood speaks in terms of "duty," one of the five principles mentioned above on which Theosophical living is based. There are certain human duties, says Ellwood, which are most likely common to all people, "but of special interest is the concept that one may have a special, personal duty—something each individual is supposed to do, something that, if one fails in this duty, will not be done and the entire world will thereby be set back by so much."[69] If one is not sure what that special duty might be, at least it is a start, says Ellwood, to know that one has such a duty and that the good of the world depends on its being fulfilled.

Will Ross, a well-known Theosophical lecturer, reinforces this theme of individuality: "All our lectures and discussions have shown that the work that has to be done is the work of the individual; it is not something that someone or the Society can do for you, it is your own particular work."[70] Ross sees the feeling of responsibility—for oneself and for all else—as the beginning of wisdom and the loss of the feeling of separateness from the rest of creation. Other Theosophists speak of the cultivation of the sense of responsibility as the process of ridding oneself of egocentricity. "Just as wisdom, compassion and peace go hand-in-hand," says Will Tuttle, a Theosophist who is also a Zen Master, "so do stupidity, egocentricity, and aggression." For Tuttle the solution to the problem of world peace can only emerge when there is widespread recognition of the value of meditation, of bringing together the rational and the intuitive, and of acceptance of the fact that "the quality of individual consciousness determines the quality of the collective consciousness that is composed of such individuals."[71]

At least in general terms, Theosophy and New Age thought share a world view—a universe in which the divine is immanent, in which there are interpenetrating levels of matter and consciousness, in which human consciousness is the most highly developed on the earthly plane and for that reason accrues to it particular responsibilities for the entire universe. But, at the level of ethical reflection, it becomes significant that Theosophy is a particular religious movement with grounding in the teachings of Blavatsky, and New Age thought is a collection of ideas that are manifested in a variety of religious movements and adaptable, up to a point at least, not just to the teachings of esoteric or occult groups but to the world view of Christianity. From all appearances, there is less systematized thinking about ethical reflection and morality than is the case in the other five groups.

This does not mean that New Age writings are not filled with references to right living, ways of being in the world that reflect the New Age concern for the life of the planet and for the development of a planetary culture. One of the most dominant themes for New Age thinking about right living is that of "community." For many New Age spokespersons the development of a higher consciousness in humankind, the belief in the sacred nature of all creation, and the movement toward a planetary culture, all of them undergirded by belief in divine immanence, dictate not just new ways of thinking, but new ways of living.

As David Spangler sees it, the emergence of communities in conjunction with New Age thought makes a kind of cosmic sense, for their formation signals "an affirmation of the spirit of connectedness; it is the living practice of communion." Spangler understands New Age communities as the "seedbed" of an emerging planetary culture, the place where the seeds can be nourished. In Spangler's understanding, these New Age communities need not be residential. He himself began his communal experience at Findhorn, in Scotland, where members lived in a single center. The Lorian Association, the community with which he is currently associated, is not residential but instead forms what Spangler calls a "community of consciousness."[72] For Spangler, community begins with one person and may expand to include the entire world, in fact, finally, must expand to include the cosmos. The seedbed communities for this vision are at present small pilot projects in New Age living.

These communities are dominated by an ethics of holism which attempts to speak to the needs of the one—defined variously as the community itself, the individual, the earth, or the Absolute, however conceived—and the many defined as the various individuals who make up the community, the regions and cultures of the world, and the limitless manifestations of the divine One. Ethical living from a New Age perspective acknowledges the reality of the many and at the same time maintains that the many are interconnected by the one. "Bad living" in the New Age view results when the many are paired off in destructive dualisms understood as cosmically antagonistic to each other—spirit-body, faith-reason, male-female, heaven-earth. The assumption of dualistic antagonism leads to exploitation of the earth, economic and political oppression of the many by the few, sexism, scientism, mental and physical illness, and narrowness of religious vision. These New Agers see as the sins of Western civilization.

In the New Age communities, efforts toward ethical living are concerned with ecology, egalitarian self-governance, a spirituality derived from a variety of sources, and with experiments in alternative methods of healing. A New Age periodical published in Indianapolis, *Earth Nation Sunrise* (now out of print), included feature stories about communities that meet some of the criteria outlined above. Designating such communities as "Living Futures Villages," the periodical required that they demonstrate attention to one or more of the following ideals: renewable energy, sustainable agriculture, respect for all life forms, medical freedom, religious freedom, educational options, and global consciousness.[73]

One such New Age community has existed outside Tahlequah, Oklahoma, since 1981, when the Reverend Carol Parrish-Harra moved from Sarasota, Florida, where she had also established a community of New Age seekers. As Parrish-Harra explains it, her motivation for moving to Oklahoma and forming Sparrow Hawk Village had little to do with her own desires ("When I was told 'Oklahoma,' my heart fell to one of those lower chakra areas") but rather with her sense of obedience to what she calls her "inner guidance." She had moved her community from St. Petersburg, Florida, to Sarasota five years earlier in obedience to that same inner guidance.[74]

Like Spangler, Parrish-Harra sees living in community as right action dictated by the New Age world view: "In all the teachings of the New Age," she says, "it is said that community is the way. . . . In the Agni books of Master Morya's you read and read about community. You read about what it's talking about . . . community . . . communion and cooperation. The keynote of the new age is that we have to be able to build as a group and no longer identify only with ourselves."[75]

Parrish-Harra sees precedent for the move to Oklahoma not just in the admonitions of Theosophy's Master Morya (along with Kuthumi one of the two primary teachers—Mahatmas—of Blavatsky). Astrologically, she understands the attempts to build New Age communities as the struggle of seekers to move from the Piscean to the Aquarian Age, but she also identifies her own move with that of the seventeenth-century New England pilgrims, who, she claims, had a vision of the new age in a different historical context. Parrish-Harra sees the founding of Sparrow Hawk Village as the further unfolding of the pilgrim vision: "The evolving heart and mind of humanity continues to seek peace and oneness with itself and nature."[76]

Theologically, the Light of Christ Community Church understands itself as esoteric Christian in perspective, drawing much of its teachings from various schools of Theosophy. But, to survey the course offerings for the seminary program,[77] which is part of the community, is to find that, in New Age fashion, Parrish-Harra draws from many eastern and occult traditions and retains vestiges of Roman Catholicism in the liturgies she and other members of the church conduct. That eclecticism is not haphazard but arises out of what Parrish-Harra sees as a moral obligation to resist pressures to adopt one particular spiritual path as the only path. In the spirit of the New Age, she sees the Light of Christ community as needing to serve the world by demonstrating that people of many different religious perspectives can live together. "Some people," she says, "feel we should be exclusively into [Alice] Bailey or [Torkom] Saraydarian, or Theosophy, etc. We feel we are into Growing. We read, study, pray, and meditate on philosophy, religions, disciplines, and seek receptivity for the approach on a day-to-day basis."

The village itself is seventy-five miles from Tulsa and is designed eventually to accommodate one hundred fifty families. Since 1981 the villagers have continued to build earth-sheltered, energy efficient row houses (owned by individuals—Parrish-Harra says the community is not a "commune")[78] and to devote some of its three hundred acres to growing crops. The community now has a school, also, but the villagers consider the church to be the center of the community. In addition to this residential community, the Light of Christ Community Church has also given rise to "communities of consciousness" in different parts of the country, including the Aquarian Light Church in Minneapolis (which is spinning off its own "satellites," as the minister, the Reverend Barbara Everett, calls them).

Another New Age community is the Institute in Culture and Creation Spirituality in Oakland, California, mentioned in previous chapters. The center itself is an academic community that is in residence at Holy Names College, and it offers both bachelors and masters degrees in Creation Spirituality. Like the Light of Christ Community Church, the ICCS has its own "communities of consciousness" around the country held together—figuratively speaking—by its founder, Matthew Fox, by workshops that are offered across the country, and by its journal, *Creation*.

ICCS was founded in 1977 by Fox, a Dominican priest, who wanted to see for himself where and how Western spirituality was being studied in the United States. "What he found," states *Creation*, "was deeply discouraging. In a time when Eastern spirituality and the human potential movement were having a profound impact on North American society the study of Western mysticism was dominated by dry, left-brain, insular, and partriarchal academic institutions."[79]

While staying within the parameters of Roman Catholic tradition, Fox describes himself as articulating a different part of that tradition—its emphasis on creation and creativity— which he interprets as having been suppressed for centuries in favor of a fall-redemption theology that has fostered the same kind of destructive dualisms that New Age thought is seeking to reintegrate. When he founded the ICCS in 1977, Fox looked for a staff that would reflect his own attempts to go beyond the strictures of Western spirituality—"artists, therapists, theologians, scientists, feminists, and social activists." The purpose of the center is threefold: to serve as "a center for innovative study, exploration, celebration, and experience of the richest elements of Western spirituality," to be "a focus for dialogue with native and Eastern spiritual traditions, the human potential movement, the new physics and the Green movement," and to enable individuals to get "in touch with their spiritual roots, their creative potential and their power to change their lives and their communities. . . . " [80]

Creation began publication in March/April 1985, its first issue subtitled "Empowerment . . . Personal, Social and Cosmic." To survey the contents of that issue as well as succeeding issues is to get a good sense of the ethical agenda of the ICCS and to become aware of the contention that ethical reflection in the New Age requires grounding in a spirituality that draws not just from traditional Catholicism but from different sources—many of them non-Christian and non-theological. Its first contributors included Starhawk, a feminist witch who is a member of the ICCS faculty, a Gestalt therapist, a physicist, a black minister and preacher, an Episcopal priest engaged in dialogue with Hindus and Buddhists, a biblical theologian, and a "feminist, activist, teacher of African dance and Priestess of Oshun in the Santeria tradition." Holding this manifestation of manyness together is the underlying assumption of the ICCS and *Creation*: that in order to give birth to the New Age, "We need a power that is rooted in creation, unafraid to let go and let be, creative and transformative."

In a subsequent issue devoted to community and subtitled "Reverencing our Interdependence," contributors speak more specifically to ethical concerns as they articulate what kind of living is appropriate to the vision of the New Age which is rooted in creation rather than fall-redemption theology. Michael Fox, scientific director of the Humane Society of the United States and writing in *Creation*, ties the understanding of the divine as it is expressed in panentheism—a reverence for the sacredness of Earth and for the inherent divinity of animals—to a moral basis for animal rights and what he calls "deep ecology" (this is reminiscent of the Theosophists' interest in animal rights). According to Fox, the Western world view which has understood that which is created as separate from the creator has fostered in Christians abusive assumptions about their powers of dominion and has led to feelings of superiority over animals and nature.[81] In panentheism, Michael Fox sees a moral imperative to include both animals and nature in the community with which we must be concerned.

In the same issue Kirkpatrick Sale, secretary of the E. F. Schumacher Society, calls for a reverence for water as that substance which "links us to the community of life." Sale speaks of the "secularization of water" as a characteristic of contemporary society in contrast with the deification of water by ancient civilizations: "Far from being a deity, water became simply a happenstance of the world, a fortuitous combination of atoms, one more of the everyday attributes of Nature." Sale goes on to say that we will not solve the water shortage problem in the world by treating it as a commodity, as has been suggested by some politicians. Instead, the ethic of the New Age, of panentheism, tells us that we must begin to understand the conservation of water as part of ecology, which Sale defines not as environmentalism, protectionism, or management of pollution but "the much deeper understanding that all these, all the forms of life, all the elements of the living planet, are connected, that there is an inescapable community of life." Sale says that in order to live out what an ecological view of the world calls us to do, "we must desire to see ourselves re-embedded in the world as a humble species."[82]

In the New Age ethical system even eating takes on cosmic significance beyond that indicated by vegetarianism. *Creation* devoted one issue to the subject of food. In "Gastronomical Musings," Jane DeCuir, a macrobiotic cook, claims that what we eat has cosmic significance because of the interrelatedness of all creation. "To eat rice," she says, "is to be empowered to grow in wisdom and to manifest God."[83] But to understand the wider significance of food and of eating goes beyond good nutrition and even spiritual enlightenment for the individual; the growing and distributing and eating of food also has political significance. "Food," says Matthew Fox, "is all entangled with global politics, economics and war—including the war on Mother Earth and her blood, the waters."[84] To change one's consciousness about food, then, and as a result to change eating habits is to make both political and religious statements of a global nature. In New Age ethics, finally, there is no moral issue that is not of global significance.

Theosophical and New Age ethical reflection have in common their inclination to be more articulate about what must be done rather than what must not be done within the framework of a world view in which we are connected with each other and with the entire universe. These two groups are more likely to speak in terms of attitudes and perspectives which must be cultivated—wisdom, compassion, love, respect for the environment—than in terms of actions proscribed. Prohibitions are certainly implied, however, and within particular communities there may be fairly rigid expectations about such things as diet, meditation and particular political persuasions (many New Agers are involved in anti-nuclear activities). Prohibitions against various expressions of sexuality do not figure prominently in Theosophical and New Age literature. Discussions of sexuality are more likely to emphasize the need for healthier attitudes about the body in general, more acceptance of the New Age understanding that, in addition to the development of higher consciousness, people need to learn that the body has its own wisdom to offer. In fact, many communities advocate "body work" as a kind of right action leading to the healing of body-soul dualism and a more authentic attitude toward sexuality.

Starhawk, who works with the Institute for Culture and Creation Spirituality and who is described in her book, *Dreaming the Dark: Magic, Sex & Politics*, as "a writer, teacher, counselor, political activist, nonviolence trainer, and witch," speaks of authentic sexuality in terms of its political implications as well as its significance for healing the body-spirit dualism which she sees as characteristic of Western culture. Starhawk claims that sexuality must serve politics rather than the other way around, and she is anxious to divorce sexuality from coercions by either Right or Left. She is no more in favor of "the New Left's demand that women practice free love (meaning sex without involvement)" than she is of the dictates of "bourgeois morality" or hierarchical and ascetic "spiritual systems that further the flesh-body split."[85] She is opposed to persecution of homosexuals, but at the same time says "we should not fall into the trap of saying one can *only* be a true feminist if one is a lesbian, or that one must be gay to be a liberated man. Desire does not follow the mind's dictates."[86] Cultural transformation will occur, says Starhawk, when we reclaim the erotic as life-giving rather than destructive and as power-from-within rather than power-over. Defined in this way and also as "energy," sexuality and the erotic are concepts that may be applied to an endless variety of human relationships, among them teaching and learning, routine work, and healing. In claiming that "the simplest aspect of polarity is the energy that flows between men and women," Starhawk insists that that same energy, the energy of the erotic, can become meaningful in the sense of "*connecting*, enabling us to bond to the world in meaningful ways, to use our power, our abilities, and to see their results."[87]

In general, New Age thought is concerned with ways to think about sexuality and about sexual relationships that go beyond the body-spirit, male-female dualisms that are deemed destructive for both individuals and the culture. In *The Aquarian Conspiracy*, Marilyn Ferguson claims that, "In new-paradigm relationships, the emphasis is not so much on sexuality as intimacy. Intimacy is prized for its shared psychic intensity and transformative possibilities, of which sex is only a part—and often a latent part at that."[88] David Toolan interprets the "letting go" of "all our holding patterns" that is necessary for coming to more truly understand how God is made known in "this messy world" as that same kind of release which is "the basic rule for good sex as for meditation and the higher reaches of prayer."[89] By this statement I understand him to mean that sexuality as much as obviously "religious" activities such as meditation and prayer must have as their source of energy that same knowledge that God is within. Toolan describes his understanding as emerging from a conviction that "the Ultimate Surd, the original Dispatcher, circulates in our common blood like some kind of high energy 'morphic resonance.'"[90]

In the New Age sources I have read, there is no hint of encouragement for sexual libertinism, for sex "without involvement," as Starhawk puts it. But there are indications of an impatience on the part of some New Age thinkers with the confines of "exclusive relationships," the most culturally validated being that of monogamous marriage. "For many people," says Marilyn Ferguson, "giving up the old need for exclusivity was the most difficult paradigm shift of all, yet necessary if they were to be true to their own mores."[91] Starhawk speaks of the need for "committed, monogamous relationships," but she defines "commitment" as implying more than heterosexual, legal marriage. "Commitment," she says, "even marriage, does not have to be based on the principle of power-over. It can be a deliberate choice to focus one's energy on another human being with depth and passion." For Starhawk, marriage can be "legal or informal, heterosexual, or lesbian or gay," but it must honor the distinctiveness of each person and the partners must also "ground the relationship by caring for all the mundane things of the earth."[92] In sum, the New Age thinker wants to define the morality of sexual relationships according to those criteria that inform the whole movement: an assumption of divine immanence, of the interconnectedness of all of us with each other and with the earth, and of the possibility of healing the alienation of flesh and spirit, body and mind, male and female, heaven and earth.

The new religions offer their thoughts about actions and attitudes they consider right or wrong, good or bad, fitting or inappropriate in response to the circumstances in which all of us find ourselves. They bring the theological imagination to bear on matters of morality, both personal and global, on those issues such as sexuality and world peace that are of concern to the whole culture, and on those concerns which are confined to particular movements. In conversation about the particular issues that have been the focus of this chapter, all of the new religions demonstrate that they have something different at stake when they engage in ethical reflection. For Mormons, there is concern for holding on to traditional values associated with family life while at the same time they acknowledge the realities of contemporary living that give a particular style to present-day ethical reflection, especially concerning matters of sexual morality. For Unificationists, there is the need to justify and interpret both for members and non-members why the movement demands what seem to many to be retrogressive practices regarding marriage and sexuality. Tying such practices to the Unification concept of "sacrifice" makes them comprehensible within the Unification world view, which says to its members and to the world that suffering and sacrifice are appropriate and necessary responses to the fallen condition of humanity and to the call to restore the original creation.

Christian Scientists engage in a kind of ethical reflection, which, as is the case with its healing practice, requires that the Christian Scientist see moral dilemmas in terms of the metaphysical claim that matter is not real. What is at stake in their ponderings is the ontological statement that undergirds the whole movement, and their effort in ethical reflection is to demonstrate the relevance of this statement both to what is happening in the world and to their own healing method. Scientology is concerned about the integrity of its technology, its auditing practices. While this movement addresses itself to topics of wider concern within the culture—drugs, psychiatric practice, the IRS—it uses the term "ethics" to refer to its own internal management and disciplinary practices. Finally, even though Theosophy and New Age thought share at least the outline of a world view based on divine immanence, these two movements display a different emphasis in their ethical reflection. Theosophy's perspective might be said to be more intellectually oriented, since its spokespersons seem particularly interested at this time in its development in speaking of the *kind* of ethical reflection that is suitable for Theosophy. New Age thought on moral matters seems much more concerned at this point with right living and not so much with defining a prescriptive and detailed ethical stance.

Even though these reflections emerge from alternative world views, none of the movements offers anything close to what could be called an alternative morality in the sense of a departure from generally accepted cultural mores. For the most part the alternative world views function to undergird traditional and even conservative norms and values. Even in the case of the Unification Church's practice of matched marriages, which flies in the face of Western custom and attitudes, the emphasis once the marriage takes place is on life-long monogamous relationships and the God-centered raising of children. In New Age thought, if there is an attempt to broaden what can be called an authentic sexual relationship, there is no urging that irresponsibility is the fitting response to the New Age. Finally, it becomes apparent that there is no escape for the new religions, any more than for the established traditions, from the need to interpret their ethical stances and moral prescriptions. There is no such thing as simply "applying" them without the need to take into consideration a variety of competing claims.

SIX

Epilogue

In the previous four chapters I have tried to provide the opportunity for six new religious movements to make their voices heard in theological conversation in as authentic a manner as possible. I have attempted to get at the heart of what these movements have to say about four topics that are vital to the theological enterprise in both Western and American culture. I have wanted, simply, to provide some answers in the cases of six new religious movements to the question articulated earlier: What is going on here, theologically speaking? It has also been my concern to demonstrate through these theological conversations that new religious movements are not outsiders to the work of theological reflection, and that the theological imagination—that capacity and inclination to order the universe in theological rather than psychological, biological, sociological or physical questions and concepts (and yet to take the psychological, biological, etc., into consideration)—does not confine its inspirations to the theologically educated members of the established religious traditions.

Nor does the theological imagination withhold its insights from those who are theologically uneducated. The insights into the nature of reality as they were revealed to or discovered by Joseph Smith, Mary Baker Eddy, Helena P. Blavatsky, L. Ron Hubbard, the Reverend Sun Myung Moon, and many interpreters of New Age thought (Matthew Fox and David Toolan are two exceptions) have emerged not from the rigors of an academically oriented theological education. Instead these founders of new religious movements were stimulated by their failure to find adequate answers to the universal questions, outlined in the previous chapters, in either the established traditions or the secular culture. This failure, they said, was due to inherent deficiencies in the theological formulations of the established traditions. As the new religions understood the situation, the established traditions were lacking in their abilities to hold together traditional theological tensions in ways that responded to human experience or even acknowledged common sense—the inconsistencies of a God depicted as both loving and angry or the lack of a reasonably articulated relationship between human effort and the achievement of salvation or enlightenment. The established religions were likewise judged wanting in their responses to contemporary intellectual currents in the culture—the rise in prestige of the sciences, for example, or psychology. And they were assessed as particularly unable to formulate doctrines of human nature that acknowledge the reality of sin without insisting on the moral helplessness of humankind. As lacking as the established traditions have been, according to the new religions, the secular culture has not done any better. It offers answers to the questions of human existence without acknowledging the reality of that which all the new religions affirm: the fundamental, ongoing, spiritual identity of the human person.

It is apparent from the previous chapters that the basic insight of the founder of a new movement, one that has its beginnings in the experience of one person and may have originated as a kind of folk religion peculiar to one region of the country (or of another country in the case of Unificationism), has the potential to elicit what might be called an imaginative response on the part of others—from believers, who perceive in the new revelation the potential for making sense of human existence. Such a response calls for an elaboration of the original insight, an expansion of its implications for answering the universal questions. If the new religion is to survive and to prosper, it must be able to put together a coherent theological system. Such systematizing may not always be accomplished by the founder; it may be left for subsequent interpreters.

There is a pattern in the religions under consideration of a withdrawing on the part of the founder to think about and study the implications of the pivotal insight. The First Vision in Mormonism occurred in 1820; this was followed by other visions, and the finding and translating of the golden tablets. The *Book of Mormon* was first advertised for sale in 1830. Eddy fell on the ice and discovered Christian Science in 1866, but the first edition of *Science and Health* was not published until 1875. Moon spent nine years after his first spiritual vision in 1936 receiving further revelations and articulating their implications. His followers wrote down these revelations. The first version of *Divine Principle* was not published until 1957, and the movement continues to describe itself as putting forth an emerging theology. Hubbard began with Dianetics and ended up with Scientology. Blavatsky spoke of twenty-five years of wandering and spiritual seeking before she published *Isis Unveiled* and *The Secret Doctrine*.

What occurs during the intervening years is a process of systematizing on the part of the founder and his or her followers and interpreters, the attempt to discover whether the basic insight can bear the weight of universal questions, whether it can generate sufficient interpretive implications to provide the foundation for a new world view.

To say that the new religions emerge from "non-elite" origins is not to say that, once systematized to a certain extent, they cannot attract the interest of an elite. By this term I mean persons sufficiently educated in a variety of ways, not necessarily theologically, to interpret the new religion in a broader context and understand what is has to offer in contrast with other systems, either new or established. The sources cited in this study indicate that this has been the case with all the religions under consideration, from Mormonism to New Age thought.

The previous four chapters have demonstrated sufficiently that the new religious movements provide a variety of answers to those theological questions that have formed the foundation for this study. In response to the stimulation of universal theological questions which, in the West and in American culture, are framed in terms of polarities, the new religions have framed their theological systems in ways that adjudicate the energy among these polarities: God and the world, God and humankind, spirit and matter, body and soul, life and death, and authority and autonomy. But they have responded, also, to another set of polarities that are more broadly cultural and less specifically theological. Thus it is not only theological issues which stimulate the imaginations of the new religions. If they are to find success in American culture, they must address themselves to a variety of competing values that are expressed in secular terms. In the remaining pages of this study, I want to look at three sets of polarities that have a long history in American culture and speculate about some of the ways in which the new religions address them and derive imaginative energy from contemplating them.

The first set, for want of more elegant terms, is concerned with "newness" and "oldness." All of these religions understand themselves as offering to their followers new models of the universe, of initiating that *novus ordo seclorum*, the new order of the ages, about which New Age thought is more likely to speak, but which is a phrase applicable to all these movements. Like the New England Puritans, like millions of others who followed in attempts to put behind them what they experienced as the corruptions, sufferings, and limitations of another culture, the new religions interpret their own beginnings as also the beginning of a new time in history, a setting forth again free from the distortions of outmoded and destructive cultural and theological systems.

Mormons speak of this beginning in terms of a new history of Christianity, one heretofore unknown, which unfolded on the American continent rather than in the Middle East. Not since biblical times, say the Mormons, have we known what God looks like and never until Joseph Smith's visions have we been aware of the fact that Jesus came to America. The Unification Church also understands itself in terms of initiating a new age. This time in history, say Unificationists, is like no other—not even that time when Jesus was on earth. Because Jesus was able to complete only the spiritual and not the physical redemption, his time on earth became only a phase in human evolution. This time is the time of the Second Advent, when the promises of history will be fulfilled. And, as the Unification Church interprets history, America has a special role to play in that fulfillment. According to the Reverend Moon, "America was formed to be the new flag bearer of God's will to move toward world salvation through co-operation between religion and state. . . . It is not by accident that America's founding spirit is described in the motto 'one nation under God.'"[1]

Christian Science and Scientology, also, emphasize the newness of their movements, but they do so not so much in terms of a pivotal point in salvation history and in the history of the American continent. Instead they use the scientific metaphor of discovery to indicate that what they offer to American culture are insights about the nature of reality and of the operation of the universe that were not available previously. They see themselves as initiating a new age of healing, a time when those ills that have plagued humankind for aeons can be put aside. In the case of Christian Science, the discovery is of a new way to understand the meaning of the Bible so as to make use of it as a testament of healing. This is not just an additional perspective on the Bible; it is a drastically new understanding with cosmic implications. Mary Baker Eddy called her religion a "new departure." Scientology offers what it calls a technology discovered and refined by its founder, L. Ron Hubbard. This technology has the power to discern and to treat the causes of unhappiness in men and women in a way that has never been possible before. In both these movements the new discoveries enable freedom from the ignorance of the past.

Theosophy and New Age thought speak in terms of evolutionary cycles, of this time in history as a genuinely new time and one in which the disciplines of science and religion will be reunited and the fragments of religious wisdom about the nature of ultimate reality will be regathered in a planetary culture. New Age thought, particularly, looks to the new order as a way of responding to those challenges which face America, even in matters of defense. David Spangler speaks of the new paradigm of reality as one which "encourages decentralization, empowering of the individual, a wider distribution of power, and the use of renewable resources as a way of living 'lightly' upon the earth." For Spangler this decentralization has potential for nuclear disarmament and national defense: "How could a foe cripple America's energy capacity without attacking every house in the country?"[2]

The imagination is also stimulated in Theosophy and New Age thought by pondering the unique role that America might play in this ongoing return of spirit and matter to the One. In *Theosophy*, Robert Ellwood mentions that some members think that "the sixth subrace of the Fifth Root Race [that phase of human and planetary history in which we are now engaged], out of which the Sixth Root Race will ultimately stem, is beginning to emerge now in the 'melting pot' of America."[3] Spangler speaks of the reasons why New Age thought has peculiarly North American overtones, even though it is a worldwide movement. America, says Spangler, was founded on a vision of transformation, and the back of the Great Seal of the United States which is printed on every dollar bill carries the words *novus ordo seclorum*. Spangler seems to be echoing Ellwood's idea of the "melting pot," a phrase which is particularly apt for the New Age understanding of a planetary culture. "To be 'new age,'" he claims, "to be a country created on behalf of the future of all humanity, is very American." Canada, according to Spangler, also shares the vision of a multicultural society.[4]

But, against this consistent theme of newness, of radical innovation, in these six religions, there is the search, also, for connection with the past and not just the recent past but the ancient past. Just as Americans have claimed parallels in their own history with that of ancient Israel, the new religions look to a knowledge of and continuity with the past in order to interpret the significance of their newness. Mormonism asserts connection with an ancient history of Christianity on the American continent. If Mormonism is a new religious tradition, it is nonetheless a religion with an ancient lineage, one that had lain undiscovered for centuries until Joseph Smith was inspired to dig up the golden tablets on which the *Book of Mormon* was written and in which the story was told. The *Book of Mormon* chronicles in its stories a battle between good and evil. It not only moves a part of the history of early Christianity to America; it adds 1,400 years to the history of America itself and ties Mormonism to biblical times and biblical history. The validation of the past and particularly of an American past, is essential to the identity of this new religion.

The Unification Church ties itself to the whole history of Judaism and Christianity, which it sees as the continuing struggle of humankind to restore the creation to its original perfection. Unificationists place themselves at the culmination of salvation history. In one sense this present time of the Second Advent, which Unificationists refer to as "good history," can only be understood in terms of that which has preceded it—"suffering history." But there is another way in which Unificationism seems to collapse history and to look on this time as similar to the time of origins: "If we think pictorially," the Unification Home Study Course explains, "we may thus say the line of history is not straight but circular, bringing us at the end to what history should have been at the beginning."[5] If the Unification Church sees itself as fostering the culmination of history, it cannot do so without reference to the past, and its emphasis on historical movement that is circular rather than linear points to its origins as a Christian movement in an Eastern culture.

Christian Science neither interprets itself as the culmination of a particular salvation history nor does it claim validation in the parallels of an ancient past. As far as the past is concerned, it offers Eddy's insistence on the revelatory truth of the Bible, but it does so along with her radical discovery about the nature of reality and of healing, which makes necessary a totally new interpretation of the Bible and particularly of the New Testament. Christian Science can be seen as a restorationist movement, but one which functions differently from Mormonism or Unificationism. It makes its claim on the biblical past but does not include in its teachings elaborations on what occurred during the centuries between biblical times and Eddy's discovery. Scientology's investment in the past is its offer of a technology that can subvert the traumas of the past and render them harmless. According to Hubbard, the technology of Scientology can reach beyond trillions of years to get at the engrams of an endless number of past lives. In Scientology, it is, in fact, the engrams that have surfaced in the auditing process from lives lived billions of years ago which are used to promote the effectiveness of the technology. In a sense, then, we might say that Scientology interprets itself as capable of redeeming the past.

Theosophy and New Age thought both claim connections with ancient wisdom, wisdom that for a variety of reasons has been lost to contemporary culture and is now being reclaimed. Because the process of evolution provides an undergirding for the self-understanding of both these movements, it is not surprising that both would see themselves as part of a continuous manifestation of spirit and matter that is dynamic rather than static. Evolutionary thinking must incorporate and integrate the past—that is one of the implications of espousing the interrelatedness of all things. The past, however, cannot be understood as an unchanging bulwark against which the present is measured. Even religious orthodoxy, says Ron Miller, director of Common Ground, no longer means "statically preserving the past but using it to sight the future."[6]

It seems to be the case, then, that most of the new religious movements in this study insist on the reality of "newness." They interpret themselves as new revelations, as providing information or insights or discoveries that either have never been available before to humankind or that have been inaccessible for centuries. America itself plays a role in giving rise to this newness or fostering it or providing the essential setting for it. But the strong desire to find connections with the past—with a salvation history or an ancient process—is present, also, and is particularly interesting to note in movements that are understood as new religions. These movements appear to qualify what has been noted as an inclination on the part of Americans to see themselves as able to step out of culture and history and to formulate something so radically new that it can escape the influences—good or bad—of the past.

In their theological systems the new religions seem, then, to be both conservators and innovators. Their new revelations serve as vehicles for preserving ancient truths and restoring lost religious knowledge. At the same time, they embrace newness and in doing so act out that same ambivalence that motivates Americans to long for the past and yet repudiate its claims, to insist on novelty and at the same time to be fearful of it.

There is another cultural polarity with which the new religions are particularly concerned—the intense interest in American culture in the competing claims of individualism and community. In *Habits of the Heart*, Robert Bellah and his colleagues claim that, no matter how much ambivalence there might be about it, "individualism lies at the very core of American culture. . . . Our highest and noblest aspirations, not only for ourselves, but for those we care about, for our society and for the world, are closely linked to our individualism."[7] *Habits of the Heart* speaks of the coexistence of individualism with "classical republicanism and biblical religion," which have historically served as a corrective for the excesses of individualism but which the authors see as losing their effectiveness in contemporary American culture. The new religions speculate about this polarity of mythic proportions in American culture in an arena broader than that of classical republicanism and biblical religion.

If there is anything that can be said without qualification about the six new religious movements in this study, it is that they place tremendous importance on the individual person—on the persistence into eternity of the "self," however defined in each movement, and on the responsibility of the individual to exert sufficient effort in order to attain salvation or enlightenment. Finally, it is the individual person who must earn salvation, find enlightenment or be transformed. And yet there is only one group among these six that is not intensely concerned, also, with the nature of community.

The whole history of Mormonism might be looked on as a struggle to understand itself in terms of "individual" and "community." Since its beginnings, there has been an on-going struggle within Mormonism on a broad scale to determine how it, as an individual community, will relate to the wider culture; in fact, as history indicates, some of these struggles have been violent.[8] But the struggle over individualism and community is not confined to the broad cultural arena, for the theology of Mormonism, too, fosters this dual emphasis. In spite of its insistence on the need for individual human effort, for Mormons there is the equally strong theme of the community of the family and of the church itself, those agencies among all other human institutions through which salvation can be attained. In chapter four, which dealt with death and afterlife, Mormon historian Truman Madsen is quoted as making a generalization about life after death in Mormonism which can also be applied to the mortal life span: "Our individual immortality is in no way contingent upon that of others. On the other hand, the highest immortality is a family affair. In that sense we are either exalted together or not at all. Thus, others are crucial to the quality and intensity of our own eternal lives."[9] In other words, we can make it on our own, but it is better with others. One might counter by saying that a statement such as Madsen's indicates the importance of Mormon community, but gives no indication of whether "community" in this movement can be defined in ways broader than that. There are some clues in this study that such may be the case, particularly when one thinks about the reality of Mormon missionary work throughout the world. Many generations of Mormons have now had exposure to a culture that is different from their own. This raises issues of responsibility, for, as L. Jackson Newell pointed out in the previous chapter, Mormon approaches to matters such as birth control must be considered in light of their appropriateness for a different culture. Mormons will no doubt continue to work out what it means to be a community within a worldwide context rather than just an American religious community.

The Unification Church, likewise, specifically calls the individual to account within its theological system, and is equally anxious to foster a sense of community with other Christian churches in America as well as a community that goes beyond cultural boundaries. Turned down in 1977 for membership in the National Council of Churches, the Unificationists continue to seek entrance to that body.[10] Part of the emphasis on community is certainly due, as it is in Mormonism, to the proselytizing that is an essential part of Unificationism. This new church does not see itself, finally, as one religion among many but as that particular revelation which will unite a fragmented Christianity, bring about a world culture, and restore the creation to its original perfection. On the way to accomplishing these things and as a means to doing so, the Unification Church practices international (and often interracial) marriages and insists that "community" must extend beyond national borders.

For Unificationists even more than for Mormons, "family" is the primary metaphor for "community." The whole church is understood as a family with the Reverend and Mrs. Moon the "True Parents." For the Unification Church, extending the family becomes the way to broaden community. In a recent issue of *Unification News*, the Reverend Moon spoke specifically of the purposes of interracial marriages, acknowledging that they are more difficult than others and require sacrificial work on the part of the spouses. In fact, says Moon, these marriages can save nations: "An international marriage is so important because it enables a true person to connect two nations and save them." For Moon these marriages are not only a means of uniting cultures; they can also unite races. Taboos against interracial marriages originated with the fall, according to Moon, and such taboos are unnatural: "Black cattle can mate with white cattle without restrictions; that is the natural way. Who opposes that?" He admonishes his followers that those who engage in international marriages will be considered pioneers who "are creating a revolution of goodness and true love."[11] For Unificationists, both "family" and "community" must be international in nature in order for the work of the church to be accomplished.

Christian Science and Scientology do not speak very specifically in their publications, at least as I have been able to discern, about the nature of community. Most of the emphasis in Eddy's writing is on the spiritual enlightenment of the individual, even though in contemporary Christian Science literature there are many references to those obligations which Christian Scientists owe to the world. In addition, there is at present an interesting phenomenon occurring in Christian Science that seems to indicate on the part of that denomination a desire for expansion of community. In two recent issues of *The Christian Century*, a liberal Protestant journal,

Stephen Gottschalk has interpreted Christian Science and its healing practices in ways that have implications for Christianity in the entire American culture. He acknowledges the "relative de-emphasis" in Christian Science in contrast with mainstream Protestantism "on the social dimension of Christian witness," but points to the contributions Christian Science has made to wartime and disaster relief and to the statement it makes about social commitment by its publication of the *Christian Science Monitor*, which in the past several years has published a series on such matters of conscience as "Hunger in Africa" and "Exiles Among Us: Poor and Black in America."[12]

As Gottschalk explains it, the social stance of Christian Scientists must be evaluated in terms of "whether spiritual healing as they understand it can really happen and whether it means what they think it means for Christianity."[13] This evaluation cannot be accomplished in isolation from the rest of American Christianity, and thus dialogue must be pursued. In *Spiritual Healing in a Scientific Age*, Robert Peel presses the same point—that evidence of the workings of Christian Science healing has implications for American Christianity as a whole and for a secular culture in which, as Gottschalk says, "medical assumptions are axiomatic." Too often, says Peel, discussions of Christian healing in general take place far from the mainstream and "at some distance from the well-groomed but constricted pastures of modernized religious thinking."[14] Christian Science does not proselytize, so these efforts to speak about the social stance of Christian Science within the perspective of its claims about healing and to initiate dialogue on the part of a religious movement that has tended to keep to itself can be interpreted, I think, as an effort at broadening what it understands as the changing parameters of its community.

It is difficult to detect efforts toward increasing community in Scientology, although as the previous chapter indicates this religious movement is involved in a variety of social efforts. Perhaps because its language is non-theological in nature and because it sees its quarrels chiefly with mental health professionals and with the United States government rather than with the established religions, Scientology has chosen to put its efforts elsewhere than on the fostering of community among other religious groups. Also, because there is still great emphasis in the movement on preserving the technology as it was developed by Hubbard, Scientology continues to give clues that it is not ready for wide-scale dialogue or broadening of its understanding of what community might mean.

To go on at length about the efforts at community in Theosophy and New Age thought would be simply to reiterate a theme that has been very prominent in all five of the previous chapters. In fact, it is one of the primary goals of Theosophy, and particularly of New Age thought, to work against what they perceive as the destructive individualism characteristic of American culture. Thus they speak of crossing boundaries of all sorts—religious, disciplinary, cultural, gender-conditioned—in order to bring about a planetary community in which all work together for the good of the whole. It may be recalled that this transformation of the alienations of present-day culture can only be brought about by the transformation of the individual person. Theosophy and New Age thought are not willing to abandon that stance in order to bring about global community, but neither are they willing to go back on their insistence that the end of individual effort is to be found in community.

Although they respond in different ways and out of the doctrines of their own systems, it is apparent that the polarities of individual and community are important in stimulating the theological imaginations of the new religions. As insistent as they are on the importance of the individual, they do not, for the most part, neglect to look at issues of community. In some ways, what the new religions define as "community" may at first glance appear to be what Bellah and his colleagues define as "lifestyle enclaves." The authors use the term "enclave" specifically to distinguish it from "community," which they define as "celebrating the interdependence of public and private life and of the different callings of all. . . . " Enclaves, they say, "involve only a segment of each individual, for they concern only private life, especially leisure and consumption."[15] In view of what we already know about the new religions, there is no way to label what they have put together as "lifestyle enclaves." They are too far-reaching in their goals for the individual member, for the particular movement, and for the overall culture to be looked at as merely affecting private life or as concerned primarily with leisure and consumption.

Leisure, in fact, does not seem at all to be one of the values espoused by the new religions. What they talk about for the most part is "work," a feature of all six groups that leads to the final set of polarities to be discussed in this chapter. I am particularly interested here in charting the relationship the new religions see between their own efforts and what they finally achieve.

The student of American religious history is familiar with a classic setting forth of the argument over the efficacy of human effort in Puritan culture—the dispute between the Puritans and the Arminians. This dispute entered American culture by way of what Sydney Ahlstrom has called "an intramural dispute of the Netherlands Reformed Church." It involves a theological tendency to emphasize free will and "works" over God's grace, and in American religious history the term "Arminian" has been applied to Methodists and eighteenth- and nineteenth-century revivalists, among others. It is a dispute that has theological foundations in the "grace"-"works" controversy of the Reformation, but it involves a set of polarities that can be described very broadly in terms of human experience and outside the confines of particular incidents of Christian or American religious history.[16] What does what we do or think, we ask ourselves, have to do with what we eventually achieve, whether materially or psychically or spiritually? "Almost everything," say the new religions. And, on the other side, what responsibility do we bear for the evil that befalls both us as individuals and the world? "Almost all," is the answer.

In respect to these answers the new religions not only accede to but go beyond the cultural drift noted by historians over more than two centuries toward an Arminian or "works" theology. It is in many ways also a common-sense theology emerging out of a common-sense wisdom—that what we achieve is what we have earned. It has little to do with discussions of fate, and it is a stance that seems particularly immune to cynicism. Chapters three and four of this study reinforce this interpretation of the new religions, but it seems a fitting note on which to conclude because when we see where the new religions fall on the continuum of a grace-works theology, we are forced to reassess the typical characterization of most new religions as "optimistic."

In the *The History and Philosophy of the Metaphysical Movements in America*, religion scholar J. Stillson Judah gives fifteen characteristics of the movements he categorizes as "metaphysical," in which he includes Theosophy and Christian Science. These characterizations of the metaphysical religions are particularly astute, and they have served students of American religion well since the book was published in 1967. But Judah's definition of "optimistic," does not seem sufficiently accurate with regard to the new religions; in fact it obscures what a closer reading of the doctrinal materials reveals. Judah claims that the metaphysical groups "stress the love of God without making explicit his judgment, and man's goodness instead of his propensity to sin." He goes on to make some accurate statements about the nature of salvation and the afterlife as involving immortality and progression, but states that "These alternative beliefs exclude the Christian doctrines of evil, grace, and providence." I would agree that the new religions, excluding Mormonism and Unificationism, do not have much to say about grace and providence, but all of them have well-developed understandings of human sinfulness and of the nature of evil. They do not ignore these matters, as became apparent in chapters two, three, and four.

That they do not ignore sin and evil and at the same time espouse a piety of responsibility is what is particularly interesting about these six movements as they place themselves on the grace-works continuum. The movements find various ways to break the traditional tension which asks us to choose between a fallen, sinful, and helpless humanity dependent on God's intervention for salvation or a sinless humanity which needs no savior but can achieve salvation or enlightenment by its own efforts. Put in secular terms, the issue deals with whether we are victims of forces beyond our control and are prevented by a variety of factors from accomplishing that which we must accomplish. In a study of Minnesota Christians conducted several years ago, one of the interpreters summed up the dilemma that seems to face traditional Christians in this respect: "If human beings are perfect, sin is impossible. If human nature is essentially weak, then perfection is impossible."[17]

The new religions say that "those are not the only choices; there are ways to break apart these tensions if we look at human nature in alternative ways from those proposed by the established traditions." Among the six religions in this study, only Unificationism speaks of the reality of original sin, but it does so at the same time that it insists upon the possibility of human perfection on this earth. It may be recalled that Unificationists believe that the offspring of blessed couples in the time of the Second Advent—now—are born without original sin, even though they may commit sins of their own by exercising free will. Even the Roman Catholic Matthew Fox refutes the idea that claiming the reality of original sin will make us better Christians or better citizens of the planet.

Nonetheless, not one of the six has given up on the fact that human persons are sinful in their actions—in what they do and in what they fail to do. Not one is hesitant on the subject of human failings. Mormons speak of sin as the result of "agency"; Unificationists talk about the fall and about disobedience and the abuse of love and the failure to honor prescribed relationships. Christian Science speaks of sin as the unreal, but it does not deny that the results of sin as error are experienced daily by men and women. As Robert Peel puts it in regard to sickness, it is unreal but it cannot be ignored. Theosophy and New Age thought ascribe sin and evil and even the slowing down of the evolutionary process to human egocentricity, a failure to understand our interconnectedness with the universe and to acknowledge that the material life is not all there is; but neither movement chooses to say that egocentricity itself is a product of original sin. Scientology speaks of human suffering and failures in terms of error and engrams rather than of sin, but it nonetheless makes what can be interpreted as a theological statement—that human nature is essentially good.

Altogether the new religions claim in various ways that to admit sinful actions and intentions without going so far as to admit a sinful nature is an acknowledgment more in keeping with the human task on earth and with human experience than to claim helplessness in the face of sin and total dependence on God's mercy for deliverance. "If we focus all our attention on fallen man," says one Mormon, "we will have difficulty ever rising above fallen man."[18] For the new religions, as we have seen, the denial of original sin or, in the case of Unificationism, at least the helplessness associated with it becomes a means to affirm human freedom and even human necessity—if we need God, God also needs us. And it has led to that universally strong insistence noted in chapter three that we must save ourselves and the planet, and, perhaps, even God.

As the new religions participate in these discussions of some of the pivotal tensions in American culture and as they derive energy for the theological imagination from these encounters, they show themselves to be involved in maintaining the tension between the old and the new and between individualism and community. In regard to the grace-works polarity, there is almost no tension at all. "Works" and responsibility will save us.

In conclusion, to look at six new religious movements in American culture provides another arena in which to understand the nature of theological reflection, another perspective from which to analyze the constructive work of the theological imagination. Because they are new, or relatively new, as in the case of the nineteenth-century movements, the religions in this study are concerned with the most basic theologcial concepts. As a result they tend to intensify those universal questions of the theological enterprise in the West and thus provide another vehicle to assess which are the most pressing theological issues in the culture. They construct their theological systems outside the boundaries of the church and of the academy and so make more credible what common sense would dictate anyway—that not all theological work of note goes on in those places. They find their way among those polarities of Western theological thought and American culture by redefining, realigning, and reinterpreting the various poles. Finally, they remind us that in what has come to be described as a secular culture the work of the theological imagination continues to abound.

Notes

PREFACE

1. At least one reason for lack of attention to the theological dimensions of new religions emerges from patterns of scholarship regarding them. Historians have been greatly concerned with religions that had their origins in the nineteenth century. There are excellent studies of nineteenth-century groups whose authors provide information about beliefs as background information, but theological concerns are not generally their focus. It has been primarily social scientists—sociologists, psychologists, anthropologists and even legal experts—who have done most of the work on religions which have emerged in American culture since the 1960s. Given the widespread assumption that the major institutions and values of the culture appeared to be in crisis at that time, it is not surprising that the emergence of new religions was understood as another among many unhealthy and frightening symptoms of cultural malaise and that we turned to sociologists, mental health professionals, and lawyers to help make sense of the proliferation of new religions. Again, their issues are not theological. More systematic description and analysis of the beliefs of the new religions has been left to spokespersons from the established faith communities who see their task as distinguishing and defending their own traditions from those of the new religions. Much of this literature has the further aim of preventing members from joining any of the new religions or else of bringing back those who have already joined. Some of this literature is vituperative in nature; some of it is quite thoughtful. But it generally does not lend itself to the kind of theological conversation in which I am interested.

2. James M. Gustafson, *Ethics from a Theocentric Perspective*, vol. 1 (Chicago: University of Chicago Press, 1981), 158–59.

3. Gordon Kaufman, *Theology for a Nuclear Age* (Philadelphia: Westminster Press, 1985), p. 19. See idem, *An Essay on Theological Method* (Missoula, Mont.: Scholars Press, 1975).

4. David Tracy, *The Analogical Imagination: Christian Theology and the Culture of Pluralism* (New York: Crossroad Publishing, 1986), 452. Originally published in 1981.

5. David Tracy, *Plurality and Ambiguity: Hermeneutics, Religion, Hope* (San Francisco: Harper & Row, 1987), 18.

ONE Introduction

1. This definition is dependent on the writings of theologians James M. Gustafson and Gordon D. Kaufman, as cited in the Preface, but it has also been influenced by the works of Peter Berger, particularly *The Sacred Canopy* (New York: Doubleday, 1967) and of Ian G. Barbour, particularly *Myths, Models, and Paradigms: A Comparative Study in Science and Religion* (San Francisco: Harper & Row, 1974).

2. Gordon D. Kaufman, *The Theological Imagination: Constructing the Concept of God* (Philadelphia: Westminster, 1981), 23.

3. Quoted from Joseph Smith's *History of the Church* in Richard L. Bushman, *Joseph Smith and the Beginnings of Mormonism* (Urbana and Chicago: University of Illinois Press, 1984), 54.

4. George Chainey, "How and Why I Became a Spiritualist," *The Independent Pulpit: Lectures by George Chainey* (Boston, 1885), 2. After leaving Methodism, Chainey became first a Unitarian and then Spiritualist, for Spiritualism promised him scientific evidence for holding to religious teachings.

5. Mark C. Taylor, *A Postmodern A/theology* (Chicago: University of Chicago Press, 1984), 8–9. On these pages Taylor includes a lengthy list of some of the polarities that have dominated Western theological thought.

6. For a helpful discussion about the limitations of American exceptionalism, see Giles Gunn, *The Culture of Criticism and the Criticism of Culture* (New York: Oxford University Press, 1987), especially Ch. 7, "American Studies as Cultural Criticism."

7. Sallie McFague, *Metaphorical Theology: Models of God in Religious Language* (Philadelphia: Fortress, 1982), 13. McFague warns that these descriptions are caricatures, but the student of religion certainly recognizes much that is accurate about them. In fact, the description of the Catholic sensibility is helpful in understanding why so many theological interpretations of New Age thinking are emerging from Roman Catholic sources.

8. Catherine L. Albanese, *America, Religions and Religion* (Belmont, Calif.: Wadsworth, 1981).

9. R. Laurence Moore, *Religious Outsiders and the Making of Americans* (New York: Oxford University Press, 1986).

10. Robert Bellah et al., *Habits of the Heart: Individualism and Commitment in American Life* (Berkeley and Los Angeles: University of California Press, 1985).

11. Jonathan M. Butler, "The Making of a New Order: Millerism and the Origins of Seventh-day Adventism," in *The Disappointed: Millerism and Millenarianism in the Nineteenth Century*, ed. by Ronald L. Numbers and Jonathan M. Butler (Bloomington: Indiana University Press, 1987), 189–208.

12. For a clear description of Mormon organization, see the Preface in Thomas G. Alexander, *Mormonism in Transition: A History of the Latter-Day Saints, 1890–1930* (Urbana and Chicago: University of Illinois Press, 1986), x–xi.

13. I find Jan Shipps's arguments in favor of interpreting Mormonism as a new religious tradition rather than simply an off-shoot of Protestantism very compelling. See *Mormonism: The Story of a New Religious Tradition* (Urbana: University of Illinois Press, 1985).

14. Gordon B. Hinkley, *Truth Restored: A Short History of the Church of Jesus Christ of Latter-day Saints* (Salt Lake City: Corporation of the President of the Church of Jesus Christ of Latter-day Saints, 1979), 4.

15. "Which Church is Right?" (Salt Lake City: Corporation of the President of the Church of Jesus Christ of Latter-day Saints, 1982), 17.

16. Sterling M. McMurrin, *The Theological Foundations of the Mormon Religion* (Salt Lake City: University of Utah Press, 1965), 6.

17. For a good analysis of the implications of literal-mindedness, both positive and negative, see Richard J. Cummings, "Quintessential Mormonism: Literal-Mindedness as a Way of Life," *Dialogue: A Journal of Mormon Thought*, 15, no. 4 (Winter 1982), 93–102. Cummings describes literal-mindedness as a "distinct mind-set which presumes facticity in scriptural accounts, interprets scripture at face value, and by extension, tends to favor one-to-one equivalence over ambiguous multivalence, a reductive simplicity over abstract complexity, the concrete over the speculative, the categorical over the tentative, and finally, the palpably material over the vaguely spiritual" (93–94).

18. See Klaus Hansen, *Mormonism and the American Experience* (Chicago: University of Chicago Press, 1981); Jan Shipps, *Mormonism: The Story of a New Religious Tradition*; Thomas G. Alexander, *Mormonism in Transition: A History of the Latter-Day Saints, 1890–1930*; and Mark P. Leone, *The Roots of Modern Mormonism* (Cambridge, Mass.: Harvard University Press, 1979).

19. Thomas O'Dea, *The Mormons* (Chicago: University of Chicago Press, 1957), 154.

20. *America in God's Providence: Two Speeches by the Reverend Sun Myung Moon* (New York: Bicentennial God Bless America Committee, 1976), 20–21.

21. Mary Baker Eddy, *Science and Health with Key to the Scriptures* (Boston: First Church of Christ Scientist, 1971), 468. This printing is taken from the version of *Science and Health* published in 1906 and further references to it throughout the book will appear in the text in parentheses.

22. Mary Baker Eddy, "The Great Discovery," *Retrospection and Introspection* in *Prose Works Other than Science and Health* (Boston: Christian Science Board of Directors, 1925), 25.

23. Stephen Gottschalk, "Resuming the Dialogue with Christian Science," *Christian Century*, 103, no. 39 (December 17, 1986), 1146–48.

24. *Basic Dictionary of Dianetics and Scientology*, from the works of L. Ron Hubbard (Los Angeles: Bridge, 1983), n.p.

25. "The Scientology Catechism," in *What Is Scientology?* Based on the works of L. Ron Hubbard (Los Angeles: Church of Scientology of California, 1978), 197–98.

26. The Dynamics are described in many of Scientology's publications. See, for example, L. Ron Hubbard, *Scientology: The Fundamentals of Thought* (Los Angeles: Church of Scientology of California, 1956), 36–39.

27. *Scientology: What Is It?* Advertising supplement to the *New York Times, Washington Post, Boston Globe, Tampa Tribune, Las Vegas Review Journal* (n.d.), 1.

28. H.P. Blavatsky, *The Key to Theosophy: An Abridgement*, ed. by Joy Mills (Wheaton, Ill.: Theosophical Publishing House, 1972).

29. Joy Mills, *100 Years of Theosophy: A History of the Theosophical Society in America* (Wheaton, Ill.: Theosophical Publishing House, 1987). See back cover.

30. Blavatsky, *The Key to Theosophy*, 22.

31. Bruce Campbell, *Ancient Wisdom Revived: A History of the Theosophical Movement* (Berkeley and Los Angeles: University of California Press, 1980), 176–78. Campbell provides historical detail about each of the three groups. For a history of the Adyar community written by a Theosophist, see Joy Mills, *A History of the Theosophical Society in America*. For a detailed history of the Point Loma Community led by William Q. Judge and Katherine Tingley, see Emmett A. Greenwalt, *California Utopia: Point Loma: 1897–1942*, Second and Revised Edition (San Diego: Point Loma Publications, 1978).

32. Mark Albrecht, "New Age Spirituality—A General Overview," *Update: A Quarterly Journal on New Religious Movements*, 5, no. 2 (August 1981), 2–5.

33. J. Gordon Melton, *The Encyclopedia of American Religions*, 2 (Wilmington, N.C.: McGrath, 1978). See chs. 16 and 17.

34. Fergus M. Bordewich, "Colorado's Thriving Cults," *The New York Times Magazine* (May 1, 1988), 36–44. Bordewich maintains that New Age thinking and practices are becoming more and more a part of the religious fare of middle America.

35. David Spangler, *Emergence: The Rebirth of the Sacred* (New York: Dell, 1984), 167.

36. Ibid., 38.

37. Ibid., 79.

38. The connections of some facets of Roman Catholic theology with New Age thought are interesting to note. In *The Aquarian Conspiracy: Personal and Social Transformation in the 1980s* (Los Angeles: J. P. Tarcher, 1980), Marilyn Ferguson cites the Jesuit paleontologist and theologian Pierre Teilhard de Chardin as "the individual most often named as a profound influence by the Aquarian Conspirators who responded to a survey," only 18% of whom identified themselves as Catholic. My own experience with members of New Age groups which lie outside the boundaries of Catholicism is that a very high percentage of them are former Catholics, a fact which may, of course, have as much to do with the demography of Minne-

sota as with anything else. Catherine L. Albanese interprets New Age thought as much more "syncretistic" in its orientation, and she takes issue with my estimate of its conceptual and numerical Catholicism. J. Gordon Melton, Director of the Institute for the Study of American Religion, suggests that because of the versatility of New Age teachings, adherents—and no doubt interpreters—often find that which is familiar; thus Catholics see Catholic elements, Jews encounter traditional Jewish themes, etc.

39. Marilyn Ferguson, *The Aquarian Conspiracy*, 23.

40. Ibid., 29.

41. See, for example, Louise B. Young, *The Unfinished Universe* (New York: Simon and Schuster, 1986) who argues that, on the basis of scientific evidence we have every reason to believe that order is increasing in the universe and that the universe is in the process of perfecting itself. One is reminded again of how the writings of Pierre Teilhard de Chardin reinforce such interpretations.

42. James Parks Morton, "Introduction," in David Spangler, *Emergence*, xi.

43. A survey of articles published since 1980 in *American Theosophist*, the official journal of the Theosophical Society in America, reveals a growing number that demonstrate this branch of Theosophy's interest in the concept of a planetary culture and in those same global issues which concern New Age thinkers. Interestingly, some recent issues of *American Theosophist* have on the back cover a statement of the "Theosophical World-View" which has a very New Age ring to it, the first tenet being, "The universe and all that exists within it are one interrelated and inter-dependent whole." See, for example, the November, 1982 issue (70, no. 10).

TWO Who or What Is God Like?

1. Gordon D. Kaufman, *God the Problem* (Cambridge Mass.: Harvard University Press, 1972), 10–15.

2. Charles Hartshorne, *Omnipotence and Other Theological Mistakes* (Albany: State University of New York Press, 1984). See particularly ch. 1, "Six Common Mistakes about God."

3. For a good discussion of this latter question see Paul Sponheim, *God—the Question and the Quest: Toward a Conversation Concerning Christian Faith* (Philadelphia: Fortress, 1985).

4. In *God the Problem*, Gordon Kaufman offers an insight that reinforces my experience that the concept of God offered by classical theism is so dominant that it cannot be ignored, whether one wants to reconceptualize this interpretation of God from within the established traditions, or, as is the case with this study, the interest is in more radically alternative concepts: "No matter how outmoded he seems, and how much we would like to write him off, we find that we must struggle with him whether we like it or not. He has been too powerful in our history—the most profound symbol in our culture—just to die easily. And so, perhaps, precisely because he is so elusive, so dubious, so problematical, he remains a serious issue for us, for our lives and culture, for our world" (14).

5. In both these movements there is potential for a feminine understanding of deity. In Mormonism God the Father lives in the "family unit" in heaven, an understanding that implies a Mother God. There is occasional mention of such a female deity in Mormon writings, but almost no institutionally encouraged devotion to her. In Unification theology, God is understood as androgynous spirit, possessed of both male and female characteristics. As in Mormonism, there is mention of this but the references I have seen to God are almost without exception to "Heavenly Father." This phenomenon has not escaped the notice of feminists in either movement. See, for example, Linda Wilcox, "The Mormon Concept of a Mother in

Heaven," in *Sisters in Spirit: Mormon Women in Historical and Cultural Perspective*, ed. by Maureen Ursenbach Beecher and Lavinia Fielding Anderson (Urbana & Chicago: University of Illinois Press, 1987), 64–67, and Patricia Zulkosky, "Women: Guilt, Spirituality, and Family," *The Family and the Unification Church*, Gene G. James, ed. (New York: Rose of Sharon Press, 1983), 175–93. For an analysis of the concept of God the Mother in Mormonism by a scholar outside the tradition, see Catherine L. Albanese, "Mormonism and the Male-Female God: An Exploration in Active Mysticism," *Sunstone*, 6, no. 2 (March-April, 1981), 52–58.

6. Bruce R. McConkie, *The Promised Messiah: The First Coming of Christ* (Salt Lake City: Deseret Book, 1978), 14. McConkie, who died in 1985, was married to the daughter of Joseph Fielding Smith, the sixth president of the LDS Church. A conservative theologian, perhaps better called traditionalist, McConkie served on the Quorum of the Twelve for many years.

7. 2 Nephi, 29:10, *The Book of Mormon: Another Testament of Jesus Christ* (Salt Lake City: Church of Jesus Christ of Latter-day Saints, 1975). All future quotations are taken from this edition and citations will appear in parentheses in the text.

8. *Divine Principle*, Fifth Edition (New York: Holy Spirit Association for the Unification of World Christianity, 1977), 9. All future quotations are taken from this edition and citations will appear in parentheses in the text.

9. *Of All Things!: A Hugh Nibley Quote Book*, Comp. and ed. by Gary P. Gillum (Salt Lake City: Signature, 1981), 1031–04.

10. Wallace Bennett, *Why I Am a Mormon* (New York: Thomas Nelson, 1958), 223. To reinforce this same point, a reader of *Dialogue: A Journal of Mormon Thought* sent a poem to the editor which acknowledges that the kind of scholarship to be found in this liberal journal has its place but is just "gaming at best." True faith, says the writer, must precede logic as is explained in the *Book of Mormon*: "Higher critics can hardly aspire/ For the case to be rested that way/ But you won't find the message thrust into view/ By rigor, no matter the day./ Just listen to Alma and try the reverse./ Believe in advance that it's true./ Forget what psychologists say of that trick/ And the message will come home to you." A.B. Leaver, "Another View of Scholarship," 18, no. 2 (Summer 1985), 8.

11. *The Principle of Creation: The Nature of God and Man, and the Purpose of Life* (The Divine Principle Home Study Course, vol. one) (New York: Holy Spirit Association for the Unification of World Christianity, 1980), 43.

12. For a helpful discussion of Joseph Smith's developing understanding of the First Vision as having more significance than personal consolation for his own religious doubts, see Richard L. Bushman, *Joseph Smith and the Beginnings of Mormonism* (Urbana and Chicago: University of Illinois Press, 1984), especially ch. 2, "The First Visions." The footnotes to this chapter contain additional useful sources on this subject. See also "Definition and Explication of Church Doctrine," in Thomas G. Alexander, *Mormonism in Transition: A History of the Latter-day Saints, 1890–1930* (Urbana and Chicago: University of Illinois Press, 1986), 272–306. In addition, in *Mormonism: The Story of A New Religious Tradition* (Urbana and Chicago: University of Illinois Press, 1985) Jan Shipps maintains that it was the "gold bible," the *Book of Mormon*, which attracted followers in the beginning of the movement and that the importance of the First Vision has been developmental. See ch. 2, "In the Beginning," 25–39.

13. Mark E. Peterson, *Moses: Man of Miracles* (Salt Lake City: Deseret Book Company, 1978), 105.

14. Sterling M. McMurrin, *The Theological Foundations of the Mormon Religion* (Salt Lake City: University of Utah Press, 1965), 39.

15. Bruce R. McConkie, *Mormon Doctrine*, 2d ed. (Salt Lake City: Bookcraft, 1966), 317.

16. In *Mormon Doctrine* Bruce R. McConkie says of the Holy Ghost, "In this dispensation, at least, nothing has been revealed as to his origin or destiny; expressions on these matters are both speculative and fruitless" (359).

17. Charles Hartshorne, *Omnipotence and Other Theological Mistakes*, 4.

18. David Yarn, *The Gospel: God, Man, and Truth* (Salt Lake City: Deseret Book Company, 1965), 4.

19. Sterling McMurrin, *The Theological Foundations of the Mormon Religion*. See pt. four, "Mormon Theology and the Problem of Evil," 91–113. McMurrin comments, however, that not only the Mormon faithful, but Mormon theologians as well, have had difficulty in seeing the potential in what he calls Mormon finitism for dealing with the problem of evil. Mormons, he says, may be just as likely as traditional Christians to interpret suffering or natural disasters as punishment from God or as something out of which good will eventually emerge.

20. Bruce R. McConkie, *A New Witness for the Articles of Faith* (Salt Lake City: Deseret Book Company, 1985), 56–57.

21. *Outline of the Principle Level 4* (New York: The Holy Spirit Association for the Unification of World Christianity, 1980), 1.

22. *Outline of the Principle Level 4*, 13.

23. John Andrew Sonneborn, ed., *Questions and Answers: Christian Tradition and Unification Theology* (New York: Holy Spirit Association for the Unification of World Christianity, 1985), 3. As Jack Corley, a member of the Unification Church, explained to me, the concept of God's heart has particular cross-cultural appeal. While those of us in the West may think of "heart" as a non-Eastern concept, Koreans and Japanese associate it with "parental heart," which is a fundamental Oriental concept. Corley speculates that this emphasis on God's heart helps to explain why Unificationism has been so well-received in Japan in contrast with traditional Christianity which has never taken hold to a great extent.

24. *The Nature of God and Man, and the Purpose of Life*, 52.

25. Ibid., 52–53.

26. There are some interesting parallels within the established traditions with the growing understanding of God as suffering along with humankind; in fact, some scholars speak of the phenomenon as a kind of "new orthodoxy." In this interpretation, however, the emphasis seems to be on the understanding that God suffers *with* us and not nearly so much that God suffers *because* of us. See, for example, Ronald Goetz, "The Suffering God: The Rise of a New Orthodoxy," *Christian Century*, 103, no. 13 (April 16, 1986), 385–89. Goetz speaks of the development of the "theopaschite revolution" as an "open secret" with enormous implications for theology which is not drawing the kind of critical theological scrutiny it requires.

27. John Andrew Sonneborn, ed., *Questions and Answers*, 8. In "The God of Principle: A Critical Evaluation," 22, no. 4 *Journal of Ecumenical Studies* (Fall 1986), 741–53, Frederick Sontag, a scholar who has written extensively on Unificationism, asks whether the revelation given to the Reverend Moon and put down in *Divine Principle* is now so binding on God that God is incapable of adopting alternative paths. In the same issue John Andrew Sonneborn, in "Unification Theology, Ecumenicity, and 'The God of Principle': A Response to F. Sontag's Essay" (754–63), responds by emphasizing that Unification theology understands God as choosing freely not to alter an overall plan.

28. John Andrew Sonneborn, *Questions and Answers*, 9.

29. Newspapers recently carried a wonderful (at least for the purposes of illustration) "Dear Abby" column devoted to the question of whether or not Mormons are Christians ("Are Mormons Christians? Some Debate It"), which illustrated on the part of one respondent, "A True Christian in Kansas," a desperate need for "conversation" with Mormons as a prelude to writing letters to newspapers (Minneapolis *Star and Tribune*, July 28, 1987, 7C).

30. It is tempting to conclude that this is just what one would expect the main difference to be between similar religious movements developed, respectively, in the nineteenth and twentieth centuries—that given the press of the secularization process, the older movement will demonstrate a much greater interest in the nature of God than the newer. But this is certainly not the case, as we have seen, with Mormonism and Unificationism.

31. Mary Baker Eddy, "Science and the Senses: Address in Chicago," *Miscellaneous Writings* in *Prose Works Other Than Science and Health* (Boston: Christian Science Board of Directors, 1925), 102.

32. Mary Baker Eddy, "The People's Idea of God: Its Effect on Health and Christianity," in *Prose Works Other Than Science and Health*, 4.

33. Mary Baker Eddy, "No and Yes," in *Prose Works Other Than Science and Health*, 6.

34. It should be noted that Christian Scientists do not denigrate the beauties of nature as a consequence of their conviction that the material world can tell us nothing of God. Mary Baker Eddy made much use of nature imagery in her poetry. See, for example, poems such as "Flowers," "Autumn," and "Spring," in Mary Baker Eddy, *Poems Including Christ and Christmas* (Boston: Trustees under the will of Mary Baker Eddy, n.d.). Also, in the "Questions and Answers" section of *Miscellaneous Writings*, Eddy speaks of the need not to deny the beauties of earth but rather to recognize that, "The pleasant sensations of human belief, of form and color, must be spiritualized, until we gain the glorified sense of substance as in the new heaven and earth, the harmony of body and Mind" (86).

35. DeWitt John, *The Christian Science Way of Life* (Boston: Christian Science Publishing Society, 1962), 39.

36. Mary Baker Eddy, *Science and Health with Key to the Scriptures* (Boston: Christian Science Board of Directors, 1971) 465. Originally published in 1875. Future references in the text are to this edition and page numbers are indicated in parentheses.

37. Ibid., 42.

38. Stephen Gottschalk, "Resuming the Dialogue with Christian Science," *Christian Century*, 103, no. 39 (December 17, 1986), 1147.

39. Robert Peel, *Spiritual Healing in a Scientific Age* (San Francisco: Harper & Row, 1987), 35. Peel's book is useful to the student of religion in a variety of ways, particularly because he discusses the relationship of Christian Science healing to that of modern medical practice as well as to that of fundamentalist faith-healing and also because he includes many accounts of Christian Science healing documented in the 1980's (although many of the healings had occurred previous to the 1980's).

40. DeWitt John, *The Christian Science Way of Life*, 35.

41. Agnes E. Hedenbergh, "Spiritual Ideals," *Christian Science Journal*, 76 (June 1958), 306.

42. Ibid.

43. *The Background and Ceremonies of the Church of Scientology of California, World Wide* (London: Krisson, 1970), 22.

44. "The Scientology Catechism," in *What Is Scientology?* Based on the Works of L. Ron Hubbard (Los Angeles: Church of Scientology of California Publications Organization, 1978), 200. "The Scientology Catechism" is arranged in question and answer format. As Scientology literature goes it is not typical, because it makes use of more traditional theological language and concepts. It was designed, I assume, to provide the basis for theological conversation with the established traditions and to indicate that Scientology addresses most of the traditional theological issues.

45. *Background and Ceremonies*, 22.

46. Ibid., 23.

47. "Dynamics," in *Basic Dictionary of Dianetics and Scientology* from the Works of L. Ron Hubbard (Los Angeles: Bridge, 1983), n.p.

48. Omar V. Garrison, *The Hidden Story of Scientology*, (Secaucus, N. J.: Citadel 1975), 52–53.

49. Ibid.

50. *20th Anniversary Commemoration of Dianetics and Scientology*, written and designed by Robert H. Thomas (Copyright 1970 by L. Ron Hubbard), I.

51. "L. Ron Hubbard Dies," *Minneapolis Star and Tribune*, January 28, 1986, 5A. Scientologists have objected to the publication of documents which would ordinarily be kept confidential, and they have likened such documents to the *Cabala* or to "sacred and confidential texts from the Vatican," to which not even all Scientologists have access. See, for example, Cathy Norman, "Scientology Scripture Held Sacred," *Austin American-Statesman*, January 11, 1986. This article appeared in the "Public Forum" section of the newspaper, but the copy given to me by the Church of Scientology of Minnesota had no page number.

52. Stephen Gottschalk, *The Emergence of Christian Science in American Religious Life* (Berkeley and Los Angeles: University of California Press, 1973), 56–57.

53. H.P. Blavatsky, *The Key to Theosophy: An Abridgement*, ed. by Joy Mills (Wheaton, Ill.: Theosophical Publishing House, 1972), 35.

54. *Introductory Study Course in Theosophy*, Part I, based on a course compiled by Emogene S. Simons (Wheaton, Ill.: Theosophical Society in America, 1967), 11.

55. Quoted in Gregory A. Farthing, *Theosophy: What's It All About?* (London: Theosophical Publishing House, 1967), 11.

56. Robert Ellwood, *Theosophy: A Modern Expression of the Wisdom of the Ages* (Wheaton, Ill.: Theosophical Publishing House, 1986), 57–58. Ellwood is Bashford Professor of Oriental Studies in the School of Religion at the University of Southern California. He is trained in the discipline of the history of religions and has written extensively on new religions in American culture. As he explains in the Foreward to this volume, "I am not a theosophist of long-standing but one who has come in midlife to the study of this tradition, activated by the sense of cosmic and spiritual wonder it has evoked for me, and by a growing sense that in it many themes and queries that have long fascinated me converge" (x-xl).

57. H.P. Blavatsky, *The Key to Theosophy*, 51.

58. Shirley Nicholson, *Ancient Wisdom, Modern Insight* (Wheaton, Ill.: Theosophical Publishing House, 1985), 40–41. In the latter statement Nicholson is quoting from Blavatsky's *Secret Doctrine*.

59. *The Mystery of Healing* by the Theosophical Research Centre (Wheaton, Ill.: Theosophical Publishing House, 1958), 26.

60. Robert Ellwood, *Theosophy*, 120–21.

61. Ibid., 150–52. In *Theosophy* Ellwood devotes an entire chapter to concepts of evil in Theosophy. It is a very cogent chapter on a subject that is hard to get a grip on in Theosophy, and Ellwood covers seven areas of Theosophical thought which have implications for understanding how this system perceives the nature of evil: the binary nature of evil, evolution, karma, initiation, black magic, religion, and Jehovah-Satan.

62. Ibid., 150.

63. Christmas Humphreys, *Concentration and Meditation: A Manual of Mind Development* (Baltimore: Penguin 1965), 124. First published in 1935.

64. H.P. Blavatsky, *The Key to Theosophy*, 125.

65. Ibid., 25.

66. Marilyn Ferguson, *The Aquarian Conspiracy: Personal and Social Transformation in the 1980's*, Foreward by Max Lerner (Los Angeles: J. P. Tarcher, 1980), 382.

67. Ibid., 383.

68. Shakti Gawain with Laurel King, *Living in the Light: A Guide to Personal and Planetary Transformation* (Mill Valley, CA: Whatever, 1986), 7.

69. David Spangler, *Emergence: The Rebirth of the Sacred* (New York: Delta, 1984), 68.

70. Matthew Fox, *Original Blessing: A Primer in Creation Spirituality* (Santa Fe: Bear, 1983), 89–91. The distinction between "pantheism" and "panentheism" is not convincing to all, however. See a letter to the editor in *Creation*, 2, no. 5 (November/December, 1986) the publication of the Center for Culture and Creation Spirituality, from Aline D. Manzi, in which she points out her uneasiness with "panentheism": "Creation centering seems a pantheism, and panentheism still is pantheism when expressing the world as part of God's being, with the attention diverted from the true center of all things" (5). For another Roman Catholic interpretation of New Age thought, see David Toolan, *Facing West From California's Shores: A Jesuit's Journey into New Age Consciousness* (New York: Crossroad, 1987). Toolan explores in particular journeys into the psyche, Eastern religions, and the new physics, and says of himself that "I was [during the experiences which he chronicles in the book] and remain a member of a Roman Catholic religious community, the Jesuit order" (xi).

71. Scott Eastham, *Nucleus: Reconnecting Science & Religion in the Nuclear Age* (Santa Fe: Bear, 1987), 177. There is a very interesting Foreword to this book by Raimundo Panikar, retired Professor of Comparative Philosophy and History of Religions at the University of California at Santa Barbara, in which he calls upon the discipline of religious studies to "offer a clearinghouse where the ultimate problems of the human world may be sifted, clarified, discussed, perhaps understood, and eventually solved. The discipline would be nothing less than the concerted essay to understand Man's ultimate predicament in a world context by all the means at our disposal" (xxxvi).

72. Brian Swimme, *The Universe Is a Green Dragon: A Cosmic Creation Story* (Santa Fe: Bear, 1984), 71–81. Swimme calls his chapter on evil "Evil from Cosmic Risk."

THREE What Does It Mean to Be Human?

1. Bruce R. McConkie, *Mormon Doctrine*, 2d ed. (Salt Lake City: Bookcraft, 1966), 575.

2. *The Principle of Creation: The Nature of God and Man, and the Purpose of Life*, vol. 1 (New York: Holy Spirit Association for the Unification of World Christianity, 1980), 25.

3. David H. Yarn, Jr., *The Gospel: God, Man, and Truth* (Salt Lake City: Deseret Book Company, 1965), 100.

4. Wallace Bennett, *Why I Am a Mormon* (New York: Thomas Nelson, 1958), 193.

5. Ibid., 192.

6. David Yarn, *The Gospel: God, Man, and Truth*, 100.

7. Ibid., 103 and 100. The second Article of Faith of the Church of Jesus Christ of Latter-day Saints states: "We believe that men will be punished for their own sins, and not for Adam's transgression."

8. Wallace Bennett, *Why I Am a Mormon*, 193.

9. Ken Miller, *What the Mormons Believe: An Introduction to the Teachings of the Church of Jesus Christ of Latter-day Saints* (Bountiful, Utah: Horizon, 1981), 64.

10. Bruce R. McConkie, *Mormon Doctrine*, 64.

11. Ibid., 63. McConkie places great emphasis in other sources on the atonement as nearly the most important doctrine in Mormon theology. The Preface to *A New Witness to the Articles of Faith* (Salt Lake City: Deseret Book Company, 1985) is McConkie's final testimony delivered at general conference thirteen days before he died in April 1985. This is the opening sentence: "I feel and the Spirit seems to

accord, that the most important doctrine I can declare, and the most powerful testimony I can bear, is of the atoning sacrifice of the Lord Jesus Christ" (xii). For a very different opinion see a letter to the editor of *Sunstone*, 5, no. 6 (November-December 1980) by Gary Ensley, in which he rejects any possibility that the doctrine of the Atonement, however interpreted, has any relevance for Mormon theology: "When will Mormons come to realize that the entire concept of the Atonement is *totally foreign* for Mormon theology? It is totally unnecessary in Mormon theology because mankind did not *faux pas* in the Garden of Eden. It did precisely what it was supposed to do" (2–3).

12. If at least some branches of traditional Christianity understand sin to be inevitable but not necessary, Mormonism seems to see sin as both: sin "is the necessary opposition and alternative to righteousness. Without sin for comparison there could be no basis for choosing salvation; and without the opportunity to reject sin, no basis for growth. . . . Under the law of opposition, the presence of sin in the world is essential to our mortality" (Wallace Bennett, *Why I Am a Mormon*, 8).

13. Wallace Bennett, *Why I Am a Mormon*, 198.

14. Ibid., 198.

15. Bruce R. McConkie, *Mormon Doctrine*, 52.

16. David H. Yarn, Jr., *The Gospel: God, Man and Truth*, 147.

17. Ibid., 100.

18. *Outline of the Principle Level 4* (New York: Holy Spirit Association for the Unification of World Christianity, 1980), 38–39.

19. "Heart of the Father," in *Holy Songs* (no publication information included), 38.

20. *The Principle of Creation: The Nature of God and Man, and the Purpose of Life*, vii.

21. For an elaboration of the consequences of the Fall, see *The Fall of Man: The Origin of Conflict and Suffering in Human Experience*, The Divine Principle Home Study Course, vol. 2 (New York: Holy Spirit Association for the Unification of World Christianity, 1980), 41–54.

22. *Outline of the Principle Level 4*, 25–30.

23. John Andrew Sonneborn, ed. *Questions and Answers: Christian Tradition and Unification Theology* (New York: Holy Spirit Association for the Unification of World Christianity, 1985), 21.

24. Unification theology understands Jesus as the Son of God but not as "God Himself," and it is specified in *Divine Principle* that "Jesus" is the name of a human person. John Andrew Sonneborn explains in *Questions and Answers: Christian Tradition and Unification Theology* (31–32) that Unification theology does not get involved in analyzing the metaphysical relationship between Jesus and the Father nor does it comment on "the great creedal formations of the early Mediterranean church, which are based in Greek philosophy, a philosophy of substances, whereas the Principle employs Oriental philosophy which is a philosophy of relationships." For a further elaboration of Unification Christology see ch. 7, *Outline of the Principle Level 4*, 137–46.

25. *The Principle of Creation: The Nature of God and Man, and the Purpose of Life*, 39–40.

26. Ibid., 40–41.

27. Ibid., 42.

28. There is a good description of the tasks of humankind during other eras of human history, which Unification theology separates into periods of 2000 years, in *The Family and the Unification Church*, ed. by Gene G. James (New York: Rose of Sharon Press, 1983): "The task during the 2000 years from Adam to Abraham was to restore communication with God through sacrifices and offerings, thereby reestablishing a foundation for the ideal family. The task during the 2000 years from

Abraham to Jesus was for the Jewish people to accept and obey the Law of the Old Testament so as to establish a foundation on the national level. The duty of people during the 2000 year period from Jesus to the Lord of the Second Advent is to believe in Jesus and to take his word to all peoples of the world, thereby establishing the foundation for the restoration on a worldwide basis" (259).

29. *The Principle of Creation: The Nature of God and Man, and the Purpose of Life*, 42.

30. Quoted in Linda King Newell, "Gifts of the Spirit: Women's Share," *Sisters in Spirit: Mormon Women in Historical and Cultural Perspective*, 134.

31. Jan Shipps, "Foreword," in *Sisters in Spirit*, xi–x.

32. DeWitt John, *The Christian Science Way of Life* (Boston: Christian Science Publishing Company, 1962), 50–51.

33. Mary Baker Eddy, "The New Birth," in *Miscellaneous Writings* in *Prose Works Other than Science and Health*, 14–15.

34. DeWitt John, *The Christian Science Way of Life*, 50.

35. Ibid., 50–51.

36. Mary Baker Eddy, "Questions and Answers," in *Miscellaneous Writings* in *Prose Works Other than Science and Health*, 79.

37. Ibid., 63.

38. Christian Science uses the traditional Christian language of "sacrifice" and "atonement," but defines atonement as "at-one-ment" with God, a demonstration of unity with God. See ch. 2 of *Science and Health* and Stephen Gottschalk, *The Emergence of Christian Science in American Religious Life*, 84–86.

39. DeWitt John, *The Christian Science Way of Life*, 62.

40. Stephen Gottschalk, *The Emergence of Christian Science in American Life*, 242.

41. Testimonies by Stephanie, Gail B., and Brian G. Pennix in *Christian Science Journal*, 104, no. 2 (February, 1986), 109–111.

42. Mary Baker Eddy, "The People's Idea of God," in *Prose Works Other than Science and Health*, 1.

43. Stephen Gottschalk, "Christian Science Today: Resuming the Dialogue," *Christian Century*, 103, no. 39 (December 17, 1986), 1148.

44. Agnes Hedenbergh, "Spiritual Ideals," *Christian Science Journal*, 76, no. 6 (June 1958), 306–307.

45. L. Ron Hubbard, *Scientology: The Fundamentals of Thought* (Los Angeles: The Church of Scientology, 1973), 63.

46. Ibid., 61. See also the definitions of analytical, reactive, and somatic minds in the *Basic Dictionary of Dianetics and Scientology*.

47. L. Ron Hubbard, *Scientology: The Fundamentals of Thought*, 86.

48. The "technology" of Scientology refers to the whole auditing process: it includes the use of the E-Meter, which is a machine that functions somewhat like a lie detector, the offices of the auditor and the discoveries of Hubbard about how the mind works that are the foundation for the questions asked in the auditing process.

49. "The Scientology Catechism," in *What Is Scientology?*, 200. As a matter of fact most of "The Scientology Catechism" is devoted to explaining Scientology in terms of language and concepts which are familiar to members, particularly, of Christianity.

50. *What Is Scientology?* in "The Scientology Catechism," 201.

51. Ibid., 202. It would be misleading to indicate that Scientologists write a great deal comparing Jesus's task of redemption with that of Scientology's technology. "The Scientology Catechism" is the only place I've encountered it. For a comparison of Scientology with a totally different religious system see Frank K. Flinn, "Scientology as Technological Buddhism," *Alternatives to American Mainline Churches*, ed. by Joseph H. Fichter (New York: Rose of Sharon Press, Inc., 1983), 89–110. Flinn

sees Scientology as a "fusion" of Buddhism and technology and elaborates on seven characteristics of Scientology to make his case. Hubbard acknowledges Buddhism as one of his sources of information. On the other hand, he also mentions Thomas Aquinas.

52. *Basic Dictionary of Dianetics and Scientology.*

53. "The Scientology Catechism" in *What Is Scientology?*, 215. See, also, some of Scientology's advertising pamphlets, such as "Purification Rundown and Atomic War." The Purification Rundown is generally advertised as useful in getting rid of the toxic effects of drugs, but in this pamphlet it is suggested that "there is the side benefit of lessening the consequences of future radiation exposure." Publication information on the pamphlet is indicated as follows: HCO Bulletin 3 Jan 80RA Revised 10 April 80 Re-revised 8 Aug 83.

54. *Basic Dictionary of Dianetics and Scientology.*

55. "The Scientology Catechism," in *What Is Scientology?*, 199.

56. Ibid., 200.

57. See William Sims Bainbridge and Rodney Stark, "Scientology: To Be Perfectly Clear," *Sociological Analysis*, 41, no. 2 (1980), 128–36. Bainbridge and Stark maintain that Clear "is not a state of personal development at all, but a *social status* conferring honor with the cult's status system and demanding certain kinds of behavior from the person labeled "clear." More importantly for my point, they maintain that in Scientology "individuals confer the title of clear upon themselves. If they privately think they aren't as clear as they hoped to be, *they* are at fault" (132–33).

58. Letter from F.P., OT III, in "Spectacular Wins," *Source: Magazine of the Flag Land Base*, no. 51 (n.d.), 18.

59. H.P. Blavatsky, *The Key to Theosophy: An Abridgement*, ed. by Joy Mills (Wheaton, Ill.: Theosophical Publishing House, 1972), 55–56. See also Robert Ellwood, *Theosophy*, 102–106, and *Introductory Study Course in Theosophy*, part I, based on a course compiled by Emogene S. Simons (Wheaton, Ill.: Theosophical Society in America, 1967), 55–59.

60. Robert Ellwood, *Theosophy*, 87. Ellwood defines the "root races" as "great cumulative stages of human development," but "they also do not parallel the anthropological levels of cultural attainment which are largely based on the type of artifacts made and the methods of food-gathering, such as the Paleolithic and the Neolithic" (88).

61. Ibid., 93.

62. H.P. Blavatsky, *The Key to Theosophy*, 41.

63. Ibid., 81.

64. Robert Ellwood, *Theosophy*, 135.

65. Ibid., 118.

66. Ibid., 100.

67. Shirley Nicholson, *Ancient Wisdom: Modern Insight* (Wheaton, Ill.: Theosophical Publishing House, 1985), 145.

68. *Handbook for Ministers, Teachers and Practitioners* (Tahlequah, Okla.: Light of Christ Community Church, n.d.), on inside of back cover.

69. David Spangler, *Emergence: The Rebirth of the Sacred*, 44.

70. Matthew Fox, *Original Blessing: A Primer in Creation Spirituality* (Santa Fe: Bear, 1983), 93. Fox speaks of "original blessing," in contrast with the traditional Christian doctrine of original sin, which he posits as the foundation of his creation-centered spirituality. According to Fox, Christianity has to its detriment overlooked creation spirituality in favor of fall-redemption spirituality, which fosters destructive dualisms and patriarchy. Fox interprets his theology as well within the bounds of traditional Roman Catholicism and not as the beginning of a new religion. "Why do I emphasize so much how creation spirituality is a *tradition?* Because what distinguishes a spirituality from a cult is precisely tradition. The Moonies have a cult

and a personality figure leading them—but not a tradition. So too with the Jim Jones movement" (21). In September, 1988, however, subscribers to *Creation*, the publication of Fox's Institute for Culture and Creation Spirituality, as well as "friends" of the Institute were informed by letter that there had been complaints to Cardinal Joseph Ratzinger of the Congregation for the Doctrine of the Faith about *Original Blessing*. Supporters were asked to respond with a positive letter campaign to Ratzinger. Later in the fall, newspapers announced that Fox had agreed to a period of silence for as long as his conscience permitted. It was also in the fall of 1988 that his most recent book, *The Coming of the Cosmic Christ: The Healing of Mother Earth and the Birth of a Global Renaissance* (San Francisco: Harper & Row, 1988), appeared in bookstores.

71. Ibid., 93. If we broaden for a moment the parameters of this conversation about humanity as the epitome of creation, we find contemporary theologians who claim that it is exactly this view of the place of humankind in the cosmos that is responsible for the present ills of the world. See particularly James Gustafson, *Ethics from a Theocentric Perspective*, vol. 1 (Chicago: University of Chicago Press, 1981). In speaking, for example, of those natural events in the history of the cosmos which have made life possible on earth Gustafson says, "To argue that these contingencies are indicators that the divine governance intentionally worked through them to bring our species into being as the crown of creation is its own leap of faith. To ponder the meaning of the forecast of the demise of the species should be sufficient to deter us from such a faith. The visions of Teilhard de Chardin of the steady development to the Omega of spirituality's dominance over biology cannot be defended" (240).

72. Brian Swimme, "The New Natural Selection," in *Fireball & the Lotus: Emerging Spirituality from Ancient Roots* ed. by Ron Miller and Jim Kenney (Santa Fe: Bear, 1987), 286. This book is a compilation of essays which emerged from the Common Ground project, a fellowship of Christians and Jews in northern Illinois. It is divided into three sections: "The American Mainline," "Encounters with Alternatives," and "New Age Models." It is particularly interesting for its inclusion of essays from Jewish, Islamic and Buddhist perspectives and the hope expressed by its authors "for the emergence of a planetary faith in the twenty-first century" (12).

73. H. Saraydarian, *Five Great Mantrams of the New-Age* (Sedona, Arizona: Aquarian Educational Group, 1975), 31.

74. Matthew Fox, *Original Blessing*, 178.

75. Ibid., 100. See also Matthew Fox, *A Spirituality Named Compassion and the Healing of the Global Village, Humpty Dumpty and Us* (Minneapolis: Winston, 1979).

76. George Trevelyan, *Operation Redemption: A Vision of Hope in an Age of Turmoil* (Walpole, N. H.: Stillpoint, 1985), 179.

77. Ibid., 194.

78. Brian Swimme, *The Universe is a Green Dragon*, 81.

79. Here, I think, is where many Catholics with a New Age orientation would draw the line. I have never encountered references to spirit guides, for example, in the publications that have emerged from the Institute for Culture and Creation Spirituality, although there is much emphasis on alternative expressions of spirituality, among them feminist witchcraft and Native American spirituality.

80. For months in Minneapolis and St. Paul cars carried bumper stickers advertising a "Visualize Peace" gathering, one part of an international celebration, at the Hubert H. Humphrey Metrodome sponsored by many New Age organizations and by established churches as well. In August,1987, many of the New Age groups, but this time not the established churches, participated in celebrations of the Harmonic Convergence. There were some serious media interpretations of this event, the Doonesbury cartoon strip notwithstanding.

81. Gordon D. Kaufman, "Reconceiving God for a Nuclear Age," in *Knowing*

Religiously, ed. by Leroy S. Rouner (Notre Dame, Ind.: University of Notre Dame Press, 1985), 148.

FOUR The Dead Learn Forever

1. Hans Kung, *Eternal Life? Life After Death as a Medical, Philosophical, and Theological Problem,* trans. by Edward Quinn (New York: Doubleday, 1984), 4.

2. There is at least some kinship among these groups with the spirit, if not the details, of the Roman Catholic doctrine of purgatory (which is not much heard of these days).

3. Charles Hartshorne, *Omnipotence and Other Theological Mistakes* (Albany: The State University of New York), 1984.

4. Truman G. Madsen, "Distinctions in the Mormon Approach to Death and Dying," *Deity and Death,* ed. by Spencer J. Palmer (Religious Studies Monograph, no. 2) (Provo, Utah: Religious Studies Center of Brigham Young University, 1978), 62.

5. Bruce R. McConkie, *Mormon Doctrine,* 2d ed. (Salt Lake City: Bookcraft), 184–85.

6. Ken Miller, *What the Mormons Believe: An Introduction to the Teachings of the Church of Jesus Christ of Latter-day Saints* (Bountiful, Utah: Horizon Publishers & Distributors, 1981), 130.

7. Boyd K. Packer, *Our Father's Plan* (Salt Lake City: Deseret Book Company, 1984), 37.

8. *Resurrection: Human History and Man's Transformation from Death to Life,* The Divine Principle Home Study Course, vol. 5 (New York: Holy Spirit Association for the Unification of World Christianity, 1980), 5.

9. Mormons distinguish paradise from heaven, the dwelling place of God. Paradise is that place where the spirits of the righteous await the Second Coming and the reuniting of their bodies and spirits. Interestingly, Unificationism also distinguishes paradise as a level of waiting in the afterlife for the Second Advent. In fact, Jesus and his followers at present inhabit paradise, since Jesus's crucifixion prevented him from fulfilling the three blessings necessary to complete resurrection while he lived on earth.

10. Duane S. Crowther, *Life Everlasting* (Salt Lake City: Bookcraft, 1967), 105–106. Crowther's book is filled with detailed information about the Mormon understanding of death, including references to the fact that life span can sometimes be determined by righteous behavior; good persons will be given the time they need to fulfill their duties on earth. On the other hand, they may be called early to a more important responsibility in the spirit world. An article on Mormon literature in *Dialogue* indicates that such after-death activities become the stuff of Mormon fiction. See Lavinia Fielding Anderson, "Making 'The Good' Good for Something: A Direction for Mormon Literature," *Dialogue: A Journal of Mormon Thought,* 18, no. 2 (Summer 1985), 104–15. See also an article by Craig R. Lundahl, "The Perceived Other World in Mormon Near-Death Experiences: A Social and Physical Description," *Omega: Journal of Death and Dying,* 12, no. 4 (1981–82), 319–27, which indicates that Mormon near-death experiences tend to confirm the Mormon concept of heaven.

11. Bruce R. McConkie, *Mormon Doctrine,* 349.

12. Even though the telestial kingdom is one of the kingdoms of glory, it is not a good place for a Mormon to end up. "It is a glorious and wondrous thing to be saved, even in the telestial kingdom," says Bruce R. McConkie, "but oh! what a course of sorrow and suffering one must travel to gain this lowest of all glories." *A New Witness for the Articles of Faith,* 145–46.

13. *Resurrection: Human History and Man's Transformation from Death to Life,* 5.

14. For an elaboration of these levels, Form-Spirit Level, Paradise, and Kingdom of Heaven, see *Outline of the Principle Level 4*, 111–15.

15. Bruce R. McConkie, *Mormon Doctrine*, 184–85.

16. It is probably the case that the average age of Unificationists in the United States and the age of the movement itself precludes their having had much experience with death. One member mentions that she had not yet experienced "ceremonies surrounding death." See "Piety and Spirituality," in *Lifestyle: Conversations with Members of the Unification Church*, ed. by Richard Quebedeaux (New York: Rose of Sharon Press, Inc., 1982), 55. The June, 1987, *Unification News* carries a picture and a notice of the death of a 23-year-old Unificationist killed in a car accident in Montana (18).

17. *The Principle of Creation: The Nature of God and Man, and the Purpose of Life*, The Divine Principle Home Study Course, volume I, 46.

18. Duane Crowther, *Life Everlasting*, 105–106.

19. Truman G. Madsen, "Distinctions in the Mormon Approach to Death and Dying," 69.

20. Duane Crowther, *Life Everlasting*, 184. Mormon work for the dead explains the Mormon interest in genealogy, for it involves the identification of Mormon families' "kindred dead" so that they may be sealed together for all eternity. See the pamphlet "Why Genealogy?" (Salt Lake City: Corporation of the President of the Church of Jesus Christ of Latter-day Saints, 1982).

21. *Outline of the Principle Level 4*, 118.

22. *Outline of the Principle Level 4*, 118.

23. *The Principle of Creation: The Nature of God and Man and the Purpose of Life*, 25–26.

24. Bruce R. McConkie, *Mormon Doctrine*, 210–211.

25. For an elaboration see *Outline of the Principle Level 4*, "Phenomena Prophesied For the Last Days," 95–98.

26. Truman Madsen, "Distinctions in the Mormon Approach to Death and Dying," 70–71.

27. In *Mormon Doctrine*, Bruce R. McConkie speaks of suicide as the attempt to escape those trials which are a necessary part of the mortal life: "No man has the right to run away from these tests, no matter how severe they may be by taking his own life" (McConkie also cautions compassion rather than judgment for those who do commit suicide), 771.

28. Mary Baker Eddy, "Is There no Death?" in *Unity of Good, Prose Works Other than Science and Health*, 37–38.

29. Thomas Linton Leishman, *Why I Am A Christian Scientist* (New York: Thomas Nelson & Sons, 1958), 125.

30. Mary Baker Eddy, "Is There no Death?" in *Unity of Good*, 40.

31. Thomas Linton Leishman, *Why I Am a Christian Scientist*, 124.

32. Ibid., 122.

33. Ibid.

34. DeWitt John, *The Christian Science Way of Life*, 114.

35. Mary Baker Eddy, "Questions and Answers," *Miscellaneous Writings* in *Prose Works Other than Science and Health*, 42.

36. Mary Baker Eddy, "Is There no Death?" 42.

37. L. Ron Hubbard, *Have You Lived Before This Life?: A Scientific Survey* (Los Angeles: Church of Scientology of California, 1977).

38. L. Ron Hubbard, *Dianetics: The Modern Science of Mental Health* (Los Angeles: Bridge, 1950), 22–23.

39. L. Ron Hubbard, *Have You Lived Before This Life?*, 31.

40. Ibid., 44.

41. Ibid., 34.

42. Chapter 3, "The Phenomena of Death," is devoted to death itself in *Have You Lived Before This Life?* and the rest of the book is concerned with reports on cases of past lives surfacing during the auditing process.

43. *What Is Scientology?*, Based on the Works of L. Ron Hubbard, 201.

44. L. Ron Hubbard, *Have You Lived Before This Life?*, 54.

45. Ibid., 3–17.

46. Ibid., 33.

47. *What Is Scientology?*, 6.

48. Anna Kennedy Winner, *The Basic Ideas of Occult Wisdom* (Wheaton, Ill.: Theosophical Publishing House, 1970), 47.

49. Quoted in Shirley Nicholson, *Ancient Wisdom, Modern Insight*, 148.

50. Anna Kennedy Winner, *The Basic Ideas of Occult Wisdom*, 51.

51. Diana Dunningham Chapotin, "Karma Re-Examined: Do We Ever Suffer Undeservedly?" *The American Theosophist*, 76, no. 2 (February 1988), 27–35.

52. Robert Ellwood, *Theosophy: A Modern Expression of the Wisdom of the Ages*, 108. For further discussions of the process of death in Theosophy, see *Introductory Study Course in Theosophy*, part I, 35–40, and H. P. Blavatsky, *The Key to Theosophy: An Abridgement*, Chs. 7, 8, and 9.

53. Robert Ellwood, *Theosophy*, 107–113.

54. Ibid., 112.

55. Ibid.

56. H.P.Blavatsky, *The Key to Theosophy*, 78–79.

57. Ibid.

58. Ibid., 85.

59. Ibid., 86.

60. Ibid., 134–35.

61. In *Beyond All Belief: Science, Religion and Reality* (Salisbury, Wiltshire: Elements, 1983) Peter Lemesurier provides a scathing criticism of Theosophy's and New Age's concept of an Ego that persists through various reincarnations. But Lemesurier presents his own New Age understanding of "Earthchild": "Humanity as a single entity, an undivided being acting in unison" (186).

62. See Dennis Klass and Richard A. Hutch, "Elizabeth Kubler-Ross as a Religious Leader," *Omega: Journal of Death and Dying*, 16, no. 2 (1985–86), 89–109. Klass and Hutch maintain that Kubler-Ross exhibits a feminine style of religious leadership which "aligns her with ancient practitioners of Greco-Roman and Near Eastern mystery religions" (89).

63. Raymond A. Moody, Jr., *Life After Life* (Covington, Ga.: Mockingbird, 1975); Elizabeth Kubler-Ross, *Death: The Final Stage of Growth* (Englewood Cliffs, N.J.: Prentice-Hall, 1975); Kenneth Ring, *Life at Death* (New York: Coward, McCann & Geoghegan, 1980).

64. Marilyn Ferguson, *The Aquarian Conspiracy: Personal and Social Transformation in the 1980's*, 383–84.

65. See Hans Kung, *Eternal Life?* and Robert Kastenbaum, *Is There Life After Death?* (New York: Prentice Hall, 1984). Both Kung and Kastenbaum (a psychologist) look at the significance of near-death experiences; both, also, are interested in putting forth interpretations of death and the afterlife which are not tied simply to the issue of "survival."

66. The Continuum exhibit began its residency in Minneapolis in a downtown bank in the late 1970s and has found a permanent home in the Minnesota Technology Center. In the summer of 1987 the large panels of the display were in the basement of the building, but a sign on the first floor indicates that they will be refurbished and displayed again and this time referred to by means of a broader and

obviously New Age title: "An Interdisciplinary Exploration of Human Consciousness and the Continuity and Inter-Connectedness of Life."

67. There is no evidence in this excerpt from Tiller that he plans to build machines to detect "spirit" substance, but I couldn't help thinking in this connection of the attempts of Robert Hare, a professor of chemistry at the University of Pennsylvania in the nineteenth century, who became a Spiritualist and built machines to detect spirit presences. See Robert Hare, *Experimental Investigations of Spirit Manifestations* (New York, 1855). The Spiritualists in general called upon scientists of the nineteenth century to put as much effort into discovering the laws of the spiritual world as they did into investigating those of the material universe.

68. Aart Jurriaanse, *Bridges* (Somerset West Cape, South Africa: Sun Centre School of Esoteric Philosophy, 1978), 153–55.

69. Carol W. Parrish-Harra, *A New Age Handbook for Death and Dying* (Marina del Rey, Calif.: Devorsee, 1982), 5–10, and 127.

70. Ibid., 43 and 126.

71. Carol W. Parrish-Harra, *Messengers of Hope* (Black Mountain, N.C.: New Age, 1983), 23.

72. Ibid., 162.

73. Brian Swimme, *The Universe Is a Green Dragon: A Cosmic Creation Story*, 113–14.

74. Ibid., 115–16.

FIVE How Shall We Live Our Lives?

1. I don't think much would be gained here by a technical discussion of the three orientations toward ethical thought which are a part of the discussion of ethics as an academic subject: deontology (duty-oriented, what is the right response?); teleology (what is the good response that will lead to desired ends?); and contextualism (what is the fitting response?). But, in another context a study of ethical reflection in alternative religions might yield some interesting patterns. For a discussion of ethics as related to alternative religions, particularly *est*, see Steven M. Tipton, "The Moral Logic of Alternative Religions," in *Religion and America: Spirituality in a Secular Age*, ed. by Mary Douglas and Steven M. Tipton (Boston: Beacon 1983) and *Getting Saved from the Sixties* (Berkeley and Los Angeles: University of California Press, 1982).

2. Five of the six religions fall rather easily into two categories outlined by sociologists Dick Anthony and Thomas Robbins in "Spiritual Innovation and the Crisis of American Civil Religion," in *Religion and America: Spirituality in a Secular Age*, ed. by Douglas and Tipton (229–48), which they call exemplary dualism and the monistic alternative. Anthony and Robbins use the Unification Church and Jim Jones's People's Temple as examples of exemplary dualisms attempting by authoritarian means to restore the moral community formerly upheld by the crumbling civil religion; they point to Meher Baba as an example of a monistic system which affirms the "harmonious relationship" of individuals to each other and to nature. While Mormonism and Unificationism are obviously examples of exemplary dualisms and Christian Science, Theosophy, and to an extent New Age thought are monistic systems with less prescriptive ethical stances (Scientology, as usual, seems to be another case and doesn't quite fit into either category), paying attention to the process of ethical reflection in each of these movements indicates that Mormonism and Unificationism are not so relentlessly authoritarian as the categories seem to indicate, nor are the monistic systems so entirely lacking in prescriptive ethical reasoning.

3. Unificationism is more uniformly conservative in its membership than is

Mormonism, partly because Mormonism has been in existence long enough to have developed an articulate liberal contingent among its members; in the Unification Church the political stance is still very much influenced by the intensely institutionalized antagonism to communism.

4. Bruce R. McConkie, *Mormon Doctrine*, 273.

5. Kenneth P. Ambrose, "Function of the Family in the Process of Commitment Within the Unification Movement," *The Family and the Unification Church*, ed. by Gene G. James (New York: Rose of Sharon Press, 1983), 23.

6. See, for example, Janet Dolgin, "Latter-Day (sic) Sense and Substance," in *Religious Movements in Contemporary America*, ed. by Irving I. Zaretsky and Mark P. Leone (Princeton: Princeton University Press, 1974), 519–46.

7. Lester E. Bush, "Ethical Issues in Reproductive Medicine: A Mormon Perspective," *Dialogue: A Journal of Mormon Thought*, 18, no. 2 (Summer 1985), 50. The First Presidency consists of the president of the Church and two counselors who are designated as "Prophets, Seers, and Revelators."

8. It would also be instructive as far as ethical reflection is concerned to chart Mormonism's history with war and peace issues. *Dialogue* devoted an issue to that subject (17, no. 4, Winter 1984). An especially helpful article by Pierre Blais, "The Enduring Paradox: Mormon Attitudes Toward War and Peace," interprets Mormon history and organization in light of what he calls a tendency toward "bellicose ideas and attitudes," and which coincides with the kind of American conservatism that favors war-promoting foreign policy. Blais calls on Mormons to be a "voice for peace" rather than war in the world and is very Mormon in his understanding of ethical perspective which ties moral action to individual choice. In a critique of authoritarian structures Blais says, "Atrocities committed at Jonestown, My Lai, and Mountain Meadows [a massacre of an anti-Mormon immigrant group from Arkansas by Mormons and Indians in 1857] were, in the final analysis, the result of individuals failing to make for themselves the correct moral choices" (64). A later issue of *Dialogue* published a letter claiming that there was only one point of view included in the "peace issue," and asked why questions about the need for nuclear weapons were not explored. See Richard H. Hart, "Peace at any Price?" *Dialogue*, 18, no. 2 (Summer, 1985), 4.

9. Ernest Eberhard, Jr., *Sacred or Secret?* (Salt Lake City: Bookcraft, 1967), 35–6.

10. The subject of gender roles in Mormonism is immense, and scholars predict that the issue of women entering the priesthood (the priesthood and its various ranks are available at least in theory to all men and denied to all women) will be much more divisive than the admitting of black males. Just as a beginning look at this issue, see Sonia Johnson, *From Housewife to Heretic* (Garden City, N.Y.: Anchor, 1983); Marilyn Warenski, *Patriarchs and Politics: The Plight of Mormon Women* (San Francisco: McGraw-Hill, 1980); the Autumn 1984 issue of *Dialogue* on Women and Priesthood; and *Sisters in Spirit: Mormon Women in Historical and Cultural Perspective*, ed. by Maureen Ursenbach Beecher and Lavinia Fielding Anderson. Several years ago I formulated some generalizations about common characteristics of nineteenth-century religious movements in which women achieved leadership status: an androgynous or impersonal concept of deity; an optimistic doctrine of human nature; either an anti-clerical stance or easy access to clerical status; and a de-emphasis on marriage and child-bearing as the primary roles for women. Mormonism has only one of these characteristics—an optimistic doctrine of human nature. Theosophy and Christian Science, at least in the nineteenth century, manifested all four. See Mary Farrell Bednarowski, "Women's Religion and Women Religious Leaders in Nineteenth Century America," *Journal of the American Academy of Religion*, 48 (Summer 1980), 207–31.

11. Lester E. Bush, "Birth Control Among the Mormons: Introduction to an Insistent Question," *Dialogue*, 10, no. 3 (Autumn 1976), 28 and 30.

12. Tim B. Heaton and Sandra Calkins, "Contraceptive Use among Mormons, 1965–1975," *Dialogue*, 16, no. 3 (Autumn 1983), 106–109. Even though higher than the rest of the nation, Mormon birth rates were at an historic low.

13. Lester E. Bush, "Ethical Issues in Reproductive Medicine, A Mormon Perspective," *Dialogue*, 18, no. 2 (Summer 1985), 46.

14. Ibid.

15. Mormonism is vehemently opposed to abortion but does not have an official doctrine stating the time when "ensoulment" takes place. There are, nonetheless, Mormons who believe that the Church has been lax in condemning abortion. See Richard Sherlock, "Abortion, Politics and Policy: Deafening Silence in the Church," *Sunstone*, 6 (July/August 1981), 17–19.

16. Lester E. Bush, "Ethical Issues in Reproductive Medicine," 58–59.

17. L. Jackson Newell, "Enlarging the Mormon Vision of Christian Ethics," *Sunstone*, 7 (March/April 1982), 31.

18. Ibid., 30.

19. Marybeth Ranes, "A Wish List: Comments on Christensen and the Ryttings," *Sunstone*, 7 (March/April 1982), 23. The title refers to two articles in the same issue of *Sunstone*: Harold T. Christensen, "The Persistence of Chastity: A Built-In Resistance Within Mormon Culture to Secular Trends," 7–14, and Marvin Rytting and Ann Rytting, "Exhortations for Chastity: A Content Analysis of Church Literature," 15–21.

20. Ibid., 24.

21. It is evident from articles in liberal journals such as *Sunstone* and *Dialogue* that other issues related to sexuality, particularly the alienation felt by single people and by homosexuals, are receiving attention. For several articles on singleness, see the Autumn 1983 issue of *Dialogue*. On homosexuality see "Solus," an anonymous article in the Autumn 1976 issue of *Dialogue* (94–99) and John Bennion, "The Interview," *Dialogue*, 18, no. 2 (Summer 1985), 167–76. "The Interview" is a short story.

22. Couples are matched by the Reverend Moon, with the help of advisors, not only in terms of compatibility, but to foster the Unification commitment to interracial and intercultural marriage. The widespread incidence of interracial marriage, at least in the American church, can be observed in the section of *Unification News* called "Goo Goo Goo," a page devoted to pictures of parents, new babies, and older children.

23. *Lifestyle: Conversations with Members of the Unification Church*, ed. by Richard Quebedeaux (New York: Rose of Sharon Press, Inc., 1982), 30. In this same volume, however, Quebedeaux remarks that in questioning leaders about birth control, he does not always encounter openness toward it as a private decision. He quoted one "high-ranking" person as saying, "We believe just like the Pope; it's our policy that artificial means of contraception are not permissible" (27).

24. Tom Walsh, "Celibacy, Virtue, and the Practice of True Family in the Unification Church," in *The Family and the Unification Church*, ed. by Gene G. James (New York: Rose of Sharon Press, 1983), 143. Walsh bases much of his interpretation of virtue on Aristotle and Thomas Aquinas, sources which give a traditional Roman Catholic flavor to the whole article.

25. Ibid., 145.

26. Arthur Eves quoted in Hugh Spurgin, Nora Spurgin and Arthur Eves, "Engagement, Marriage and Children," *Lifestyles: Conversations with Members of the Unification Church*, 26.

27. Tom Walsh, "Celibacy, Virtue, and the Practice of True Family in the Unification Church," 144.

28. Hugh Spurgin, Nora Spurgin and Arthur Eves, "Engagement, Marriage and Children," *Lifestyle: Conversations with Members of the Unification Church*, 12. Nora Spurgin mentions further that it may be more sacrificial for an interracial couple—

black and white—to live together in Harlem rather than to be separated: "They may be struggling and suffering and working just as much as the couple that is working on separate missions."

29. Ibid., 32.

30. Ibid., 14.

31. Ibid., 14.

32. See "Women's Caucus," in *Lifestyle: Conversations with Members of the Unification Church*, 113–24.

33. Marian Flew, "Being a 'Bottomless Pool of Love,'" *Unification News*, 5, no. 5 (May 1986), 18.

34. See Michael L. Mickler, "Crisis of Single Adults: An Alternative Approach," *Lifestyle: Conversations with Members of the Unification Church*, 161–73.

35. See Hugh Spurgin, Nora Spurgin, and Arthur Eves, "Engagement, Marriage, and Children," *Lifestyle: Conversations with Members of the Unification Church*, particularly 38–46.

36. "*Conservative Digest* Interview with President Bo Hi Pak of the *Washington Times*," in *Unification News*, 6, no. 4 (April, 1987), 5. The *Unification News* carries many articles about CAUSA meetings which are attended by members of conservative and pentecostal churches. CAUSA also publishes many documents which are helpful for understanding more about the Unification interpretation of communism. See, for example, the journal *CAUSA*, which is published four times yearly by the CAUSA Institute.

37. "Some Questions and Answers about Christian Science," *Christian Science Sentinel*, 87, no. 35 (September 2, 1985), 1508–9.

38. Beulah M. Roegge, "Morality Uplifting Sexuality," in *The Christian Basis of Morality* (Boston: Christian Science Publishing Society,1982), 13.

39. See the chapter called "Marriage" in *Science and Health* or the section called "Wedlock" in *Miscellaneous Writings*.

40. Ibid., 15–17. This oblique reference to disapproval of homosexuality receives reinforcement from another source. In "Some Questions and Answers about Christian Science (*Christian Science Sentinel*, 87, September 2, 1985) the response to the question "How does your Church view homosexuality?" is as follows: "Our Church has always regarded homosexuality as something that calls for compassionate healing rather than condemnation of persons on the one hand or acceptance as a Christian way of life on the other. Our religion is Bible-centered, but our position on this rests not just on Leviticus but on the whole Bible, specifically and especially the New Testament" (1508).

41. William E. Moody, "Peace that lasts—building from the heart up," in *Waging Peace: The Spiritual Basis* (Boston: The Christian Science Publishing Society, 1985), 2. This booklet is one of two on the subject of world peace made up of articles which appeared primarily in the *Christian Science Sentinel*. The second, with the same title, was published in 1986.

42. Grant C. Butler, "Why Pray for Peace?" in *Waging Peace: The Spiritual Basis*, 11–12.

43. Cynthia Howland, "Peacemaking and Prayer," in *Waging Peace: The Spiritual Basis*, 13.

44. Carolyn B. Swan, "Watchwords of Peace," in *Waging Peace: The Spiritual Basis*, 2d series, 23.

45. Robert Peel, *Spiritual Healing in a Scientific Age*, 38. Peel quotes from *A Century of Christian Science Healing*, published in 1966, which suggests that, "In some cases a relatively minor physical ailment may require a longer struggle with ingrained traits of character than does an acute need which turns the individual more wholeheartedly to God."

46. Stephen Gottschalk, "Spiritual Healing on Trial," *The Christian Century,* 105, no. 20 (June 22–29, 1988) writes of legal action, particularly the manslaughter charge against the Christian Science parents of Robyn Twitchell, a two-year-old who died of a bowel obstruction while being treated by spiritual means, and what significance these actions have for Christian Science healing and for First Amendment rights. Gottshalk points out that Robyn Twitchell is the only child to have died under Christian Science care during this decade in Massachusetts, where Christian Science membership is strong.

47. Peel is actually quoting a letter written by parents who sought surgery for an infant daughter; they, in turn, are quoting Eddy (109).

48. Robert Peel, *Spiritual Healing in a Scientific Age,* 41.

49. Ibid., 110.

50. Ibid., 110–11.

51. L. Ron Hubbard, *The Way to Happiness* (Los Angeles: Regent House, 1981).

52. Mary Sue Hubbard, *Marriage Hats* (Los Angeles: Bridge Publications, 1970).

53. "Scientology Ethics," in *What Is Scientology?,* 79.

54. L. Ron Hubbard, *Introduction to Scientology Ethics* (Los Angeles: Bridge Publications, Inc., 1968). See particularly the chapter called "The Ethics Codes" (45–68).

55. See Ron Wallis, *The Road to Total Freedom: A Sociological Analysis of Scientology* (New York: Columbia University Press, 1977), particularly 142–145. Wallis includes in these pages copies of documents or letters sent to suppressed persons by Scientologists disconnecting from them. He draws parallels with the period in the history of Christian Science during which Eddy sought to insure that her own interpretation of Christian Science healing prevailed in the future. I agree that there is a parallel in the historical development of these two movements, but question Wallis's use of sources such as Georgine Milmine, who was notoriously hostile to Eddy in a series printed in *McClure's Magazine* in 1906 and 1907.

56. L. Ron Hubbard, *Introduction to Scientology Ethics,* 80.

57. *Scientology: What Is It?,* 13.

58. Ibid.

59. Joy Mills, "Man: Radical Element in Evolution," *American Theosophist,* 71, no. 4 (April, 1983), 88.

60. John Algeo, "The Golden Stairs: Ethics in the Ancient Wisdom Tradition," *American Theosophist,* 72, no. 10 (November, 1984), 357. See also idem, "A Theosophical View of War and Violence," *The American Theosophist,* 70, no. 9 (October 1982), 278–87.

61. Bruce F. Campbell, *Ancient Wisdom Revived: A History of the Theosophical Movement* (Berkeley and Los Angeles: University of California Press, 1980), 201–204. Campbell mentions two incidents involving C.W. Leadbeater, one of the early leaders of the movement, in which ethical ambiguity became problematic. The Adyar Society lacked criteria to judge some of Leadbeater's ideas as non-Theosophical even though they obviously departed from Blavatsky's teachings; and, when Leadbeater was accused of pedophilia and at one point ousted from the Society there was no stated reason for keeping him from reinstatement. In contemporary times Campbell sees the need for Theosophists to be vigilant about a non-prescriptive ethical stance, since a claim of religious neutrality may convey a false sense of universality and discourage periodic reformation.

62. John Algeo, "The Golden Stairs," 357.

63. Robert Ellwood, *Theosophy,* 189–210.

64. Ibid., 202, 204.

65. John Algeo, "The Golden Stairs," 358.

66. Ibid., 367.

67. Geddes MacGregor, "Changing Ethical Attitudes: An Evolutionary Process, *The American Theosophist*, 72, no. 10 (November 1984), 355. Geddes MacGregor is not identified as a Theosophist but he frequently writes on the implications of Eastern spirituality for Western religion. See, for example, *Reincarnation in Christianity: A New Vision of the Role of Rebirth in Christian Thought* (Wheaton, Ill.: Theosophical Publishing House, 1978).

68. Ibid.

69. Robert Ellwood, *Theosophy*, 190–91.

70. Will Ross, "Application of Theosophy," *American Theosophist*, 70, no. 3 (March 1982), 51.

71. Will Tuttle, "Meditation and Conflict Resolution: Toward Developing a Peace Ethic," *American Theosophist*, 74, no. 7 (July 1986), 241.

72. David Spangler, *Emergence: The Rebirth of the Sacred*, 126–129.

73. "Sparrow Hawk Village," *Earth Nation Sunrise: Printing News of the Peaceful Planet*, no. 8 (Fall 1984), 6.

74. Carol Parrish-Harra, "Carol Parrish-Harra Discusses Community" (no publication information). This is an excerpt from a talk given by Parrish-Harra about her reasons for leaving Sarasota and establishing Sparrow Hawk Village. For an elaboration of her understanding of "inner guidance" and of her movement from Roman Catholicism to esoteric Christianity see an autobiographical work, Carol W. Parrish-Harra, *Messengers of Hope* (Black Mountain, N.C.: New Age Press, 1983).

75. Ibid., 4.

76. Ibid., 2.

77. See Handbook for Ministers, Teachers and Practitioners.

78. During the days that I visited Sparrow Hawk Village in August, 1985, two women from San Francisco drove in with a U-Haul trailer, ready to move into the house they had had designed and built after a visit to the community the previous summer. One of them, a teacher for many years, told me that she simply wanted to change the way she lived in a way that made more sense with what she believed about the universality of all religions.

79. "Institute in Culture and Creation Spirituality," *Creation*, 2, no. 4 (September/October 1986), 42.

80. Ibid.

81. Michael Fox, "Panentheism: Where Animal Rights and Deep Ecology Meet," *Creation*, 2, no. 3 (July/August 1986), 16–17.

82. Kirkpatrick Sale, "Planet Water: It All Starts Here," *Creation*, 2, no. 3 (July/August 1986), 11.

83. Jane De Cuir, "Gastronomical Musings," *Creation*, 3, no. 1 (March/April, 1987), 19.

84. Matthew Fox, "Dancing the Orange," *Creation*, 3, no. 1 (March/April 1987), 26.

85. Starhawk, *Dreaming the Dark: Magic, Sex & Politics* (Boston: Beacon, 1982), 140–41.

86. Ibid., 142.

87. Ibid., 146.

88. Marilyn Ferguson, *The Aquarian Conspiracy*, 397.

89. David Toolan, *Facing West from California's Shores: A Jesuit's Journey into New Age Consciousness*, 316.

90. Ibid., 314.

91. Marilyn Ferguson, *The Aquarian Conspiracy*, 397–98.

92. Starhawk, *Dreaming the Dark*, 142.

sıx Epilogue

1. *America in God's Providence: Two Speeches by the Reverend Sun Myung Moon* (Bicentennial God Bless America Committee, 1976), 20–21.

2. David Spangler, *Emergence*, 136.

3. Robert Ellwood, *Theosophy: A Modern Expression of the Wisdom of the Ages*, 99.

4. David Spangler, *Emergence*, 140.

5. *Consummation of Human History: God's Goal in History, Biblical Prophecy and the Present Day*, 7.

6. Ron Miller, "A Road Map to Religious America," in *Fireball and the Lotus: Emerging Spirituality from Ancient Roots*, ed. by Ron Miller and Jim Kenney, 28.

7. Robert Bellah, et al., *Habits of the Heart: Individualism and Commitment in American Life* (Berkeley: University of California Press, 1985), 142.

8. For an interesting discussion of how one historian sees Mormonism as fostering an identity as "outsider" in American culture in the nineteenth century in order to forge an identity as a people, see the chapter on Mormonism in R. Laurence Moore, *Religious Outsiders and the Making of Americans* (New York: Oxford University Press, 1986), 25–47.

9. Truman Madsen, "Distinctions in the Mormon Approach to Death and Dying," *Deity and Death*, ed. by Spencer J. Palmer, 69.

10. Jonathan Wells, a faculty member at the Unification Seminary in Barrytown, New York, who holds a Ph.D. from Yale, has written a response to the 1977 decision: "Excommunication Without a Trial: The 1977 National Council of Churches Critique of The Theology of the Unification Church" (May 1988).

11. Reverend Moon, "The Importance of International Marriage," part I, vol. 7, no. 5, *Unification News* (May 1988), 3. This article is an excerpt from a sermon given in Belvedere, New York, on July 5, 1987, which was a celebration of the 8,000 couple marriage held five years previously.

12. Stephen Gottschalk, "Christian Science Today: Resuming the Dialogue," *The Christian Century*, 103, no. 39 (December 17, 1986), 1148. See, also, Stephen Gottschalk, "Spiritual Healing on Trial: A Christian Scientist Reports," *The Christian Century*, 105, no. 20 (June 22–29, 1988), 602–605.

13. Stephen Gottschalk, "Christian Science Today: Resuming the Dialogue," *Christian Century*, 103, no. 39 (December 16, 1988), 1148.

14. Robert Peel, *Spiritual Healing in a Scientific Age*, vii-viii.

15. Robert Bellah, et al., *Habits of the Heart*, 72.

16. Martha Nussbaum has recently dealt with the general theme of human efficacy and its relationship to the good life as it is articulated in Greek philosophy and tragedy of the fifth century B.C. Nussbaum maintains that a preoccupation of Greek thought is that "the good human life is dependent upon things that human beings do not control" and that Greek tragedy and philosophy provide a variety of responses to this understanding. See *The Fragility of Goodness: Luck and Ethics in Greek Tragedy and Philosophy* (New York: Cambridge University Press, 1986), especially ch. 1. My point here is that the general question is a universal human question which is a subject for discussion in nearly every culture; it is certainly not confined to American culture but the responses in American culture, particularly in the new religions, take on a particular flavor.

17. Joan D. Chittister, OSB, and Martin E. Marty, *Faith and Ferment: An Interdisciplinary Study of Christian Beliefs and Practices*, ed. by Robert S. Bilheimer (Minneapolis and Collegeville, Minn.: Augsburg Publishing House and Liturgical Press, 1983), 84–85.

18. David Yarn, *The Gospel: God, Man and Truth*, 104.

Annotated Bibliography

This selective bibliography includes items that are useful in answering the theological questions addressed in the four central chapters of this book. Most of the sources cited are already referred to in the Notes (although not every item in the Notes is included in the Bibliography). Except for the first section, I have arranged sources according to particular groups. In the first section, I have included general works on new religions, as well as some volumes which are concerned with new ways of looking at the nature of theology at this time in the history of American culture. Although the book does not emphasize a sociological perspective, a few references to sociological works are included. I have annotated only where I think some point about the reference needs explanation or clarification.

GENERAL SOURCES

Albanese, Catherine L. *America: Religions and Religion*. Belmont, Calif.: Wadsworth Publishing Co., 1981.

Beckford, James A. *Cult Controversies: The Societal Response to the New Religions*. London: Tavistock Publications Ltd., 1985. Beckford is a British sociologist who deals primarily with new religions in England and Western Europe, but the similarities and differences are instructive for a student of new religions in American culture.

Bromley, David G., and Anson D. Shupe, Jr. *Strange Gods: The Great American Cult Scare*. Boston: Beacon Press, 1981.

Ellwood, Robert S. *Alternative Altars: Unconventional and Eastern Spirituality in America*. Chicago: University of Chicago Press, 1979.

———. *Religious and Spiritual Groups in Modern America*. Englewood Cliffs, N.J.: Prentice-Hall, 1973.

Fichter, Joseph H., ed. *Alternatives to American Mainline Churches*. New York: Rose of Sharon Press, Inc., 1983.

Gaustad, Edwin Scott. *Dissent in American Religion*. Chicago: University of Chicago Press, 1973.

Gustafson, James. *Ethics from a Theocentric Perspective*, vol. I. Chicago: University of Chicago Press, 1981. Gustafson's discussions of what theology is from his own perspective and his interpretations of the encounters of theology and culture are helpful to the student of religion who is interested in new religions as emerging theological systems. Gustafson, however, is not concerned with new religions.

———. *Ethics from a Theocentric Perspective*, vol. II. Chicago: University of Chicago Press, 1984.

Judah, J. Stillson. *The History and Philosophy of the Metaphysical Movements in America*. Philadelphia: Westminster Press, 1967. This book includes chapters on Christian Science and Theosophy.

Kaufman, Gordon D. *Theology for a Nuclear Age*. Philadelphia and Manchester: Westminster Press and Manchester University Press, 1985. This small volume deals with the contemporary emphasis on the "contextualizing" of theology and contains references to some of Kaufman's other work on the need to reconceptualize the work of theology at this time in history.

Kerr, Howard, and Charles L. Crow, eds. *The Occult in America: New Historical Perspectives*. Champaign-Urbana: University of Illinois Press, 1983.

Melton, J. Gordon, and Robert L. Moore. *The Cult Experience: Responding to the New Religious Pluralism*. New York: Pilgrim Press, 1982.

Moore, R. Laurence. *Religious Outsiders and the Making of Americans*. New York: Oxford University Press, 1986.

Needleman, Jacob, and George Baker, eds. *Understanding the New Religions*. New York: Seabury, 1978.

Robbins, Thomas. "The Transformative Impact of the Study of New Religions on the Sociology of Religion." *Journal for the Scientific Study of Religion*, vol. 27, no. 1 (March 1988), 12–31. This article includes a very useful bibliography of social science sources.

Shinn, Larry D. *The Dark Lord: Cult Images and the Hare Krishnas in America*. Philadelphia: Westminster Press, 1987. *The Dark Lord* deals with a new religious movement not discussed in this book. However, the author, a religious studies scholar, provides a good model for the study of new religions. At the same time he provides a careful critique of the anti-cult model which has been so prevalent in the analysis of new religions.

Stark, Rodney, and William Sims Bainbridge. *The Future of Religion: Secularization, Revival, and Cult Formation*. Berkeley and Los Angeles: University of California Press, 1985.

Tracy, David. *Plurality and Ambiguity: Hermeneutics, Religion, Hope*. San Francisco: Harper & Row, Publishers, 1987.

———. *The Analogical Imagination: Christian Theology and the Culture of Pluralism*. New York: Crossroads, 1981.

Zaretsky, Irving, and Mark Leone, eds. *Religious Movements in Contemporary America*. Princeton: Princeton University Press, 1974.

MORMONISM

Alexander, Thomas G. *Mormonism in Transition: A History of the the Latter-day Saints, 1890–1930*. Urbana and Chicago: University of Illinois Press, 1985.

Arrington, Leonard J. *Brigham Young: American Moses*. New York: Alfred A. Knopf, 1984.

Arrington, Leonard J., and Davis Bitton. *The Mormon Experience: A History of the Latter-day Saints*. New York: Alfred A. Knopf, 1979.

Beecher, Maureen Ursenbach, and Lavinia Fielding Anderson, eds. *Sisters in Spirit: Mormon Women in Historical and Cultural Perspective*. Urbana and Chicago: University of Illinois Press, 1987.

Bennett, Wallace F. *Why I Am a Mormon*. New York: Thomas Nelson & Sons, 1958.

The *Book of Mormon*. It is not easy to start reading the Book of Mormon without some sense of its general history, structure, and themes. For two helpful sources see Richard Bushman, "The Book of Mormon," in *Joseph Smith and the Beginnings of Mormonism* (cited below), especially 115–19; and Thomas O'Dea, "The Book of Mormon,'" in *The Mormons* (cited below), especially 26–37 on "themes."

Bushman, Richard L. *Joseph Smith and the Beginnings of Mormonism*. Urbana and Chicago: University of Illinois Press, 1984.

Hansen, Klaus. *Mormonism and the American Experience*. Chicago: University of Chicago Press, 1981.

Johnson, Sonia. *From Housewife to Heretic*. New York: Anchor Press / Doubleday, 1983. This book is different from others listed in that it is an autobiography and also in the nature of an exposé; but it contains very useful information about the "little tradition" of Mormonism, the everyday living within its world view especially for women.

Leone, Mark. *The Roots of Modern Mormonism*. Cambridge: Harvard University Press, 1979.

McConkie, Bruce R. *A New Witness to the Articles of Faith*. Salt Lake City: Deseret Book Company, 1985.

———. *Mormon Doctrine*, Second Edition. Salt Lake City: Bookcraft, 1966.

———. *The Promised Messiah: The First Coming of Christ*. Salt Lake City: Deseret Book Company, 1978.

Miller, Ken. *What the Mormons Believe: An Introduction to the Teachings of the Church of Jesus Christ of Latter-day Saints*. Bountiful, Utah: Horizon Publishers and Distributors, Inc., 1981.

McMurrin, Sterling M. *The Theological Foundations of the Mormon Religion*. Salt Lake City: University of Utah Press, 1965.

O'Dea, Thomas F. *The Mormons*. Chicago: University of Chicago Press, 1957.

Shipps, Jan. *Mormonism: The Story of a New Religious Tradition*. Urbana and Chicago: University of Illinois Press, 1984.

CHRISTIAN SCIENCE

Eddy, Mary Baker. *Prose Works Other than Science and Health with Key to the Scriptures*. Boston: First Church of Christ, Scientist, 1925.

———. *Science and Health with Key to the Scriptures*. Boston: First Church of Christ, Scientist, 1971. [First copyrighted by Mary Baker Eddy in 1875.]

Gottschalk, Stephen. *The Emergence of Christian Science in American Religious Life*. Berkeley: University of California Press, 1973.

———. "Christian Science Today: Resuming the Dialogue." *Christian Century*, vol. 103, no. 39 (December 17, 1986), 1146–48.

———. "Spiritual Healing on Trial." *Christian Century*, vol. 105, no. 20 (June 22–29, 1988), 602–605.

John, Dewitt. *The Christian Science Way of Life*. Christian Science Publishing Society, 1962.

Peel, Robert. *Mary Baker Eddy: The Years of Discovery*. New York: Holt, Rinehart and Winston, 1966.

———. *Mary Baker Eddy: The Years of Trial*. Boston: Christian Science Publishing Society, 1971.

———. *Mary Baker Eddy: The Years of Authority*. New York: Holt, Rinehart and Winston, 1977.

———. *Spiritual Healing in a Scientific Age*. San Francisco: Harper & Row, 1987.

THEOSOPHY

Besant, Annie. *Esoteric Christianity*, Abridged Edition. Wheaton, Ill: Theosophical Publishing House, 1970. First published 1901.

Blavatsky, Helena P. *An Abridgement of The Secret Doctrine*, ed. Elizabeth Preston and Christmas Humphreys. Wheaton, Ill: Theosophical Publishing House, 1966. *The Secret Doctrine* first published in 1888.

———. *The Key to Theosophy, An Abridgement*, ed. Joy Mills. Wheaton, Ill: Theosophical Publishing House, 1972. Original Complete Edition published in 1889.

Campbell, Bruce F. *Ancient Wisdom Revived: A History of the Theosophical Movement*. Berkeley and Los Angeles: University of California Press, 1980.

Ellwood, Robert S. *Theosophy: A Modern Expression of the Wisdom of the Ages*. Wheaton, Ill.: Theosophical Publishing House, 1986. In Appendix B Ellwood presents a brief discussion of "Theosophical Classics."

Johnson, Raynor C. *The Imprisoned Splendor: An Approach to Reality, Based upon the Significance of Data Drawn from the Fields of Natural Science, Psychical Research, and Mystical Experience.* Wheaton, Ill.: Theosophical Publishing House, 1971. First published in 1953.

Mills, Joy. *100 Years of Theosophy: A History of the Theosophical Society in America.* Wheaton, Ill.: Theosophical Publishing House, 1987.

Murphet, Howard. *When Daylight Comes: A Biography of Helena Petrovna Blavatsky.* Wheaton, Ill.: Theosophical Publishing House, 1975.

Nicholson, Shirley. *Ancient Wisdom-Modern Insight.* Wheaton, Ill.: Theosophical Publishing House, 1985.

Winner, Anna Kennedy. *The Basic Ideas of Occult Wisdom.* Wheaton, Ill.: Theosophical Publishing House, 1970.

SCIENTOLOGY

The Background and Ceremonies of the Church of Scientology of California, World Wide. The Church of Scientology of California. Printed by Krisson Printing Ltd., 1970.

Bainbridge, William Sims, and Rodney Stark. "Scientology: To Be Perfectly Clear." *Sociological Analysis,* vol. 41, no. 2 (1980), 128–36.

Hubbard, Ron L. *Basic Dictionary of Dianetics and Scientology.* Los Angeles: Bridge Publications, Inc., 1983.

———. *Dianetics: The Modern Science of Mental Health.* Los Angeles: Bridge Publications, Inc., 1978. First published in 1950.

———. *Have You Lived Before This Life?* Los Angeles: Church of Scientology of California Publications Organization. Copyrights 1950–1977.

———. *Introduction to Scientology Ethics.* Los Angeles: Bridge Publications, Inc., 1968.

———. *Scientology: The Fundamentals of Thought.* Los Angeles: The Church of Scientology Publications Organization, 1956.

Wallis, Roy. *The Road to Total Freedom: A Sociological Analysis of Scientology.* New York: Columbia University Press, 1977. Wallis is a British sociologist, but his is one of the few book-length, scholarly studies of Scientology; his analysis is useful for the student of American religions. At the end of the book, Wallis includes a rebuttal of his study written by a Scientologist.

What Is Scientology? Based on the Works of L. Ron Hubbard. Los Angeles: Church of Scientology of California, 1978.

Whitehead, Harriet. "Reasonably Fantastic: Some Perspectives on Scientology, Science Fiction, and Occultism." *Religious Movements in Contemporary America,* ed. Irving Zaretsky and Mark Leone. Princeton: Princeton University Press, 1974.

THE UNIFICATION CHURCH

Barker, Eileen. *The Making of a Moonie: Choice or Brainwashing?* Oxford: Basil Blackwell Publisher Ltd., 1984.

Bryant, M. Darrol, and Susan Hodges. *Exploring Unification Theology.* New York: Rose of Sharon Press Inc., 1978.

Bryant, M. Darrol, and Herbert W. Richardson, eds. *A Time for Consideration: A Scholarly Appraisal of the Unification Church.* New York: Edwin Mellen Press, 1978.

Bromley, David G., and Anson D. Shupe, Jr. *"Moonies" in America: Cult, Church, and Crusade*. Beverly Hills, Calif.: Sage Library of Social Research, no. 92, 1979.

Divine Principle. New York: Holy Spirit Association for the Unification of World Christianity, 1973. Although the Reverend Sun Myung Moon's picture appears in the beginning of the book, and the contents is understood to be an interpretation of what has been revealed to the Reverend Moon, he is not designated as the author of the text. The contents of *Divine Principle* with sections arranged in the same order can be found in other publications with illustrations that may be somewhat easier to follow. For example, there is the six-volume *Home Study Course* (1980) published in paperback by the Holy Spirit Association for the Unification of World Christianity.

Hargrove, Barbara. "On Studying the Moonies as a Political Act." *Religious Studies Review*, no. 8 (July 1982), 209–13.

James, Gene G. *The Family and the Unification Church*. New York: Rose of Sharon Press, Inc., 1983.

Kim, Young Oon. *The Types of Modern Theology*. New York: Holy Spirit Association for the Unification of World Christianity, 1983.

———. *Unification Theology and Christian Thought*. New York: Golden Gate Publishing Co., 1975.

Kliever, Lonnie D. "Unification Thought and Modern Theology." *Religious Studies Review*, no. 8 (July, 1982), 214–21.

Outline of the Principle Level 4. New York: Holy Spirit Association for the Unification of World Christianity, 1980. Here is another presentation of the doctrines in *Divine Principle*.

Quebedeaux, Richard. *Lifestyle: Conversations with Members of the Unification Church*. New York: Rose of Sharon Press, Inc., 1982.

Sonneborn, John Andrew. *Christian Tradition and Unification Theology*. New York: Holy Spirit Association for the Unification of World Christianity, 1985.

Sontag, Fred. *Sun Myung Moon and the Unification Church*. Nashville: Abingdon, 1977. This is one of the earliest scholarly publications which looks at the Unification Church in the United States, Europe, and Asia. Chapter 5, "What Does the Doctrine Teach?" provides a useful, preliminary overview of Unification doctrines.

Thompson, Henry O., ed. *Unity in Diversity: Essays in Religion by Members of the Faculty of the Unification Theological Seminary*. New York: Rose of Sharon Press, Inc., 1984.

NEW AGE THOUGHT

It is impossible to cover the many facets of New Age thought in a brief bibliography. The following selections are intended to provide some variety of perspective on what can be called a "New Age world view," and the implications of that world view for the basic theological questions referred to in this book. I have cited only fairly contemporary works rather than the works of authors whose perspective could certainly be considered compatible with New Age interpretations—e.g., Pierre Teilhard de Chardin, whose influence is frequently referred to by New Age thinkers—but whose writing preceded the articulation of the contemporary New Age movement.

Eastham, Scott. *Nucleus: Reconnecting Science and Religion in the Nuclear Age*. Santa Fe: Bear & Company, 1987.

Ferguson, Marilyn. *The Aquarian Conspiracy: Personal and Social Transformation in the 1980s*. Los Angeles: J. P. Tarcher, Inc., 1980.

Fox, Matthew. *The Coming of the Cosmic Christ: The Healing of Mother Earth and the Birth of a Global Renaissance.* San Francisco: Harper & Row, Publishers, 1988.

————. *Original Blessing: A Primer in Creation Spirituality Presented in Four Paths, Twenty-Six Themes, and Two Questions.* Santa Fe: Bear & Company, 1983.

Miller, Ron, and Jim Kenney. *Fireball and the Lotus: Emerging Spirituality from Ancient Roots.* Santa Fe: Bear & Company, 1987.

Parrish-Harra, Carol W. *A New Age Handbook on Death and Dying.* Marina del Rey, Calif.: Devorss & Company, 1982.

————. *Messengers of Hope.* Black Mountain, N.C.: New Age Press, 1983.

Smith, Huston. *Beyond the Post-Modern Mind.* Wheaton, Ill.: Theosophical Publishing House, 1982.

Spangler, David. *Emergence: The Rebirth of the Sacred.* New York: Dell Publishing Co., Inc., 1984.

Swimme, Brian. *The Universe Is a Green Dragon: A Cosmic Creation Story.* Santa Fe: Bear & Company, 1984.

Toolan, David. *Facing West from California's Shores: A Jesuit's Journey into New Age Consciousness.* New York: Crossroad, 1987.

Young, Louise B. *The Unfinished Universe.* New York: Simon and Schuster, 1986.

JOURNALS AND PERIODICALS

In attempting to understand theological themes in new religious movements, contemporary issues of particular interest, concerns about identity, and interpretations of teachings, I find it helpful to read journals and periodicals published by the groups I am studying. The following list provides a sampling. I have included two New Age journals in order to convey some sense of the variety of publications available.

The American Theosophist. This is the official journal (monthly) of the Theosophical Society in America, but the Theosophical Society warns that it is not responsible for what is contained therein unless it appears in an official document. The journal contains articles by Theosophists and those outside the movement devoted to the interpretation of Theosophical teachings and to the application of a Theosophical perspective to contemporary issues. Like *Dialogue* and *Creation* this journal publishes special issues (spring and fall) devoted to such topics as "The Spiritual in the Arts" and "Science and Ancient Tradition." As of September 1988, *The Quest* (a quarterly publication) replaced the special spring and fall issues.

Christian Science Sentinel (weekly) and *The Christian Science Journal* (monthly). Both these periodicals contain articles about Christian Science as it relates to matters of theological understanding or current issues, editorials, poetry, and testimonials.

Creation. This journal emerges (bi-monthly) from the Institute in Culture and Creation Spirituality. It is useful in that it provides an obviously theological orientation for the discussion of New Age issues, and its content illustrates particularly well the great variety of global, social, and personal issues with which New Age thought is concerned and the multiple perspectives it applies to these matters. The "Response" section provides an arena for theological conversation from those who disagree with the periodical's general stance as well as for those who affirm it.

Dialogue: A Journal of Mormon Thought. Dialogue (quarterly) specifies that it "has no official connection with the Church of Jesus Christ of Latter- day Saints." There is no doubt that this journal emerges from the liberal sector of Mormonism, but it is particularly helpful because it contains such a variety of articles—about historical, doctrinal and social issues—as well as fiction, poetry, and book reviews. *Dialogue* occasionally features issues dealing with such matters as Mormonism and blacks, women and the priesthood, and war and peace. The lengthy "Letters" section makes possible the articulation of more conservative voices in this journal.

Freedom. This is a monthly periodical founded by the Church of Scientology in 1968. Its feature articles are not theologically oriented but devoted to what might be called "exposes" of those aspects of government and culture to which Scientology takes particular exception—among them the IRS, the CIA, and the use of drugs in the treatment of mental health patients. *Freedom* also contains book and movie reviews and advertisements.

Meditation. This is another example of a New Age periodical, one which provides a less obviously theological orientation than that of *Creation*. *Meditation* is published quarterly by Intergroup for Planetary Oneness in Van Nuys, California. Its masthead describes the publication's purpose: "To explore and promote meditation as a consciousness-expanding activity and to be a source of reference for meditation activities and organizations." The purpose of meditation is understood to be both personal and planetary transformation, and the articles, editorials, illustrations, book reviews and advertisements reflect the typically broad New Age understanding about how such transformation can be accomplished.

Unification News. This newspaper-format publication appears monthly and contains news items about the activities of the Unification Church around the world—everything from international conferences to regional picnics—occasional presentations by the Reverend Moon, a page on "Divine Principle Study," other doctrinal discussions, editorial and news columns, and book reviews. There are general advertisements and classified ads as well.

Index

Abortion: Mormonism, 159n

Absolute: Theosophical concept of God, 36

Agency: Mormon doctrine of human nature, 49–50

America: Unification Church, 10–11, 129–30; New Age and Theosophy, 130–31; Mormonism and ancient history, 131; newness and new religions, 132. *See also* Culture, American

The Aquarian Conspiracy: near-death experience, 93

Arminians: grace-works controversy, 136, 137

Astrology: New Age communities, 120

Atonement: Mormon doctrine of human nature, 48–49; Mormonism and gender roles, 54; Mormon view of death and the body, 77; Mormon theology, 149–50n; Christian Science, 151n

Auditing: Scientology and death, 88, 89; Scientology and technology, 151n

Basic Dictionary of Dianetics and Scientology: parts of the mind, 60; definition of Clear, 62

Bible: Mormonism, 21; Unificationism, 21–22

—Christian Science: death, 84; sexuality, 109; healing, 130; past, 131–32; homosexuality, 160n

Birth control: Mormonism, 99, 100–102; Unificationism, 103–104, 159n

Blavatsky, Helena P.: history of Theosophy, 13, 14; concept of God, 35, 36, 38; doctrine of human nature, 64–65; prayer, 65–66; death and afterlife, 90, 91, 92

Body

—Death: Mormonism, 76–77; Unificationism, 82; Theosophy, 90–91

—doctrine of human nature: Mormonism, 47, 54, 71–72; Unificationism, 54, 72; Scientology, 60, 64; Christian Science, 64, 72; Theosophy, 65, 70, 72; New Age, 70, 72

Book of Mormon: Joseph Smith and history of Mormonism, 8; Bible and revelation, 21; publication, 128; ancient history, 131

Catholicism: interpretations of New Age thinking, xii; New Age concept of God, 40; New Age and Matthew Fox, 121–22; connection with New Age, 143n–144n

Celibacy: Unificationism and marriage, 104–105

de Chardin, Pierre Teilhard: influence on New Age, 143n, 144n

Christian Science: sources, xii; cosmology and Scientology, 7; history of, 11–12; concept of God, 27–32, 34–35, 43; doctrine of human nature, 55–60, 63–64, 72–73, 138; death and afterlife, 82–86, 89, 97; ethical and moral issues, 107–12, 125–26; newness, 130; Bible and connection with past, 131–32; individualism and community, 134–35; beauty of nature, 147n; atonement, 151n; monistic system, 157n; homosexuality, 160n; healing and legal action, 161n

Christian Science Monitor: social issues, 135

Christianity: definition of theology, x; Mormonism and Unification Church, 27; Christian Science concept of God, 28; Theosophical concept of God, 36; new religions and human nature, 45; death, 76; Theosophy and afterlife, 92; new religions and salvation, 97; Mormonism and ancient history, 131

Church of Jesus Christ of Latter Day Saints. *See* Mormonism

Classical theism: concept of God, 19–20, 21, 144n; Mormon concept of God, 24

Clear: Scientology doctrine of human nature, 61–62, 63; as social status, 152n

Communism: history of Unification Church, 10; Unificationism and conservative politics, 106–107, 158n

Community: history of New Age, 15–16; New Age and ethics, 119–23; and individualism as theme of new religions, 133–36

Confidence: New Age doctrine of human nature, 68–69

Conservatism: Mormonism and Unificationism, 99, 106–107, 157–58n

Cosmology: new religions, 6–7; Mormonism, 8–9; Unification Church, 10; Christian Science, 11; Scientology, 12–13; Theosophy, 14; New Age, 16–18; gnosticism and Scientology, 34; ethical and moral issues, 98

Creation: New Age and moral issues, 122

—concept of God: Mormonism, 24; Christian Science, 29, 34–35; Theosophy, 36

Creation: New Age and ethics, 122–23

Culture: theological imagination and religious traditions, 1–2; new religions as participants, 6

—American: theological imagination and universal questions, 1; nineteenth-century religious pluralism, 2; twentieth century and new religions, 2–3; dyadic thinking and religion, 4–5, 129; new religions and human nature, 45; near-death experience,